PHANTOM BOYS

PHANTOM BOYS

TRUE TALES FROM THE UK OPERATORS
OF THE McDONNELL DOUGLAS F-4

RICHARD PIKE

GRUB STREET • LONDON

Published by
Grub Street
4 Rainham Close
London
SW11 6SS

A CIP record for this title is available from the British Library

ISBN-13: 9-781-909808-22-5

Design by Sarah Baldwin
Edited by Natalie Parker

Printed and bound by Finidr, Czech Republic

Grub Street Publishing only uses FSC (Forest Stewardship Council) paper
 for its books.

CONTENTS

For Lizzie, Alan and Sally. I am justifiably proud of them.

AUTHOR'S NOTE

With sincere thanks to the contributors to this book as well as to Grub Street Publishing who have allowed me rather more latitude than is probably traditional for the genre. Their openness and enthusiasm have been illuminating. With sincere thanks, too, to aviation artist Chris Stone whose painting appears on the front jacket cover of this book.

CHAPTER 1

POSTAL DROP

JACK HAMILL'S BAD BREAK

'Please', I thought, 'Don't look at me like that.' It really wasn't entirely my fault. Or maybe it was; I wasn't altogether sure at that stage. In either case, the situation seemed surreal as the two of us, my navigator and I, laid on the ground whilst discussing what had gone wrong. The postman himself stood there trembling as he gazed down at us. Clearly flummoxed, he looked as if he was in a greater state of shock than either of the aircrew who must have seemed to him like creatures from outer space. While I stared up at him, a light breeze ebbed and flowed within the pillar of smoke that rose from the nearby wreckage of our Phantom. "Are you two okay?" he asked tentatively, his facial expression one of sheer disbelief.

"We appear to be," I said simply in the absence of a more elaborate remark that came immediately to mind. "That's all right then," said the postman in his Scottish accent. He glanced at us again before, disconsolately, he started to wander off, back to his postal van which was parked on a road that led to the small Scottish town of Kirriemuir. Promptly galvanised into action, I decided that a courteous move in the light of our mutual amazement might be to stand up and follow him. I would try to talk calmly to the poor postman – try to ease his obvious state of alarm and despondency.

After all, I reckoned, I'd become quite good at coping with anxious types, a skill picked up as a qualified flying instructor at RAF Valley, Anglesey. I'd spent three years there in the early 1970s as an instructor on the Folland Gnat, a small, agile machine whose qualities of sensitive handling and high manoeuvrability had made the aircraft well-suited as an advanced trainer. I'd greatly enjoyed flying the Gnat, which was the type used by the Red Arrows when the aerobatic team was formed in 1964. The year before that, a group of flying instructors had instigated the Yellowjack aerobatic team, although higher authority had evidently disliked the colour yellow and had disapproved of the team's reputation for maverick tendencies.

*

Before Valley, I had been a pilot on the Avro Vulcan, the iconic delta wing strategic bomber which became the backbone of the United Kingdom's airborne nuclear deterrent for much of the Cold War period. During my time on the Vulcan force, the policy of relying on high speed, high altitude flight to avoid interception was changed to one of low-level tactics, a move which, from the pilots' point of view, made life a little more interesting. The two pilots sat on Martin Baker ejection seats, unlike the rear crew members who, in an emergency, had to abandon the aircraft through the entrance door.

This highly controversial policy was maintained despite a practical scheme to fit ejection seats for the rear crew and despite, too, a tragic case in October 1956 during a ground-controlled approach to London's Heathrow Airport. Vulcan XA897, the first Vulcan B1 to be delivered to the Royal Air Force, had been on a flag-waving round-the-world tour and had returned to Heathrow in foggy conditions.

Instead of diverting to another airfield, the Vulcan continued to Heathrow where a reception party waited. A few hundred yards short of the runway, the Vulcan hit the ground before bouncing back into the air. The two pilots, Squadron Leader D R Howard and his co-pilot Air Marshal Sir Harry Broadhurst the commander-in-chief of Bomber Command, now had just seconds in which to decide whether to stay with the badly damaged aircraft and attempt an emergency landing, or whether to eject thus saving themselves but committing the rest of the crew to certain death.

The pilots chose to eject. Perhaps, as the four rear crew members on that flight heard the firing mechanism of the pilots' ejection seats, if the men perceived, then, a sudden and terrible instant of doom, maybe as they sat in their non-ejection seats ready to be thrust helplessly, pathetically, inevitably towards the abyss, perhaps, if time twisted to turn seconds into an eternity and, even with eyes tight shut, colours of red, white, blue, green and black flashed, flashed, flashed across the screens of those closed eyes, their final thoughts were less of mounting panic in the midst of reckless endangerment, more, one can only hope, of an ultimate, mysterious sense of concord beyond, in the imminence of death, the realms of normal conscious comprehension.

If Sir Harry Broadhurst's reputation took a downwards plunge after this tragedy, I could, in a curious way, empathise, although for entirely different reasons. After five years on the Vulcan fleet, I was invited for an interview for a possible job as an aide-de-camp. When the air vice-marshal asked me why I wanted to become his aide-de-camp, I merely said: "I don't." This response, if admirably succinct, nonetheless failed to impress the senior officer. It was a case, therefore, of: "For you, my lad, it's off to Training Command!" and I packed my bags as ordered. Of the forty students on my course at the Central Flying School, the institution where people were taught how to be flying instructors, just four were selected for the Gnat. Despite grumbles from former fighter pilots that a Bomber Command type such as myself should pinch one of the valued Gnat slots, this was, from my perspective, an incredible opportunity which would alter the entire progression of my thirty-two-year flying career.

For after the three-year stint at Valley, in July 1973 I was posted to fly the Phantom FG1 with 43(F) Squadron based at RAF Leuchars in Scotland. This was the start of an unbroken eight-year period on the Phantom fleet for me, with a posting after 43 Squadron to 19(F) Squadron at RAF Wildenrath in Germany followed by two years at RAF Coningsby in Lincolnshire – initially on 29(F) Squadron, then as an instructor on the Operational Conversion Unit. At that point, in 1981, I went to fly Hawker Hunters with the Sultan of Oman's Air Force (re-named in 1990 the Royal Air Force of Oman) until returning to Coningsby and the Phantom fleet in 1984 for a further two years.

It was one day in the latter period, during an instructional sortie with my student in the Phantom's front seat, that our aircraft developed undercarriage problems. The undercarriage nose-wheel was stuck in the up position and, despite our efforts to coax the thing down, the nose-wheel refused to budge (we later learned that a 2 cm bolt in the undercarriage system had sheared). As my student was inexperienced on the Phantom (this was his second sortie on the type), I took control of the aircraft despite the problems of restricted vision from the back seat. The emergency drills stipulated that before landing we should fly out to sea to jettison the gun pack which was fitted beneath the aircraft. However, in the hope of saving the expensive gun pack I was ordered, instead, to jettison the pack near the air traffic control tower. 'Are you mad?' I thought, but refrained from saying so.

I flew 'low and slow' towards the air traffic control tower. The timing was critical, as was the line of flight. While the air traffic control tower grew closer and larger, I reflected that it was not every day that we had an opportunity to bomb our own airfield. Anxiously, my finger hovered by the gun pack's jettison button. Tension rose until, just as the Phantom drew level with the air traffic control tower, I pressed the button. There was a slight noise, an almost infinitesimal pause before, to the amazement of those involved (apart from one or two, including me), a grotesque hole adjacent to the air traffic control tower suddenly appeared while, simultaneously, a column of debris rose majestically up into the sky. Another pause ensued before the debris, which included shards of metal from mangled pieces of wrecked gun pack, began to descend with shocking grace to fill up the hole. I heard these details later, of course, for by this stage the Phantom had flown well beyond the scene.

I now had to set up for an approach and landing minus nose-wheel. My head moved restlessly from side to side in order to obtain the best view and I was aware of my student's anxiety as, poor fellow, he sat apprehensively in anticipation of a crash landing. He may have said little but perhaps, like me, with the mind emptied of anything but the vacuum of resignation that afflicts those threatened with imminent peril, an intense atmosphere dominated our cockpits. With no wish to add to my student's trepidation, I did not mention that we were in a novel situation – that this was the first case of a British Phantom having to land without a nose-wheel.

While I concentrated on setting up the approach, on the downwind leg I cast a last gloomy glance at the undercarriage indicator. Nothing had changed; the nose-wheel remained implacably stuck. With the flat Lincolnshire countryside stretching to the horizon, the familiarity of local features was somehow reassuring when I turned the Phantom onto finals. The restrictive rear cockpit view, however, meant that the ideal runway perspective was hard to maintain. I strived to focus on the near end of the runway, therefore, and carefully monitored the aircraft's airspeed. As the touchdown point loomed, suspense was palpable. Now we crossed the runway threshold, shortly after which, with a thump, the Phantom's main wheels touched the tarmac. Quite quickly, even though I held the stick fully aft, the aircraft settled with a startlingly nose-down attitude on the runway. As the Phantom came to a rapid stop, I brought back the twin throttles to close down both engines. With the realisation that we had landed safely, I felt a great sense of relief; indeed, I experienced a warm, almost metaphysically pleasant feeling – we had made it!

Later, even the acid approval of higher authority was shown in the form of a 'Good Show' certificate. Even so, the desk wallahs at headquarters couldn't resist a comment that I should have thought about jettisoning the rear canopy before landing. In fact, I had thought about it, but was wary from a previous experience of the disagreeable impact of buffet in the Phantom's rear cockpit when flying without a canopy.

Perhaps the nearly-ten years' worth of experience I had gained by the time of this incident had helped to achieve a successful outcome. This was not the case, however, in 1975 when, as a relative newcomer on the Phantom fleet, I was faced with a situation which was both drastic and dramatic. I had felt delighted to be invited to fly as number four in 43 Squadron's four-ship formation team due to take part the RAF Leuchars' Battle of Britain events over the weekend of 20/21 September 1975. The rehearsal on 18 September, had, as usual, been briefed by the team leader, the squadron's commanding officer, known for his somewhat cavalier approach to flying.

Having signed the necessary pre-flight paperwork, the four pilots with their navigators walked out to the aircraft. I glanced up at the sky; the weather looked reasonable and I felt a surge of excitement at the prospect of a challenging, action-

The first UK Phantom to land with the nose-wheel stuck up.

packed flight – although naturally at this juncture I had no inkling of just how challenging and action-packed. While my navigator strapped into his ejection seat in the Phantom's rear cockpit, I carried out the necessary ritual of external checks. When satisfied with these, I climbed the access ladder to the pilot's cockpit where a ground crewman assisted as I strapped into the Martin Baker ejection seat. He confirmed that the seat safety pins were removed before he stepped down to man a fire extinguisher while he supervised the start procedure.

My mind was entirely focused on the task in hand as I carried out the pre-start cockpit checks and soon, as we looked at the leader to receive his signal, all four pilots were cleared to start engines. With a thumbs up sign from my ground crewman, I looked inside the cockpit again to initiate the start cycle of the Phantom's first Rolls-Royce Spey engine. When this engine had settled, I initiated the starting sequence of the second engine and before long, with all four aircraft 'turning and burning', the leader spoke to air traffic control. The controller, who sounded a little edgy, then cleared the formation to taxi out to the runway-in-use. A distant figure behind extensive panes of glass in the Leuchars' air traffic control tower, the local controller now cleared us to line up and take off. We moved swiftly onto the take-off spot where, as briefed, we arranged ourselves into two pairs.

As number four in the formation, I moved to an echelon starboard position on the leader of the second pair. The first pair now took off as a separate unit at which, with a hand signal from the second pair's leader to increase engine power, I edged the Phantom's twin throttles forward. I kept my eyes firmly on the leader anticipating a positive nod of his head. I did not have to wait long. When the signal came, I released the Phantom's brakes and started to ease the throttles forward to maintain a good formation position. My navigator called out airspeed as we accelerated...80 knots...100 knots...120 knots...soon, as I continued to concentrate on the leader, I could see his wheels leave the runway, after which, on a further nod of his head, I operated the undercarriage 'up' switch.

My leader now applied bank to catch up with the first pair before, quite quickly, we all slotted into pre-briefed positions. The four-ship formation leader then rolled out onto a northerly heading to take us towards the Firth of Tay. He would fly to the west of the city of Dundee beyond which, near the town of Kirriemuir – the birthplace, incidentally, of J M Barrie, the creator of *Peter Pan* – we could practise our Battle of Britain Day routine in an area of relatively open airspace.

For the next forty or so minutes, I used my navigator to do the tasks which, normally, I would carry out myself – to keep an ongoing check of our position, to note any potential weather problems, to maintain a good look-out. As well, no doubt, as keeping a close eye on the others in the formation, from force of habit his head would move from one side to the other as, almost mechanically, he searched the sky. Meanwhile, I would focus on the leader's Phantom while I held an accurate position in the number four slot. The formation members relied wholly on the leader's judgement to present an exciting yet safe display that would retain observers' interest. From time to time, if he called a formation change, the team members would react slickly in a swirl of well-rehearsed manoeuvres.

The final planned manoeuvre, known as a Canadian break, entailed all four aircraft starting from an echelon formation. On the leader's order, each aircraft would break away individually at two- to four-second intervals then turn

Four Phantoms in box formation.

downwind in preparation for landing. However, unlike a normal break when the leader would turn first, in this case the outside aircraft would break first, rolling through some 270 degrees **under** his colleagues. The others would follow in sequence so that all aircraft ended up downwind with suitable separation before landing. This so-called Canadian break was a flamboyant, and some would say fairly pointless, exercise which could cause problems. As I'd expressed reservations, the leader, who had experience of the procedure as a former member of the Canadian Snowbird aerobatic team, had decided that the two of us, at the conclusion of the main rehearsal, should practise the manoeuvre together while the others flew back to base.

We set up for the first practice with the leader on my right side in an echelon position. We flew at an altitude of between 2,000 and 3,000ft. The weather conditions remained cloud free with generally good visibility; the area below was open countryside with a mix of green, brown, light and dark yellow patchworks of early autumn colours. I did not know this at the time, but the local postman was watching us while he conducted his mail rounds.

The scene was set. In this tranquil part of Scotland with its unusual if unspectacular place in history, a location where nothing much ever happened, it would have seemed inconceivable to the genial inhabitants that quite so much trouble was about to descend quite so quickly. The leader now initiated the Canadian break. He called: "Breaking...GO!" and in a snappy, aggressive turn, he rolled his Phantom under mine. I counted two seconds then, with the application of full aileron, I followed his move. After a roll through 270 degrees I expected to spot the leader...but he was nowhere in sight. Instinctively, therefore, I pulled back hard on the stick; I wanted to climb out of a situation of possible collision. As I snatched the stick back, however, the aircraft nose reared violently upwards. Later, I discovered that a Phantom with full roll control applied would depart from controlled flight even with as little as 1.7 g applied. My navigator recognised the problem immediately and promptly ejected. Meanwhile, I took the 'unload for control' action at which the aircraft nose sliced down. I swiftly realised, though, that my altitude was far too low for any hope of a successful recovery.

Now, with both hands, I grasped the ejection seat bottom handle and tugged it hard. Nothing happened; at least, it appeared as if nothing happened. 0.3 of a second can seem like an eternity when you are a mere 1,000ft up and pointing vertically downwards in a twenty-ton, out-of-control aeroplane. Abruptly, though, I heard a bang and felt a jolt as I was unceremoniously propelled from Phantom XV580. I felt myself falling...falling...falling until the parachute billowed out and the straps jerked hard between the fork of my legs. The ensuing silence was sudden and great. The wind blew on my face and, just as I looked down at the fields and hedges and trees of the surrounding countryside, one of the fields – a large brown one – came up and hit me. I'd had no time to adopt the ideal parachute landing position – the position so carefully briefed at endless practise sessions – and instead, I slammed into the ground like the proverbial tent peg.

So it was that, before I could really catch up with what was happening, I found myself lying on my back in a ploughed field. My body was tangled in a mass of chords and white parachute silk. I breathed deeply and sighed. I released the parachute harness but continued to lie on my back, not exactly in a relaxed state but reckoning that there seemed little point in moving just yet. After the recent frantic cockpit activity everything seemed so peaceful, so elemental. It would be nice to stay put and rest – to try to pretend that none of this had actually happened. With a forefinger, I poked at the mud of the field in which I lay. I looked up to see my navigator in his parachute while he made a more leisurely descent than my own. Not too far away I spied the smoke and fireball of the crashed Phantom. Suddenly it struck me that he was drifting into the fireball. Horrified, I wanted to yell a warning, "*Tim... Watch out!*" It was too late, though, and he drifted through the smoke before he landed, as if by design, just three to four yards from my position. His landing, if better than mine, nevertheless was hardly textbook and, like me, he ended up lying on his back.

I paused for a second or two to reflect on this bizarre situation. Eventually I managed to sit up and lean on one elbow. "Tim," I said, "some highly paid help is going to want to know about this." The remark, which to the casual observer might appear a little inane, elicited no response that I can recall, although I became aware of another voice in the vicinity, a strange voice: "Are you two all right?" asked the voice. I glanced up and slightly behind me at a figure that peered down at us. The figure was dressed in a postman's uniform. Despite the temptation to say all sorts of things, I replied: "We appear to be." "That's all right then." At this, he turned around and began to wander off.

On instinct, I decided to stand up and chase after the poor fellow who appeared to be in a worse state of shock than either of the two aircrew. "Hey!" I cried at which he stopped and the two of us began to chat. Meantime, a small crowd started to gather. Excitedly, folk looked this way and that, pointed with fingers, discussed possibilities. It was not long, though, before we heard the clatter of a rescue helicopter which swooped down to land nearby. Men with stretchers now emerged from the helicopter; I was strapped into a stretcher and so was my navigator before the two of us were whisked off to hospital. At the hospital they discovered three smashed vertebrae in my spine and I didn't fly again for six months. My navigator was declared fit and he flew the next day. When, finally, I was allowed to return to flying, it was, for me, a poignant moment.

Poignant, too, was the news some four years later that the same Canadian break manoeuvre had been attempted in a Phantom and with the same result. On that occasion, however, the crew did not survive. If there was an unhappy link between the Vulcan tragedy at Heathrow and the Canadian break in a Phantom – if the Vulcan had been suitably equipped and the Canadian break banned, then unnecessary loss of life would surely have been avoided. In both cases, dark forces were darkened further by questions whose answers lay within the cloudy intellect of dubious decision makers.

CHAPTER 2

BASTILLE BLUES

ALAN WINKLES CAME ACROSS CLOSURE
OF AN UNWELCOME KIND

The French, without doubt, are proud of their way of life and French folk will usually be eager to claim the virtues of their *je ne sais quoi* factor. Sometimes, however, the *quoi* in question can cause a problem or two for everyone else. I discovered this myself in July 1987, on a day known as Bastille Day or *La Fête Nationale*. The day when the storming of the Bastille prison on 14 July 1789 is remembered as a symbol of the modern nation and thus a cause of considerable celebration all over the place.

The day for me and for my navigator started well enough. It was an unexceptional Tuesday with the two of us on duty with another pilot/navigator crew. We were supported by a team of squadron engineers in the quick reaction alert (QRA) set-up at RAF Leuchars. Two Phantoms, kept at readiness to be airborne in a matter of minutes when ordered by the ground radar controller at RAF Buchan, were in a special hangar next to a couple of crewrooms, one for the aircrew and one for the engineers. As the commanding officer of 43(F) Squadron at the time, I was not often on QRA duty although I liked to ensure that I was rostered for the occasional stint. If, as the saying goes, all was quiet on the western front, it was, for one thing, an opportunity for me to catch up on irksome paperwork from HQ whose staff seemed to relish the distribution of documents and texts notable for introductory flannel, adjectival overkill, unrestrained use of abbreviations and curious, multi-syllable military terms which contained no obvious meaning although, admittedly, they did sometimes help to enliven proceedings by mangling old-fashioned common sense out of recognition.

While we waited for a call to action, we listened to the steady background tick of a 'telebrief' device with its direct connection to the Buchan controller. As I concentrated on the HQ and other paperwork, my colleagues read newspapers, listened to the radio and discussed squadron issues as well as more general affairs including, I seem to recall, last month's general election victory by Mrs Thatcher's

Conservative party and the intriguing challenge by US President Ronald Reagan to Soviet Premier Mikhail Gorbachev to tear down the Berlin Wall. It was during such discussions that the telebrief's monotonous tick suddenly quietened, a sign that the controller was about to make an announcement. Crewroom conversation ceased at once and we all stared in anticipation at the telebrief, an insignificant looking box in one corner of the room. Perhaps we were about to hear news that Mr Gorbachev had called the American bluff and was about to demolish the Berlin Wall by swamping that divided city with tanks, but no, Berlin's wall would stand for another couple of years yet, and the controller's voice announced instead: "Leuchars, this is Buchan...alert one Phantom."

Now all hell was let loose as we reacted. The Q2, back-up, pilot operated the scramble claxon while my navigator and I, as the nominated Q1 crew, dashed to our aircraft. We skipped up the side of our Phantom's cockpit access ladders, wriggled slickly into the Martin Baker ejection seats, eased bone domes (flying helmets) over our ears and in practically no time at all we were ready to speak to the controller. "Two zombies have been identified heading towards the Iceland/ Faroes gap," she said in dulcet tones, "remain at cockpit readiness and standby for further instructions." Unlike the Lightning force when QRA scrambles normally involved an almighty scramble, the QRA Phantoms at Leuchars often received long-range warning of 'zombie' (i.e. Soviet) activity thus allowing a more leisurely pace.

This, though, was not always the case and my mind, while we waited, went back to one such unusual situation the previous year. As part of a naval co-operation exercise, I'd been on combat air patrol to the east of the Shetland Isles when the radar unit at RAF Saxa Vord, situated on the northern tip of the Shetlands, had given orders to intercept a civilian airliner which was off-track and not responding to air traffic control's messages. On his airborne radar, my navigator had swiftly spotted the relevant radar return and, as he called out appropriate directions, it was not long before I could pick up the aircraft visually. Soon, as I closed onto the target from astern, my navigator agreed with the assessment that it was an Ilyushin Il-62, NATO codename 'Classic', a Soviet long-range jet airliner with a capacity for almost 200 passengers and crew, and which looked similar to the Vickers VC10 aircraft. The Classic, which had Aeroflot markings, was flying at an altitude of 35,000ft at an airspeed of around .85 Mach and the machine was flying directly towards the area of our naval exercise.

Maintaining the Phantom's position astern the Ilyushin, I closed up to about 100 feet directly below the intruder. While discussing with my navigator our next course of action, suddenly, to our amazement, a fairly large square panel on the Classic's underside began to open. Like lustful sets of prying eyes, three enormous camera lenses were now revealed. No sleuth was needed to work out that the Aeroflot's crew members had been ignoring air traffic control deliberately in order to overfly and photograph the ships of the United States fleet and the carrier group involved with the exercise. The situation was as blatant as it was outrageous.

Normally, to fly in close proximity to another aircraft without the captain's knowledge would be wholly contrary to the practices of good airmanship. In this case, however, I realised that the Ilyushin captain would need to fly a steady height and airspeed in order to achieve good photographic results. I decided, therefore, to fly even closer to the Ilyushin – some 30 or 40 feet beneath it – so as to block the recalcitrant cameras' view. Keeping the Phantom in that position for about six or seven minutes, my navigator and I grinned at the cameras, struck the tops of our bone domes lingeringly and flamboyantly, offered thumbs up and other gestures until, eventually, the Classic captain, doubtless still oblivious of our presence, made a classic turn onto a south-easterly course when, at last, he obeyed air traffic control's instructions to head off into the wide blue yonder. Later, I could picture the Soviet intelligence people when they summonsed the Classic captain, pointed at the jaw-dropping photographic triumph, then put hands on hips and made every effort not to smile or laugh – a laugh that might start with a rumble to grow rapidly into a belly-roar – while the shame-faced captain wrung his hands, bit his lip then made a hasty, embarrassed retreat. Maybe at that point the room filled with unwelcome applause.

"Maintain cockpit readiness," the controller's voice cut through my reminiscences, "standby for an update of intelligence information." "Understood," I said and continued to wait patiently.

If, I mused, that close encounter with a Classic had been of an unwelcome kind, then there'd been an even more unwelcome event quite recently that involved an aircraft on our own side – an English Electric Canberra. The incident had occurred on one dark and dirty night when a Phantom from my squadron had been programmed to fly a sortie designed to hone the anti-electronic counter measure (ECM) skills of the crew, a junior squadron pilot with, as his navigator, an exchange officer from the United States Air Force. The ECM-equipped Canberra would deliberately apply radar and radio-jamming techniques in order to confuse and attempt to throw off the attacking fighter. It was a difficult and challenging exercise.

The Phantom's crew conducted a number of complex practise interceptions then, on the last one, the navigator mistakenly selected the wrong range scale on his airborne radar. The Phantom, as a consequence, ended up behind the Canberra on a rapidly closing collision course. At the last second, the navigator realised his error and shouted a warning. Immediately, his pilot applied a high angle of bank and turned away hard. During this manoeuvre a slight bump was felt as the Phantom passed through the Canberra's slipstream.

Back at base, when engineers carried out turn-round procedures, it was realised that the slight bump reported by the aircrew had turned out to be rather more than slipstream effect. A large mark on the Canberra's wingtip fuel tank matched a scar of equivalent length and size running along the underside of the Phantom. When the news of their unintended brush with fate was revealed, the crews of both aircraft must have felt a sense of numbness in the pits of their stomachs.

Suddenly, the Buchan controller called: "We've received updated information on the zombies; they've altered course...standby..." she hesitated before, with renewed urgency, she went on: "...climb to flight level 300, steer 340 zero degrees to patrol due east of the Faroes...scramble, scramble, scramble, acknowledge."

Within moments I had initiated the start cycle of the first Rolls-Royce Spey engine, quickly followed by the second, after which I received clearance from air traffic control to taxi out and take off. When I engaged reheat during the take-off run, the 20,515lbs of thrust from each of the Rolls-Royce Spey 201 turbofans provided an accustomed punch in the back as the aircraft accelerated. While we climbed, the incandescent sunlight of that mid-July day began to highlight the natural splendour, the sweeping vistas, of the Scottish Highlands as we headed north-west. Below, people might have looked up at the distinctive sound of engine noise as the Phantom flew above.

Eventually the stretches of land changed to sea and we could spot fishing and other boats which appeared as black specks upon the surface. "Turn left ten degrees," said the controller, "two zombies are currently range one hundred and twenty miles ahead." Using the remarkable facility of his Pulse Doppler radar, it was not long before my navigator cried, "I think I've got them!"

Sure enough, as if my navigator had stood up, placed two fingers in his mouth and whistled to gain their attention, the zombies, according to his radar, had turned before persisting with their predictable course en route to Castro's Cuba. In order to stay in radio contact with the controller I maintained our altitude for as long as practicable but at length it was necessary to commence a descent down to the zombies' height. It could seem incongruous as we flew towards the sea's surface which glittered an apparent welcome in the summer sun but which could lead us unwittingly towards a clash with those we'd learnt to regard as potentially hostile.

For the Soviet Union, despite admirable technological achievements, including the launch of the first ever satellite and the world's first human space flight, and notwithstanding current policies of glasnost and perestroika, was without doubt a mercurial state with malevolent policies. The dangers of the Cuban missile crisis of 1962, the resultant risk of nuclear confrontation, and the hazards of the ongoing Cold War were among issues that weighed on our minds when we intercepted zombies. Beneath the veneer of political rhetoric lay genuine peril.

In the year 2013, with the release of classified documents under the United Kingdom government's thirty-year rule, it was revealed that in the perilous circumstances of 1983 officials had prepared a putative speech to be delivered by Queen Elizabeth II in the event of World War III breaking out:

'I have never forgotten the sorrow and pride I felt as my sister and I huddled around the nursery wireless set, listening to my father's inspiring words on that fateful day in 1939 at the start of World War II. Not for a single moment did I imagine that this solemn and awful duty would one day fall to me. But whatever terrors lie in wait for us all, the qualities that have helped to keep our freedom intact twice already during this sad century will once more be our strength.'

Tensions in the year of 1983 had run high when US President Ronald Reagan enraged and alarmed Moscow with the denunciation of the Soviet Union as the 'evil empire'. Reagan had announced plans for a Star Wars ballistic missile shield in space and the deployment of US nuclear cruise missiles to Europe. Further international strains had been caused when the Soviets shot down a South Korean airliner that had strayed into Soviet airspace. All 169 passengers and crew on board the airliner were killed. Now, four years on from that difficult year, these and other incidents ensured that my navigator and I remained more than a little circumspect as we approached the zombies.

Soon my navigator began his patter as he set up the intercept geometry: "The targets are passing from right to left," he said, "for displacement turn starboard thirty degrees." He was an experienced fighter navigator and I had every confidence that the flight lieutenant's instructions would lead to an efficient interception. "Maintain this height and airspeed," he went on, "standby for a port turn onto the targets' heading." Suspense rose as we flew closer to the zombies and apart from the navigator's terse intercept instructions, silence dominated our cockpits. "Standby…" he said, followed by: "turn left now." By this stage we had glimpsed the zombies and while I turned the Phantom as directed we were able to confirm the aircraft type. Two Tupolev Tu-95RTs (*Razvedchik Tseleukazatel*) four-engined turboprop-powered maritime reconnaissance aircraft, NATO code-named Bear D, now loomed ahead.

The aptly-named Bear aircraft, with its distinctive and, for a propeller-driven machine, unusual swept-back wings (the contra-rotating propellers, incidentally, were reported to rotate faster than the speed of sound which arguably made the Bear the noisiest aircraft on earth), first flew in 1952 and seemed to represent the very essence of the Cold War era. Compared to the Phantom's relatively modest wingspan of just over 38ft and length of 63ft, the Bear's wingspan was over 164ft and the length was more than 151ft. The Bear D carried a crew of six or seven which included two pilots, a flight engineer, a communication systems operator, a tail gunner, a navigator and sometimes a second navigator. The actions of these individuals could prove less than friendly on occasions.

When I'd confirmed good visual contact with the Bears, my navigator ceased his patter and we both concentrated on looking outside the cockpit. As we approached the first Bear I prompted him to write down the aircraft's nose-wheel door number, airframe details, notable features, other particulars including crew reaction – especially from the tail gunner who we could see peering out from his Perspex 'bubble'. Perhaps ostracised by other crew members, I surmised him, probably unjustly, to be a glum individual stranded in the rear of the Bear, solitary, neglected, his face as emaciated as that of a saint in a sarcophagus.

At least today, I reflected, we'd not have to contend with the tail gunner problem I had experienced a couple of years ago – a problem caused during a night flight when, for identification, I'd had to fly very close to a Bear, considerably closer than normal. It had been one of those nights when darkness had turned from grey-black to black, from black to jet black, from jet black to pure liquid blackness when our only hope of discerning the Bear's number was to wait for a break in the clouds to reveal a lighter patch of night sky. I'd asked my navigator to switch his radar controls to mapping mode in order to verify our range and bearing from the Scottish islands as, simultaneously, I glanced down at the fuel gauges. This was as well, for at that precise moment, just as our eyes were not directly focused on the Bear, a brilliant red light from the tail gunner's bubble had suddenly illuminated us; a light so brilliant, in fact, that I thought there had been an explosion. At once, I'd applied full left aileron and rudder to pull away before levelling the Phantom about half-a-mile from the Bear and 1,000ft below it. I'd reported this dangerous turn of events to the ground radar controller who'd then ordered us to return to base.

If some of the Bear crews had hostile tendencies, those we came across today appeared to be benign – although at this point we were unaware of surprises in store. Having moved from the rear Bear to the forward one and having noted all necessary details, we now remained in a loose formation with the Soviet machines for the next thirty or so minutes without any sign of zombie-like belligerence. Perhaps, I mused, in the struggle for a better world, the current trends of perestroika were more *stroika* than we'd all reckoned.

At length, though, it was time to leave our unusual travelling companions and head for home. I therefore initiated a climb and turned onto a south-easterly heading. Any sense of winding down after a job well done, however, was swiftly dispelled when the controller at Benbecula Radar announced that our task was not yet complete and that we were to rendezvous with a VC10 in-flight refuelling tanker in anticipation of further 'trade'. At this, our pulses quickened at thoughts of more Soviets heading our way bent on anti-perestroika activity.

Soon, on completion of in-flight refuelling, our controller ordered: "Vector one-eight-zero, standby to re-intercept those zombies." It seemed that our recent

Bear travelling companions, far from setting course for Cuba after we had left them, had flown instead along the west coast of Ireland and currently appeared to be heading for the Bay of Biscay.

The Benbecula controller now handed us over to Portreath Radar in Cornwall where the new controller confirmed that, having re-intercepted the Bears, we were to continue to shadow them on their southerly course. Meanwhile, another VC10 in-flight refuelling tanker was on its way to support us. My navigator, as before, used his Pulse Doppler radar to spot the Bears at a considerable range, and commenced his commentary to set us up for a 120-degree interception (i.e. to make a final turn though 120 degrees onto the targets' heading). The intercept geometry worked well and before long, having spotted our Bears visually, we closed up to hold a position to one side of them. By this juncture the Bears themselves were in a loose formation on each other and eventually, when the VC10 tanker had joined us from a training task over the North Sea, our unofficial formation consisted of four aircraft – two Bear Ds, a Phantom FG1 and a Vickers VC10.

Proceedings appeared to be moving along quite happily until, at a distance of around 150 miles south of the Cornish coast, my navigator sheepishly announced in a small voice that his navigational charts no longer covered this area. The news sent a worried shudder down my spine. I stared at the bleak expanse of sea beneath us, at the waves which disintegrated into sheets of white foam and which seemed to accentuate our sense of isolation. I could hardly blame my navigator; we were well beyond our normal operating area and it would be unreasonable to expect him to carry navigational charts that covered the entire world. In any case, before too long we would be close to the French city of Brest and the northern reaches of the Bay of Biscay so we could expect our shadowing duties to be taken over by Mirage fighters of the French air force.

By now we were no longer in radio contact with Portreath or any other radar unit; our sole means of radio communication was with the VC10 crew. A further blow to our prospects, therefore, came with the announcement from the VC10 captain that this was Bastille Day in France and that, consequently, we could not anticipate any form of relief from Mirage units. Far be it for me, I reasoned, to deny the French their day of Bastille celebrations, but surely there were other considerations too. I could not avoid a feeling of irritation when I pictured our Mirage colleagues as they attended their Bastille barbecues on this hot mid-summer's day. I imagined, nonetheless, them wiping perspiration from their foreheads and I hoped that some, surely, would look up and say: "Permit us to come and help," but any such form of *beau geste* seemed unlikely and I knew that fanciful optimism had to be banished from my thoughts.

At this point the VC10 captain said that his crews' efforts to line up suitable diversion airfields in case we got into trouble were proving fruitless as none of the airfields in France would reply to radio calls; all of them, apparently, were closed. Moreover, said the captain, his VC10 was getting short of fuel, he could offer us a bit more fuel but then he'd have to return to base. "They're trying to organise another VC10 to take over from us," he added, "we're not sure of the timescale but hopefully relief should arrive in another thirty or so minutes."

As vexed calculations worked their way through my mind, including notions, as Robert Browning would have it, of how a man's reach should exceed his grasp, at this moment I had to admit to a sense of impotence. We had no maps of the local area, no specific diversion airfields, no current meteorological information, no radio contact with anyone apart from a retreating VC10. Our gallant Bears, however, persisted to soldier on.

It was at this stage that, in an odd twist, relief from our difficulties appeared to come from a most unlikely source: the Bears themselves. For having, no doubt, monitored our radio calls and become aware of our plight, the Bears promptly began to turn. Instead of pursuing their course towards the Bay of Biscay, the two Soviet machines now started to retrace their route back towards Ireland – a route that would take us towards our home base.

Perhaps, in an unspoken common bond between aviators, they had decided to react to our predicament. We'll not know, of course, but I do know that our situation soon became less precarious thanks to the actions of our official adversary. Maybe there was an element of self-interest – after all if one of the Bears encountered, say, a technical problem and was forced to ditch in the sea, then we'd be in a position to alert the rescue services and to circle the spot until help arrived. In that respect, perhaps the zombies welcomed our presence. I sometimes speculated what might happen if the scene was reversed – if we were the ones in need of assistance – and maybe today we glimpsed the answer.

As the White Cliffs of Dover started to loom in the distance, with each passing mile our circumstances began to improve. At length, another VC10 tanker turned up as promised and eventually we were able to hand over 'our' Bears to Norwegian fighters who escorted the Soviet machines on their way back to Murmansk in the north-west corner of Russia. Meanwhile, my navigator and I, older and wiser after our five-hour marathon, flew back, finally, to Leuchars.

When the post-flight paperwork had been completed, I knew that a number of issues had to be tackled. My mind seemed filled with visions, questions, contradictions. Our situation on this day had been in the hands of others and for one thing I continued to feel needles of irritation about the problems created by our French allies. Any form of *beau geste* appeared to be a conditional gesture and the concept of 'bon voyage' would seem less than appropriate when it came to Bastille Day.

CHAPTER 3

DISTANT HORIZONS

JOHN WALMSLEY'S RECORD-BREAKING FLIGHT

As the world began to breathe the early morning air and watch the first rays of the sun, this, I knew, was one of those rare moments in life when everything seemed to be unaccountably fine. Such sights were meant to be the privileged preserve of astronauts and, certainly, a couple of hundred miles above the earth's surface, astronauts could wonder at simultaneous spectacles – sunrise ahead, sunset behind – whereas in our Phantom, at five or so miles high, we had to wait six-and-a-half hours between sunset and sunrise. The feeling of exhilaration, nonetheless, was potent.

It was, as the Phantom flew across the Indian Ocean at longitude ninety degrees east, that I was able to observe the serene beauty, the vivid colours and the sweeping vistas of dawn. While I watched the horizon, and as a corner of the sky began to blossom gradually from crimson into subtle hues of orange and yellow, it was hard not to feel awed by nature's pageantry. Nature, though, had offered other recent surprises, too, as we'd progressed our planned flight from RAF Coningsby to Tengah in Singapore.

For this marathon task, four Phantoms (plus spares) from 54 Squadron (motto: 'Boldness endures anything') had been allocated. Two Flights of two Phantoms were involved, with the first Flight's departure on 18 May 1970 followed the next day by the second Flight. In my own case, I was in the second Flight as number two to a 54 Squadron flight commander. Victor tanker aircraft provided in-flight refuelling, while Avro Shackleton maritime patrol aircraft operating from Masirah Island in Oman and Changi in Singapore offered search and rescue facilities for the long and desolate flight across the Indian Ocean.

With the chief aim of proving that the Royal Air Force could deploy fighter aircraft rapidly to the Far East, an intriguing sideline of the exercise was to try to set a new world record for the non-stop flight between London and Singapore. For this, a Fédération Aéronautique Internationale competitors' licence was required

25

(mine was No 2628 signed by the secretary-general of the Royal Aero Club). In order to verify that the aircraft which arrived in Singapore were the same as those which had taken off from Coningsby, a lead seal was attached to a pipe in each of the Phantoms' rear cockpits. In addition, all of the Phantoms' engines, including those of the spare aircraft involved, were fitted with lead seals. Royal Aero Club observers were pre-positioned at Coningsby, Heathrow Radar and Tengah.

In the event of a Phantom having to ditch in the sea beyond helicopter range, the Shackletons planned to home onto our SARBE personal locator beacons before dropping dinghies along with water and food. Meanwhile, any friendly shipping in the area would be diverted to rescue us. In view of the urgent need for drinking water and because of the possible delay before the Shackletons could reach us, each Phantom pilot and navigator carried a solar still, a simple device designed to use the sun's rays to convert small amounts of sea water into distilled water (it was estimated that on a good day the solar still could produce over two litres of drinkable water). As no room was available in the tightly-packed ejection seat survival packs, the solar stills had to be carried in special holders underneath the torso harnesses on our chests.

As for flying dress, we were permitted to dispense with the immersion suits normally required for flights over the sea and to wear comfortable flying suits instead. When it came to the call of nature, so-called 'piddle packs' were supplied – a flat plastic bag arrangement which contained a compressed sponge to absorb fluid. Personally, I managed without one; perhaps the excitement of taking off from Lincolnshire to land in Singapore was sufficient incentive to go the whole way.

So it was that, at 11:49 on Tuesday 19 May 1970, a month and two days after the seemingly miraculous return to earth of the crippled Apollo 13 moon mission, our Flight of Phantoms took off. The start was not without difficulty: a faulty hydraulic pressure gauge in my aircraft meant a hasty change to a spare Phantom (XV482). Soon, though, the mission could commence as briefed. We conducted an echelon pairs formation take-off to climb up to an altitude of 30,000ft in order to rendezvous with two Victor tankers. In view of the rule that any world record attempt from London must begin within 50 km of Hyde Park Corner, we headed south initially so as to overfly London before turning left towards the Channel and the first in-flight refuelling session.

To ensure minimum loss of time, special techniques for in-flight refuelling had been agreed. Both Phantoms, having reduced their indicated airspeed to the required 290 knots, would refuel simultaneously before, on completion, accelerating again to a nominal cruise speed of Mach 0.9 at an altitude, ideally, of 33,000ft – parameters that would give the Rolls-Royce Spey engines the best chance of lasting the near-fifteen hours of continuous flight.

On completion of the initial refuel of 4,800lbs each, the first Victor tanker

John Walmsley (second from left) and crew before their flight.

peeled away to return to base while his colleague flew with us in a loose formation across France and towards Italy. Approaching the Mediterranean Sea the two Phantoms took on another 4,400lbs of fuel each so that both aircraft were fully fuelled by the time we reached a position just north of Corsica. At this stage the second Victor turned away and as the Phantoms continued on towards Cyprus, it was without an escort. Flying above the Mediterranean I was aware of the painful clarity of the light. Screwing up my eyes at the sun, I thought about the benign nature of the spring weather below. Before long the countryside could become unbearably hot but at present the weather would be balmy with light breezes and gentle rain in the night. Wild flowers would bloom in impossible places; across Cyprus, the sweet smell of orange blossom would be potent.

"The next rendezvous with Victor tankers should take place in one hour and ten minutes." My navigator Aubrey's voice cut through my reflective moments as he performed calculations. "Okay," I said. "That will be 120 miles west of Cyprus and we're due to meet up at an altitude of 27,000ft."

Using our high frequency (HF) radios we had, as pre-briefed, already made radio contact with the Victors some two hours before the planned rendezvous time. By making contact in this way we could take advantage of opportunities to adjust the original schedule, a flexibility which helped us to gain time wherever possible. Just south of Crete, for example, we had worked out that our fuel reserves were sufficient to permit an acceleration to low supersonic airspeed for a period.

In order to share the added strain of flying in a formation position, albeit a loose formation, the two Phantoms alternated as leader from time to time. We used a system of hand signals to indicate fuel state: a thumbs up meant a fuel state above 10,000lbs (the Phantom's maximum with three external tanks fitted was 22,500lbs); a thumbs down meant less than 10,000lbs, then fingers were held up for each 1,000lbs less than the planned amount.

When, eventually, Aubrey confirmed that he had radar contact with the Victors, at the appropriate point we descended for the briefed rendezvous procedure. Initially heading directly towards us, at a pre-calculated range of eighteen miles from our position the Victors turned onto a reciprocal heading. The Phantoms could then close with minimum delay onto the twin refuelling baskets by now trailing behind the allotted Victor tanker. At this juncture we needed a considerable quantity of fuel: 17,500lbs for each Phantom and by the end of the refuelling, the fuel-exhausted Victor turned away to land back at Akrotiri in Cyprus. The second Victor, meantime, accompanied the fighters for a while as we flew north towards Turkey.

As our flight above Turkey progressed, the sunset at 16:45 was marked by a riot of colours that began to spread across the horizon. The sight seemed somehow full of surprises; the more I looked, the more I saw. Below, remote villages faded as if refusing to acknowledge the end of the recent winter's hibernation. From a safe distance I could imagine the earthbound routines of daily life, of school schedules, of newspaper circulation, of food preparation, of small scenes of irony and tragedy.

By the northern reaches of Turkey the Victor had delivered a further 8,900lbs of fuel to each Phantom before turning back for Akrotiri. At this night-time stage of the flight, with light from a full moon glinting on the surface of Lake Van ahead, I turned on my cockpit lights and adjusted them to a suitable level of brilliance. I'd consumed a packed meal and, fatigued now, strived to avoid the temptation to fall into a doze followed by suddenly jolting awake. The moonlight's convenient gleam helped us to read our maps, and at a distance of over two hundred miles flare stacks from Persian Gulf oil fields shimmered and flickered in the night sky."The next tanker rendezvous will be over Masirah Island," Aubrey reminded me.

Thus it was that we continued on a south-easterly course towards Bahrain, Qatar, Abu Dhabi and the flare stacks, before we flew above Muscat and Oman where, incidentally, Qaboos bin Said, with the help of British military force, would stage a successful coup in a couple of months' time (he'd use the oil wealth to modernise and develop his country which would be renamed 'The Sultanate of Oman'). Beyond Muscat and Oman, our night-time rendezvous with two Victors over

Masirah Island at 19:32 worked well, and although in-flight refuelling in the dark could involve particular hazards, conditions were good and each Phantom took on 17,500lbs of fuel without difficulty before the first Victor left us.

Now, though, as we headed for the vastness of the Indian Ocean, a strong sense of isolation became predominant, even if our loneliness was appeased for a period as we held company with the remaining Victor tanker. This tanker eventually off-loaded 8,600lbs of fuel to each Phantom before it turned around to leave us on course for the fourth and final rendezvous – overhead Gan, a RAF station with the apposite, if uninspiring, motto of 'En Route' and positioned on the southernmost island of Addu Atoll, part of the larger group of islands which formed the Maldives. Having made contact with air traffic control at Gan, the controller cleared us to proceed south of latitude ten degrees north for the rendezvous with two more Victors. Proceedings worked out as arranged, but the smooth progress of events thus far was about to change. Trouble was brewing – big trouble.

It began with the radio. Sporadic crackles and intermittent interference heralded the approach of a storm while we took up an easterly heading beyond Gan. Events happened slowly at first and, as planned, we commenced another large fuel transfer. Mounting levels of turbulence, however, hinted at the tribulations that lay ahead. It was still dark but the moonlight was sufficient to make out some of the surrounding pandemonium before we entered thick cloud. An adjacent tower of cumulus was far from still; moonlight revealed that early streaks of cloud draped across the skies at insouciant angles were hastily hustled away as the storm advanced. Nature can put on a thrilling show, a paradoxical mix of violence and splendour, and the spectacle was dramatic. Even though I could not see the surface of the sea, I could imagine the waves in riotous crowds that raged, frothed, boiled and reached up with their white foam to be caught by the wind and whipped along the surface. A shiver of angst went through me. The thought of having to use my Martin Baker seat to eject in these conditions filled me with dread, as did the prospect, if matters turned seriously pear-shaped, of nothing but a small rubber dinghy to cope with the elements. Better, I reckoned, to think of something else; to hope and pray that, apart from anything else, the Rolls-Royce engines would keep going.

At this point, as we began to penetrate ever-thicker layers of cloud, we started to enter an increasingly wild and worrying world. Curious events followed one upon the other. The Phantom's cockpit canopy began to be bathed in an eerie blue glow. This, for me, was a spectacle as unbelievable as watching the moon burst into flames. The blue light of St Elmo's Fire seemed to quiver quietly as if in anticipation of its next performance which, when it came, involved an erratic dance across the windshield. The phenomenon looked extraordinary – especially as I had not experienced it before – and I learnt later that a St Elmo's event can sometimes be accompanied by a distinctive hiss or buzzing sound, although this could not be heard through the soundproofing of my bone dome helmet. If I pointed a finger at the windscreen's metal surround, static electrical discharges would jump from digit to metal (or was it from metal to digit?) – a rare and bizarre sight. Bizarre, too, was the luminous blue plasma display of St Elmo's Fire which began to flicker across the wings and airframe of our Victor tanker.

To accompany the fire, now we experienced the water. In positively biblical proportions rain was driven past the aircraft in horizontal sheets, like marauding waves of black liquid. The rain grew stronger and the turbulence increased as we progressed towards the heart of the storm. Out of the darkness, water was hurled against the Phantom's windscreen like a river rushing towards a boulder. Visibility was reduced to the point that it became impossible to see the Victor's wing lights. I was forced to hold formation on lights designed to highlight the rim of the refuelling basket – a technique that's not recommended, especially in heavy turbulence. I tugged at my seat straps to ensure that I was secured as firmly as possible into the Martin Baker seat.

As the Phantom was buffeted from side to side, a sense of tormented giddiness was hard to ignore. The Phantoms were hurled ferociously while cacophonies of crackles from lightning and booms of thunder, as if from great bass drums, burst from the heavens. Again and again the aircraft were thrown upwards, downwards, sideways; again and again, as our machines leapt and lurched like frenzied, demented creatures, we struggled on. Even so, and despite the occasional application of full dry (non-reheat) power to our Rolls-Royce engines (almost unheard of when in-flight refuelling), the battle was lost eventually when both Phantoms were propelled ignominiously, as if mere puppets at the deity's whim, from their refuelling baskets.

But we had managed to take on some fuel, sufficient at least to persist on an easterly course to fly through the storm. Between us we swiftly arranged height separation until, after what felt like an interminable period, all aircraft, battered if not bruised, were released from nature's clutches. The feeling of relief was startling, as if an unsettled monster's mighty fist had decided to slam us clear of trouble. Later, Aubrey (who at one stage during the storm had disconnected his cockpit intercommunication system in order to eat an apple which, he said, helped him to maintain a semblance of sanity) raised an index finger in the air, like a punctuation mark, as if to emphasise the point when he swore that he saw the other Phantom apply up to ninety degrees angle of bank while the pilot struggled to cope with the conditions.

Now, however, it was time to continue with the refuelling. The post-storm refuel was carried out in clear skies and uncannily benign conditions which enabled the Phantoms to take 17,500lbs of fuel each before the Victor returned to Gan. For the next 400 nautical miles, the other tanker accompanied us before the final refuel of 6,700lbs to each Phantom. As this Victor turned around to fly back to Gan, I was conscious of a somewhat sombre sense of silence caused by the absence of our tanker colleagues; without them, the undertaking would not have been possible.

Before long, more or less at the point that Aubrey confirmed that we were close to longitude ninety degrees east, the darkness started to melt away from the sky to reveal dawn's stunning display. I experienced unforeseen, strange emotions as the genesis before us seemed to arouse an awakened appreciation of our surrounds. The night's efforts had been conscientiously made, even though the results were more the product of perseverance than of good fortune, and now a fresh mood of optimism would dissolve earlier fears and trials. It was like entering a vast room filled with applause. Six-and-a-half hours had elapsed since the sunset over Turkey; now, with the arrival of a pristine dawn, a new determination prevailed.

While the sun persisted to pull the curtains on the day, the air was filled with light as if from a great chromatic symphony, a colour canvas of supernatural proportions. Eagerly, I scanned the horizon which became a neat, sharp line. All about me the flatness and infinity of the Indian Ocean appeared as an endless panorama of sea and sky. There was nothing to block the view, a hugeness which hit me like a blow in the stomach having become accustomed to six-and-a-half hours of night-time concealment. Below, I thought that I could detect a patch of oil that glimmered on the sea's surface. To one side, my colleagues flew along happily in their Phantom. Ahead, in the distance, I could spot the outline of a ship.

It was not long before we picked up on the aircraft high frequency radio something unexpected: the sound of a very British voice. Balanced, as I felt, on the cusp of the routine and the sublime, it was a sobering moment. A small thing, a mere detail, yet the airwaves brought a new sense of reality as I discerned the dulcet tones of a crew member of a Vickers VC10 transport aircraft – an aeroplane, which, during its long service between the first flight in June 1962 and retirement from the RAF in September 2013, achieved the fastest crossing from London to New York by a subsonic jet airliner (only the supersonic Concorde was faster), although it was not a contender in today's race. The airliner's radio was more powerful than ours so I was keen to take advantage of a useful relay facility. "Can you radio ahead to Tengah and Changi for weather forecasts?" I asked the VC10 captain. "No problem," came the reply, "standby."

The subsequent reports revealed good weather, furthermore the VC10 captain had obtained clearance from air traffic control for both Phantoms to carry out a high-speed, low-level fly-past at Tengah airfield. The senior controller at Tengah, nominated by the Royal Aero Club to act as their official timekeeper there, would press the stopwatch for our world record attempt. I breathed deeply and sighed. The marathon was drawing to a conclusion. As we commenced a high-speed descent from overhead Sumatra, we were told that a Lightning F6 from 74 Squadron would intercept and accompany us for the final stages of the flight.

Soon, when Singapore loomed, I was intrigued to observe this island country — a nation made up of sixty-three separate islands and positioned less than a hundred miles north of the equator. We'd been briefed that, on landing at Tengah, we should anticipate the tropical rainforest climate, the high humidity, the lack of distinctive seasons, and the abundant levels of rainfall. Also as part of pre-flight briefings, we'd learnt about, or been reminded about, some of Tengah's background.

Commissioned as a RAF base in 1939, in frantic and terrible scenes following Japan's entry into World War II, Tengah had been subjected to so-called 'carpet bombing' by Japanese bombers during the first air raid on Singapore shortly after the start of the Battle of Malaya. After the war, as part of Britain's military commitment to the Southeast Asia Treaty Organisation (SEATO, which was dissolved in 1977 when a number of members withdrew from the organisation), V bombers were stationed at Tengah. (Years later, I learnt that, according to classified documents declassified in the year 2000, Red Beard nuclear weapons were stowed there in a highly secret and secure weapons facility.)

From the mid 1960s, 74 Squadron, with the feisty motto of 'I fear no man' and equipped with equally feisty Lightning F6 aircraft, was based at Tengah where the squadron operated alongside Hawker Hunters from 20 Squadron and English Electric Canberras from 81 Squadron. All of this was about to change, however, and next year, in March 1971, the RAF would pull out of Tengah after which, over the next two or so years, the base would be handed over to the Singapore Air Defence Command (later the Republic of Singapore Air Force).

For the low-level fly-past at Tengah we flew at 540 knots, an airspeed which ensured that the Phantoms' presence was duly declared to one and all. It was as we broke into the airfield circuit and carried out checks before landing that I was struck, suddenly, with the notion that it was all over. The stopwatch had been pressed; the flight had been completed; in a single hop we had departed from Lincolnshire and arrived at Singapore – but had we broken any records?

The answer came as we taxied to the dispersal area after landing. The senior controller announced on the radio that our time, at 14 hours 6 minutes and 55.6 seconds, had beaten the previous day's timing of 14 hours and 14 minutes which had been achieved by a single Phantom (his colleague had been forced to land and remain at Gan following an undercarriage problem). Later, we worked out a few more statistics: the distance covered was recorded at 10,789.765 kilometres and the average speed was 764.266 kilometres per hour (474.89 miles per hour). Instead of the shortest 'great circle' route we had been required to fly the diplomatically cleared military route. No such constraint, however, applied to a civilian Boeing 707 which, with two crews and ferry tanks on board, a few weeks later flew the great circle route and thereby managed to beat our time, albeit only by minutes. The new world record meant that our own record had stood for just a matter of weeks.

In spite of this, we were presented with certificates by Prince William of Gloucester at the Royal Aero Club. Some members of our Boeing 707 competitors were present and, in a most convivial atmosphere, they treated us to a slap-up dinner after the ceremony. Our position as record holders had been brief but then, I mused, it was surely the taking part that mattered. Despite the anxieties and the hazards, the flight, for me, had been something which I would not have missed for the world.

John Walmsley (second from right) and crew with
HRH Prince William of Gloucester (centre).

CHAPTER 4

BLEAK CHOICE

STEVE GYLES' DILEMMA

The situation was hard to take in. Fire trucks rushed about, vehicles negotiated potholes and ridges carved within the rough airfield grass, Land Rovers raced here and there. No-one, though, came to my aid; those converging on the scene acted as if I was not there – as if I was invisible. Even the station commander, when he sallied forth in his car, disregarded me as he swept by. All and sundry seemed determined to ignore me, leaving me alone and bewildered by what had taken place.

Just a few moments ago, when a Land Rover fire truck had driven towards the scene, I'd pointed to the prostrate body of my navigator, and the truck had veered off in that direction. As if watching a slow motion replay of a horror movie, I now saw a fireman turn from the truck as he dashed across to drape a blanket over the navigator's body. In a split-second, gut-churning instant it occurred to me that my navigator was dead. The implications began to rush across the surface of my brain. One moment the two of us were performing routine, professional tasks until, quite promptly, matters had started to go wrong – seriously wrong. And now he was dead. I had killed him. Before today, we had not even met, let alone flown together. On my kneepad aide-memoire I'd even scribbled down his name in case I should forget it. It was my fault; I had forged his demise. Overwhelmed with a sense of unrestrained guilt, certain that I had betrayed the trust of a brave soul, I felt the kind of abject depression that must come, I imagine, to a soldier who realises that he has been fighting on the wrong side; a sensation of wretchedness that causes the mind to feel hollow and the cavity of the chest to become a vacuum. My distracted thoughts surmised the grieving of a family, the angry shouts, the aura of infraction.

While my feelings of despair persisted, eventually a large fire truck drew up and the driver yelled down to ask if I needed assistance. At last, I thought, someone's trying to help me. "Thanks," I said and went to climb up into the cabin. An agonising surge of back pain, however, foiled my attempts. With further savage twinges and with notions that I had foregone any justification for a tranquil future, I sank to the ground, lay down and waited for the ambulance.

Of course, it was not meant to have been this way. As far back as my schoolboy days I had always liked aircraft and been interested in aviation-related affairs. Indeed, I had boasted to my peer group of the intention to become a pilot. One day, when I was studying in the school library at Enfield Grammar School (a north London boys' school founded in 1588), a friend of mine announced that he had applied to join the Royal Air Force as an engineering officer. This news struck me like a thunderbolt. At that point still mulling over what to do, I had not contacted the recruiting authorities. However, intensely annoyed that my friend, so it seemed, had overtaken me (if I was to apply to join the service, how dare he beat me to it?) I sent off my application that very day. When summonsed to the recruitment centre, I managed to last the full five days of assessment (unlike my friend who was sent home after one day) at the end of which I was one of six to be accepted out of a total, I believe, of sixty applicants.

Good fortune continued for me when, after flight training, I was posted in 1968 to 11 Squadron at RAF Leuchars to fly Lightning aircraft. This proved, in a number of ways, a valuable precursor to my later posting onto F-4 Phantoms, and it was at an early stage of my time with 11 Squadron that I learnt in a most sobering manner of the need, one might say, to expect the unexpected, a key quality for successful operation of the versatile and demanding Phantom. For it was in the spring of 1970, when the Soviet air force (*Voyenno-Vozdushnye Sily*) decided, sillily, to celebrate the centenary of the birth of that amazing gremlin in the Kremlin, Comrade Vladimir Lenin, that by chance I became involved in this heroic event. On QRA duty over the night 22/23 April 1970, I awoke with a start in the small hours, at around 04:00, when an inconspicuous-looking 'squawk' box in one corner of the pilot's crewroom started to make strange sounds. At once, I tumbled out of bed – pilots on QRA duty were allowed to sleep as long as they remained in flying gear – and dashed across the room to listen closely. The controller's detached voice now reverberated from the box: "Leuchars, Leuchars, this is Buchan...alert two Lightnings."

As the nominated Q1, the first to go in the event of a scramble, the other pilot, despite looking as bleary-eyed as I felt, ran with admirable élan out to his aircraft. As the Q2 pilot, I set off the scramble alarm, acknowledged the Buchan controller's call, scribbled down the time, then sprinted to my Lightning. For a brief period, both pilots sat in their individual cockpits before the controller's voice crackled through our bone dome earpieces when he ordered the Q1 Lightning to scramble. When my colleague was safely airborne, the controller stood me down from cockpit readiness but by that stage I was too worked-up to think of going back to sleep. I therefore made myself a cuppa and sat quietly in the crewroom to await developments. Developments soon began to develop. I was aware of frenetic activity as squadron personnel were summoned to their places of duty, and surrounding hustle and bustle became increasingly hectic as more Lightnings were made ready for QRA back-up duties. In the meantime, a series of conversations with the Buchan controller kept me updated with the overall scenario.

My colleague returned just as dawn was breaking. He explained how, in pretty much pitch-black conditions, he had shadowed two Soviet bombers which he reckoned were Tu-95 Bear D aircraft. As we talked about his flight, suddenly the squawk box came to life again. "Leuchars, this is Buchan," said the controller, who sounded a bit breathless this time, "alert two Lightnings." A small but significant hesitation followed after which, most unusually, he went on: "and as many more as you can manage." The controller's tone sounded almost plaintive when he continued: "we have eighty plus unidentified tracks coming round the North Cape."

For a second or so we two pilots stared at each other in astonishment. We said nothing, but our thoughts seemed to coincide: eighty plus? Is he bonkers? Has he lost the plot? Has World War III broken out? This, though, was no moment to prevaricate and as we set off the scramble alarm I made a dash for my aircraft (the Q1 machine was in the process of engineering turn-round). My carefully placed bone dome, judiciously laid-out cape leather flying gloves and thoughtfully positioned seat straps facilitated rapid progress as I leapt into the cockpit, plugged-in my personal equipment connector (PEC) and buckled up the seat straps. Very soon, when I spoke with the controller, he gave height, heading and other details as he ordered me to scramble and to maintain radio silence.

The start-up and take-off procedures went without a hitch and before long, just as pale shafts of dawn sunlight began to emerge across the area, I flew the Lightning in a north-easterly direction. With my airborne radar, navigational aids, and 'identification friend or foe' system switched off to thwart the possibility of tactical information being passed on by eavesdroppers, I had to keep a good lookout for other aircraft. Old-fashioned navigational techniques were needed to plot the Lightning's position and from time to time this could be verified by peering down at fixed-position North Sea oil installations. After thirty or so minutes, when approaching the general area briefed by Buchan, I reckoned it was about time to break radio silence. Glancing inside the cockpit, I therefore switched on the identification friend or foe system, the navigational aids and the AI23B airborne radar. The radar took some moments to warm up but when it had done so, and when I squinted through the fold-up rubber viewing shade of the radar's B-scope display, what I saw made my pulse start to race and my brain cells to go into overdrive. The radar revealed mass contacts too numerous to count up. I had expected something unusual, but this was overwhelming; my mind became a turmoil of conflicting thoughts as I struggled to absorb the implications of such a mass of hostile images.

While the mass contacts of 60...70...80 (who knows?) contacts which, as if raging bulls bent on widespread death and destruction, bore down on my sole Lightning, I spoke with the controller at RAF Saxa Vord. The controller confirmed that my radar information was correct and that the incoming hordes now ranged from twenty to sixty miles from my current position. "Copied," I tried to sound nonchalant but my voice had become annoyingly shrill. I swallowed hard, continued to study the radar screen and wondered what the hell to do next.

In a way, though, the dilemma was resolved for me when I visually spotted the first wave of Soviet aircraft. From that moment, more or less, my radar became redundant as I concentrated on the visual picture outside the cockpit. The Soviet hordes, mainly Tu-16 Badger and Tu-95 Bear aircraft, seemed to have organised themselves into groups of finger-four formation. Selecting a nearby group, I manoeuvred the Lightning for an interception and visident (visual identification) procedure. My nerves, as may be expected, were on edge; every move appeared to assume excessive significance. Having closed onto the selected group of Soviet machines and identified them as Tu-16 Badger aircraft, it was time to take photographs. Using a special 35mm camera with an automatic wind-on facility and plenty of film, I moved to the rear of the formation, took a photograph of both sides and underneath Badger number four, then moved on to the next machine.

Just as I completed the photo shoot of the formation's third Badger, my peripheral vision picked up a shadow passing over the Lightning's cockpit. I glanced up to see another formation of four Badgers cross about 500ft above me. This seemed suddenly to emphasise the surreal nature of what was happening around me; as if caught up in some kind of crazy dream, I felt the need to pinch myself to return to reality. A small voice within me whispered, "Well I'll be darned."

The situation, though, was no mere flight of fancy. There was a job to be done and before long, when I was joined by a Victor in-flight refuelling tanker, my Lightning's fuel tanks were filled to full. For the next one-and-a-half hours, as I moved from one Soviet formation to the next, I was able to photograph proceedings for posterity. Never before had we seen such masses and never, hopefully, were we likely to do so again. The reaction of Soviet crews was intriguing: some would studiously ignore us and these Bears and Badgers presumably had political observers on board.

Crews on the non-political machines seemed to react altogether differently –

almost festively – with chicken legs, drink cans, maybe even the odd tumblers of vodka waved around happily. After all, I had to remind myself, this was supposed to be some kind of bizarre birthday bash. If, from time to time, I asked Saxa Vord for 'pigeons' (i.e. heading and distance) to base, some of the Soviet crews would helpfully hold a map against one of their side windows and point. I became increasingly amazed by the turn of events. I had become embroiled in the affair by chance and, ridiculously, I seemed, along with the Victor crew and another Lightning that eventually entered the fray, to represent the entire people of the Western world.

It was the following day, as I thumbed through the pages of various newspapers, that I came across a copy of one of my photographs in *The Daily Telegraph* with the caption: 'Strike Command pilots are becoming increasingly adept at "Bear hunting" and although unable to communicate with the Russian aircrews, appropriate hand signals are invariably exchanged.'

Without doubt, all of this provided appropriate background experience for some years later when, following a further tour in the Lightning force and a tour as an instructor at the Tactical Weapons' Unit at RAF Brawdy in South Wales, I was posted to fly the McDonnell Douglas F4 Phantom FG1 with 43(F) Squadron based at RAF Leuchars. The Phantom was different to the Lightning in a great many respects. Some eight feet longer than the Lightning and with a wingspan that was nearly four feet greater, the Phantom was a two-crew machine with the advantage of a more advanced radar system, carried considerably more fuel, and could be equipped with eight air-to-air missiles instead of just two. Although a Lightning F7 with extended fuselage, improved radar and missile systems, variable geometry wings and other novel features had been considered, the machine was never built and government decision-makers evidently opted for the versatile Phantom as an alternative.

The Phantom, although it lacked variable geometry wings, nonetheless had a complex – some would say over-complex – system of boundary layer control to facilitate lower airspeeds for approach and landing. The Phantom had other quirks too, and from the ex-Lightning pilot's point of view, a key issue was the concept of working with a navigator – of crew co-operation – an area which some Lightning pilots found difficult having been drilled for years in the art of self-sufficiency.

It was in November 1977, with a faint wintry sun hovering on the horizon, that I prepared with my navigator for a training flight in Phantom FG1 XV571 ('A') with another Phantom as leader of the pair. It could seem that pre-flight briefings in the Phantom world went on and on much longer than for Lightning flights but eventually, when all four crew members were satisfied, we signed the necessary paperwork then walked out to our aircraft. Looking back, I clearly recall a sense of anxiety, a fine, high-drawn tension – a disquiet within my mind as if by some premonitory process I knew that trouble lay ahead.

Before long, after start-up routines, I began to follow the other machine as we taxied to the take-off point. In order to ground manoeuvre the Phantom, the pilot had to press a small button on his control stick which, when combined with appropriate rudder movement, turned the nose-wheel. This nose-wheel steering system was generally reliable but on occasions could give trouble. I had no idea at that moment, of course, that its malfunction was about to force dire spilt-second decisions.

At 09:30, as the lead Phantom commenced its take-off run, I pressed my stopwatch. The leader accelerated with a roar down Leuchars' long runway and climbed out towards Balmullo quarry. After thirty seconds, I released my Phantom's brakes, and eased both throttles forward with my left hand in order to select full power on the twin Rolls-Royce Spey engines. Although my main focus was outside the cockpit, I glanced occasionally at the instrument panel to check the indications. At 70 knots, all appeared fine. At 90 knots the aircraft still felt okay until, just as the airspeed indicator reached about 100 knots, the Phantom began to veer to the right. I checked the engine dials; both engines were synchronised; nothing wrong there. However, my heart missed a beat when, despite a judicious application of rudder, the aircraft persisted to swing right. I dabbed firmly at the left brake to try to control the swing, but without success. Then, quite abruptly, the aircraft snapped sharply to the right. By now the Phantom's airspeed was around 130 knots, but despite full left brake and full left rudder, the machine continued to slide to starboard. At once, I brought both throttles back to the idle position to abort take-off.

At this point, time seemed to go berserk. My brain cells became clogged with a rapid and chaotic overload of data. There was a shocked silence in the cockpit; perhaps my navigator and I pondered our imminent destruction; the touch-paper had been lit, now we had to hold our breath and wait for the detonation. This came quite quickly. As the Phantom left the runway, the 20-or-so ton machine hit the grass at an airspeed of around 100 knots. Suddenly, in my left rear view mirror, I spotted an explosion of flame. Glancing over my left shoulder I expected to see the left wing on fire but immediately realised that my navigator had ejected; the ball of flame had been caused by his canopy ejector igniters.

With a sinking sensation, I knew the need was for an extremely quick decision. "I hope you know what you're doing," said a small voice within me. Curious, haphazard thoughts raced through my head and three, in particular, printed themselves firmly on the memory cells. I still recollect them to this day. Firstly: what did the navigator know that I did not? Secondly: a board of inquiry would be convened whether I ejected out of the aircraft or not. Thirdly: I had always wanted a 'Martin Baker' tie (awarded by the ejection seat manufacturers to aircrew who escaped by means of a Martin Baker seat).

Thrust into an obscure, disembodied timescale, I now had further worries. Aware of a previous F-4 accident when the navigator had been killed when hit by the pilot's canopy during an ejection sequence, I felt compelled to delay my own ejection. However, the brain, it seems, will transmit complex information with greater-than-normal rapidity in high-stress situations – what might be described as an exponential rate of cerebral activity. For it was later, as the duly convened board of inquiry examined the evidence, that board members discovered a remarkable fact: a period of a little less than half-a-second had elapsed between my initial observation of flames, the three main thought processes that went through my head, the deliberate attempt at delay, and the ejection procedure itself.

As I pulled the bottom ejection seat handle, the force of the seat's movement threw my head down sharply. Now, in bizarre and random images, I experienced snapshot pictures including, I recall, one of the Phantom's canopy arch. This was followed by a sense of blackness. I was aware of a general roaring sound, a series of violent jerks which reminded me of a London Underground train at high speed in a tunnel, then briefly nothing. My eyes must have been closed but when I opened them it was to glimpse a view of forest above my head before the parachute swung over to place me the right way up with feet pointing towards Mother Earth. Oddly, I realised that before me was a rather fine view of the St Andrews Old Course ninth hole which was enjoyed by the golfing fraternity. Any illusion of enjoyment, however, was quickly dispelled. In another snapshot image, I spotted my navigator's parachute and realised that I was overtaking him fast. I became aware that the ejection seat's bottom handle remained in my grasp. Then I realised that I was still attached to the seat itself and that my parachute, therefore, would have to cope with the equivalent weight of two bodies. With a 16ft diameter parachute, a single body would result in a firm landing, but with two bodies...

I hit terra firma very firmly. I landed on my backside on the runway itself and never before or since has 'terra' ever felt 'firma'. Later, I likened the impact to landing on one's backside after jumping onto concrete from a 10ft high wall – ouch! Indeed, the shock of landing had fractured my spine, although I did not appreciate this at the time. I lay motionless on the runway for what felt like ages; the force of impact had knocked air from my lungs and I struggled to find breath. Eventually, though, I was able to sit up before attempting to release the parachute. This caused difficulty as the Americans, always keen to do things differently, had designed parachute Koch fasteners whose operation bore absolutely no resemblance to the familiar British 'turn and twist' system. At length I remembered what to do, released the parachute and the dinghy pack, then disconnected and removed my bone dome before struggling to my feet.

The situation seemed increasingly surreal. Maybe I sought that moment of grace when decisions appeared of their own volition. The reality, though, was altogether different as my mind absorbed the surrounding scene with a growing sense of bewilderment. About 40 yards away, where the Phantom was bogged down in long grass, the aircraft emitted a peculiar whining sound like a wounded creature. Before ejecting, I had managed to stopcock one engine but the other Rolls-Royce Spey continued on its merry way as if unclear what else to do. I turned around to spot, about 60 yards distant, some parachute silk and my navigator's legs. Then, above the racket of the Rolls-Royce Spey, I heard another sound, that of engine noise from a fast approaching Land Rover fire tender. When the driver saw me, I gave a thumbs up sign to indicate that I was okay. I pointed at my navigator while simultaneously attempting to run towards his prostrate body, though my efforts to run were restricted by back pain. The Land Rover sped towards the navigator, attendant crewmen leapt out, then one of them returned for a blanket which he draped over the navigator's body.

Convinced that my navigator was dead and that it was my fault, I turned round and began to walk away slowly. With emotional tripwires adding to the turmoil in my head, I experienced a mounting sense of desolation. As if imprisoned within a sure and timeless torment caused by inconceivable acts, it seemed impossible that I should ever be able to forgive myself. An abyss loomed: liberation from this form of purgatory would be beyond my reach.

By now, as numerous vehicles converged on the scene, the wilderness of Leuchars' normally quiet and remote runway had been turned into the equivalent of London's

XV571 'A' well-bedded down in the snow. The squadron commander
wasn't happy as it was his aircraft.

Hyde Park Corner in rush hour. While I hardly anticipated the attendance of a beautiful girl with skirts that swayed about her hips as she hurried to help me, neither did I expect an apparent land of wolves and wild dogs as everybody raced in every conceivable direction apart from mine. When he swept by grandly in his car, the station commander did not even glance in my direction. This, thankfully, was not the case for the driver of a large fire engine who, when he drove by, shouted down to ask if I wanted a lift to the medical centre. "Thanks," I said but my attempt to climb into the vehicle's cab was thwarted by savage twinges of back pain; I was unable to lift my foot above knee height. I therefore sank to the ground, lay down and waited for the ambulance.

Although I felt a sense of relief at the eventual arrival of the ambulance, my tortured thoughts almost expected a medical attendant to jump out and poke me with a foot. Perhaps my distracted state might have reckoned the attendant to be an old hag with strands of hair tied behind her head, her mouth wide open to reveal but a single tooth, though in reality the medic proved to be competent and kindly. I was strapped into a metal stretcher before the ambulance driver set off for Ninewells Hospital in Dundee. Crossing the Tay Bridge, I was aware of a conversation between the driver and the medic about money needed for the bridge toll. Both men claimed to be without cash at which the driver said: "No problem," and activated his ambulance siren and flashing blue lights thus allowing us to pass through the toll station without delay or cost.

At Ninewells Hospital – reputed, incidentally, to be the largest teaching hospital in Europe and an establishment internationally renowned and respected for introducing laparoscopic (keyhole) surgery – I lay disconsolately in bed for some two or three hours until a doctor turned up to reveal the news of multiple fractures to my lower spine and a dislocated coxis. "And your navigator," he added, "has a broken leg."

My mind went into overdrive. "A broken leg?" I asked. "Yes." If my navigator is dead, I thought, then a broken leg would seem to be something of a detail. "And I'm glad to say," went on the good doctor, "that your navigator has regained consciousness." "He has?" I was aware that my eyebrows might have lifted almost to the back of my head. Seized by a new mood of optimism, for the first time in about three-and-a-half hours I actually smiled.

The following day, the president of the board of inquiry told me that I was not to blame for the accident. "The evidence shows," he said, "that moisture in the nose-wheel steering system caused an electrical short as a result of which the nose-wheel ran away some 70 degrees to starboard." Many years later, I learnt by chance of an additional problem which was not discovered until the Phantom FG1 was taken out of service. A gyro designed to feed information to the nose-wheel steering system was found in aircraft XV571 ('A') to be flapping about loosely on its mounting system. There were no signs of the retaining bolts. It seemed that although the system usually coped, on that particular day I hit the jackpot, as they say – information which gave me a sense of closure over an issue which had niggled at my mind for years.

After a week in Ninewells Hospital, the navigator, Flight Lieutenant Andy Moir, and I were both transferred to the Royal Air Force Hospital at Ely. "Ah - Flight Lieutenant Moir," said the pretty ward nurse at Ely, "you're the young man who ejaculated." Flight Lieutenant Moir, of course, let out a spontaneous guffaw which caused the nurse's face to redden before she left in a fluster. When she returned, avoiding my navigator's amused stare, the nurse said: "Flight Lieutenant Gyles? I believe that you are the other one who ej… ej…baled out over Scotland."

Four months later we were both declared fit to fly. My check-out with the squadron's qualified flying instructor had to be curtailed shortly after take-off when one of the engines suddenly emitted a loud bang before it surged and had to be shut down. After this, the squadron's navigators began to think that I was jinxed and no-one seemed too happy to fly with me for a while. Other than that, I managed to complete my tour without further dramas. When I was posted from the squadron, my regular navigator, Flight Lieutenant Lawley, crewed-up with another pilot. One day in January 1981, almost exactly a year after I had left the squadron, a nose-wheel steering problem on take-off caused Bob Lawley to eject from his Phantom. This time, the pilot did not abort but performed the Phantom's first-ever soft ground take-off. The machine's stabilators carved gouges along the airfield grass which provided proof enough of the narrowness of his escape. Did he make the right decision? As some might say: 'You pays your money and you takes your choice…" In both this case and mine, it was a bleak choice indeed.

CHAPTER 5

TRUE WITNESS

PHIL OWEN'S DISAGREEMENT WITH HQ

I sensed a sudden surge of adrenaline. Dawn had crept away and now, as I took up a north-easterly heading across the North Sea, an air of anticipation dominated the atmosphere in the cockpit of our 111 Squadron Phantom FGR2 XV401. It was early on a clear and cloudless morning in 1978, the fine autumnal colours of the Scottish mainland had faded into the distance and now, as my navigator searched ahead for the reported Soviet aircraft, he was operating his radar system with the touch of the true professional. We worked together as a constituted crew (we remained 'paired' for almost two years) which doubtless contributed to our common competency. He instructed me to make occasional heading changes then he cried abruptly: "Hold it there!" and from the tone of his voice I knew that he reckoned to have picked up the required radar return.

At this stage an interlude of speculation was inevitable. I stared in front to try to spot the 'intruder' visually although this would take a while yet as the Soviet machine was still a considerable distance away. From our height of around 30,000 feet, I glanced at the sea's surface and noted the position of isolated North Sea oil installations. These provided useful navigational aids for aviators – a peripheral benefit, of course, and from the larger perspective I could recollect how, in the mid 1960s and just a year or so before I joined the RAF, British Petroleum's rig *Sea Gem* had discovered gas in the West Sole Field, a cause of much excitement and conjecture. The celebrations, though, had been short-lived because the *Sea Gem,* as it was moved away from the discovery well, had capsized when two of the support legs crumpled and broke. Equipment and personnel had been thrust into the sea's dire winter temperatures with the consequent loss of over a dozen lives. The hazards of North Sea exploration had been highlighted, nevertheless activity continued apace especially after the oil crisis of the early 1970s when the price of oil quadrupled.

At present, when I stared down at the installations and the way that their numbers appeared to grow exponentially, I could comprehend the significance of their presence. Naturally, though, I could not appreciate at this stage the unexpected and curious way in which they would affect our immediate task. "I'll hold our current height and heading, Al," I said to my navigator. "Okay," he muttered, clearly engrossed, "that's fine."

Apart from the uncertainties of the situation, I had other concerns too. A few minutes ago, just as we'd completed an in-flight refuelling session with a Handley Page Victor tanker, the controller had announced that we'd be taken off our planned training sortie in order to intercept and identify a Soviet aircraft flying past Norway's North Cape. The Soviet machine had been tracked by NATO radars and was now heading in our direction. However, as our Phantom was not on QRA duty, the aircraft was not armed and we were not equipped with the obligatory QRA camera. These accoutrements were reserved for the aircraft formally assigned to QRA duty at our base at RAF Leuchars. On the plus side, at least I had the benefit of a couple of tours of experience on the English Electric Lightning. Both of these tours had been at RAF Gütersloh in Germany, a base close to the border between West Germany and the German Democratic Republic. My background experience there had been useful in a general sense, although I was conscious that the scenario in Germany had been altogether different from my present one.

I could recollect, for instance, how the short distance to the border (a matter of minutes of flying time in a Lightning) had meant that the QRA commitment (known locally as 'battle flight') at Gütersloh had involved particular demands. When ordered to scramble, the Lightnings were expected to be airborne in double-quick time, usually within a couple of minutes. This meant that the iniquitous Iron Curtain, more correctly known as the Inner German Border and which stretched for nearly 900 miles to separate east from west, had to be approached with considerable precision. For this man-made obscenity, which comprised massive rolls of barbed wire, minefields, floodlights, special dog-runs, carefully combed sandy strips, anti-vehicle ditches, booby traps, automatic alarms and a series of tall watchtowers manned by some 50,000 armed guards, could be the cause of an almighty rumpus if crossed by one of our aircraft. Unless ordered to do so, we were not allowed to enter a so-called buffer zone let alone cross the border itself.

Towards the end of 1976, when the Lightning squadron (19[F] Squadron) on which I served was about to disband before reforming with Phantoms, we were visited by a legendary figure of the Lightning world. I'd heard about this man when I was a youngster, perhaps at around the time when I'd realised that my destiny was not to sit in an office to work at a desk. The man was Roland Prosper 'Bee' Beamont CBE, DSO and bar, DFC and bar, Croix de Guerre (Belgium – awarded posthumously in 2002), retired wing commander, fighter ace shot down in 1944 and made a prisoner of war after his 492nd operational mission, chief test pilot at the British Aircraft Corporation, chief test pilot of the P1/Lightning test programme, Lightning ace *extraordinaire* and all-round good egg, and with whom, fortunately, I got on well. To prove the point I have a photograph taken after our flight together in a twin-seat Lightning T4 trainer. Although I was the safety pilot for the flight, he flew the sortie from start to finish with little input from me. He had not flown a Lightning for some years but it was evident that he had lost none of his core handling skills. After the flight he presented me with a pair of gold Lightning cufflinks as a thank you.

Unlike the battle flight set-up at Gütersloh, the QRA scrambles from Leuchars tended to be more leisurely affairs; it was not uncommon for crews to receive advance warning of a scramble when NATO radars tracked the progress of Soviet aircraft flying from the direction of Norway. Due preparations could be made and sometimes the controller would state a time by which the aircraft were to be manned. This, though, was not always the case and sometimes, in unplanned circumstances, the controller might announce abruptly: "Leuchars alert two Phantoms" at which point all hell would be let loose as everyone reacted. Unplanned, too, was today's exceptional task.

"Target now 15 miles ahead," said Al, my navigator, as he continued to count down the range. My heartbeat began to quicken. Soon he would order a turn as he continued to work out an accurate intercept geometry. I re-checked around the cockpit...flight instruments, engines, fuel, oxygen, warning panels. Confident that all was in order, I returned my focus to the scene outside the cockpit for I hoped to pick up the target visually at any moment now.

"For displacement, turn left through 30 degrees," said Al. I turned the Phantom as instructed and persisted to search the sky. It was not long before Al went on, "Standby for a right turn onto target's heading." A tense silence followed this announcement. Perhaps in the ensuing seconds I went over in my mind the intriguing, if potentially hazardous, prospects. Then, after his next command, "Turn right now," I spotted something: juxtaposed against the morning sky, a small dot on the horizon wavered and began to materialise slowly into the shape of an aircraft. Gradually, as the dot enlarged, I was able to work out that this was a fairly large aircraft with dimensions similar to those of a Handley Page Victor.

My navigator continued to call out our range from the target until eventually, in a confident tone, I told him to look away from his radar to make a visual assessment of the type; our combined evaluation should provide a correct analysis. "It's a Badger 'G'," he said, a judgment with which I agreed. I stared at the Tupolev TU-16's (NATO code-named Badger) swept wings which spanned just over 100ft (the Victor's wingspan was 110ft), the twin engines close to the fuselage behind the pilot's cockpit, the large red stars daubed on the wings and tail, the remote gun turrets with AM-23 cannon built into the dorsal and ventral, the manned and massive-looking gun turret in the aircraft's tail.

Under each wing the Badger carried Raduga KSR-2 (NATO code-named AS-5 Kelt) air-to-surface missiles. These missiles, each of them nearly 30ft in length and with a wingspan of over a dozen feet, looked enormous, absurdly so, and not dissimilar to WWII V1 'doodlebugs'. At briefings given by our squadron intelligence officer some of this dated Soviet equipment could seem like a joke but now, face-to-face with the real thing, it appeared less amusing for the Kelts could be fitted with one-megaton nuclear warheads. "We'll hold a position to the starboard side of this bugger," I said to Al, "and see what develops." So it was that for some time the two aircraft, Badger and Phantom, remained in a loose formation like two hostile sharks each waiting for the first to stir up trouble.

The Badger made the first move. At a range of about 150 miles from the United Kingdom coastline the bomber initiated a descent. Maintaining our position on the right side, we followed the Soviet machine as it slowly reduced height. While we descended, and as I searched for signs of crew members taking photographs of us, I was conscious of some of my previous experiences intercepting Soviet Tu-95 (NATO code-named Bear) aircraft. Certain versions of the Bear had prominent observation blisters on the fuselage sides which offered photographic opportunities for the crews. This in turn offered the interceptors good, sometimes comical, opportunities too. For the Bear photographers, who tended to use tripod-mounted cameras, took a fair amount of time to assemble their apparatus. From my cockpit I was able to judge the moment when the photographer, having completed necessary preparations, was about to take his picture. At that point I'd move to the Bear's other side and the photographer would be obliged to re-arrange his tripod. When he was settled, I'd move back to the other side again. After a few cycles of this pantomime the photographer's abusive gestures were a sight to behold.

Today, though, I saw no sign of a photographer's tripod and while we continued down I chatted with my navigator as we tried to anticipate the bomber's actions. We were aware that it was not unusual for a Badger to go through the motions of the launch of an AS-5 Kelt missile before simulating the post-launch profile of the weapon. After about ten minutes in the descent, we reached an altitude below 5,000ft by which stage I moved in to hold a closer formation position off the Badger's right wing.

"I reckon he's heading for one of the oil rigs," said Al as he monitored his radar picture. By this point we expected the Badger to level off but the machine carried on down to end up, much to our surprise, well below 500ft. "He's aiming for the gap between those oil platforms ahead," said Al. "We're below the height of the main decks," I said, "I think we'd better ease back." It was evident that if the Badger turned to the right and I held the current formation position we could end up in the sea. Indeed, when the Soviet machine finally levelled off at a height below 250ft to fly between the oil platforms, the Badger was lower than the height of the platforms' helidecks. Like castaways on a far-flung island, oil workers could be seen staring down at the aircraft. At length, when the Badger had completed the profile, the machine set a heading for its home base which was our cue to head for ours.

Before long, after landing the Phantom at Leuchars, we were required to complete paperwork which included an intelligence report to send off to headquarters as swiftly as possible. It was fanciful, of course, but I speculated on the anonymous type who would receive and analyse our intelligence report. I pictured a man in a room darkened by a lowered lamp shade through which thread-like rivulets of light streamed, someone whose eyes roved as he spoke and who rubbed a nervous thumb and forefinger together as he contemplated our account. He'd be a crafty type, I decided, outwardly keen on things like pelmanism and calisthenics, although in reality he'd be a clumsy individual, a man who, the more he tried, the clumsier he would become. Worried by the thrust of our report, he would bite his lip theatrically and stare straight ahead.

A few days elapsed before we heard back from HQ but when we did, my navigator and I were stunned. For some moments we were speechless: perhaps, after all, my surmise had been correct. 'Your account is an exaggeration,' stated the intelligence fellow from the clean, white building that housed HQ, 'Soviet pilots are extremely well-disciplined and would never fly such low profiles.'

"This is outrageous," said Al. "Appalling," I agreed. "How dare HQ doubt our word?" Aghast, aflame with thoughts of David and Goliath, I was fired to positively biblical levels of indignation. "We should contact the oil rig workers. They saw what happened. They'll confirm our report." Still in a state of high dudgeon, we talked the matter through but at length decided that it would be unrealistic to try to trace the oil workers. Furthermore, as we had no photographic evidence, how could we prove to others what we had seen with our own eyes?

"HQ have not listened," I said shaking my head woefully. "The bastards just have not listened." "Maybe they prefer not to listen. It seems that the intelligence people are not very intelligent." "But we saw what we saw," I felt deflated, as if dropped like a shot bird.

Yet something still pulled at me, not as if someone had grabbed my arm, but something subtler and less physical. I continued to feel a burning irritation that our report, truthful and accurate as it was, had been so summarily dismissed. Then it occurred to me that the Soviet pilot himself could verify our account. A meeting under current circumstances would be impractical, of course, but perhaps one day such a meeting could take place. In a bizarre twist, it was this thought which eventually helped to calm me down and allow my sense of outrage to abate.

CHAPTER 6

SHORT TRIP

DAVID ROOME'S QUICK DECISION

It was March 1977 and darkness had fallen already. I was about to undertake a late-night sortie but when I glanced outside the airfield lights showed up a steady stream of fine drizzle. In spite of the conditions I was determined that my enthusiasm should not be dampened; as a member of 23 Squadron I would adhere to the spirit of our squadron motto: '*Semper Aggressus*' ('Always on the Attack'). Perhaps I was conscious that among the squadron's famous forbears of more than forty-five or so years ago was Group Captain Sir Douglas Bader. Back then, despite orders that forbade unauthorised aerobatics below 2,000ft, Bader had decided that such orders should be treated as advisory. In December 1931 he had performed low-level aerobatics at Woodley airfield, Berkshire in a Bristol Bulldog, apparently on a 'dare'. His aircraft had crashed when the tip of its left wing touched the ground and in his logbook Bader had made the laconic entry: 'Crashed slow rolling near ground. Bad show'. Even though he lost both legs in the accident which very nearly killed him, Bader went on to become one of the RAF's highest scoring aces in World War II and therefore a role model to us all. I was not to know, of course, the extent to which his examples of quick reactions were about to be needed in my own case.

Based at RAF Wattisham in Suffolk from the mid 1970s, 23 Squadron had been re-equipped with the Phantom FGR2 following a period at RAF Leuchars where the squadron had operated the English Electric Lightning. As an ex-Lightning pilot myself, I had gained experience in the squadron's role of air defence – experience which, in a general sense, was about to prove more than a little useful. My time on the Lightning force had included a tour in the Far East where, based at RAF Tengah, I'd been a member of 74 (F) Squadron equipped with the Mark 6 version of the Lightning. One day, following some practise interception exercises in co-operation with a high-flying RB-57F aircraft of the United States Air Force (USAF),

I was offered an unplanned chance to in-flight refuel to full tanks. On completion of the refuel the Lightning was positioned off the east coast of Malaysia and some 300 miles north of Tengah – ideally placed for a high-speed, high-altitude dash back to base. I called air traffic control and was cleared to proceed. Now I was about to embark on a remarkable and unusual voyage of opportunity.

Having selected full cold power on the Lightning's throttles, I initiated a climb to the aircraft's subsonic service ceiling of 50,000ft. When settled at that height, I rocked the twin throttles outboard and pushed them fully forward to select maximum reheat on both of the Rolls-Royce Avon engines. As the Lightning accelerated without fuss through the sound barrier, I had to watch the Machmeter carefully for at such altitudes there was nothing outside the cockpit to offer an impression of relative speed. Mach 1.4...Mach 1.5...Mach 1.6...before long the indicator was edging up towards Mach 2.0 at which speed I smoothly, and rather gingerly, pulled back the control column. When the Lightning climbed up through 60,000ft, then on up to 65,000 – 70,000 – 75,000ft, this was, for me, new and exotic territory.

Nevertheless, on the basis that, as they say, you can't make an omelette without breaking eggs, I decided to keep going. However, various unfamiliar symptoms, some subtle, some not so subtle, started to make me feel increasingly ill at ease. In order to hold the climb attitude I had to bring the stick further and further back. Eventually, just shy of 88,000ft when the Lightning at last ran out of steam, the stick was firmly on the backstops; I had no further elevator control and the nose lowered of its own accord. The ailerons, though, remained responsive and when I rolled the aircraft to look down vertically I suffered a strange, disconcerting sensation – a bit like being balanced on the ferrule of an infinitely long umbrella. Above me, the sky was pitch black and to either side the curvature of the earth was clearly visible. I'd felt awed by that solitary opportunity but I had the uncomfortable feeling that I did not belong there; it was as if someone was saying with a finger held to the lip, "Sssh! Go quietly, be on your guard, go back down!"

The experience was one that I could not forget, which was true, too, of the events about to unfold at Wattisham on one dismal, overcast night in the early spring of 1977. As I walked with my navigator to the engineering line hut to sign our Phantom's technical log, in my mind I went through the potential hazards of the night's flight. Normally, the squadron aircraft flew with just two underwing fuel tanks, 308-gallon 'Sargent Fletchers' (with 'Sargent' spelt the American way), but tonight an additional 500-gallon centre-line tank would be fitted and the heavier Phantoms would require a longer than usual stretch of runway for take-off.

When we entered the line hut, I listened vaguely to the hum of voices inside the room. The duty engineers seemed weary and a little deflated, a state of mind in part fostered, perhaps, by the foulness of the weather. Glancing around, it could seem that an invisible curtain separated the engineering world from that of the aircrew. The Phantoms' complex maintenance requirements consistently plagued the aircraft despite great efforts by the engineers who, I sensed, were inclined to feel undervalued. Maybe we assumed too much, I thought, as I strode towards a row of technical logs lined up on top of a desk. "You'll have to fix that kite," said the line 'chiefie' to one of his men.

"Fix it?" said the airman. An edgy silence ensued. In the background, The Carpenters' *Top of the World* seemed less than apposite as it beat out from an old radio. "Yes, fix it," went on the chief technician sharply. He then turned to me and said: "Your aircraft's okay, sir. Ready to go." His change of tone cut through my rush of thoughts. "Thanks, chief," I said, "good work!" He grinned and I turned around to make for the line hut door.

Outside, the flow of drizzle persisted as I walked towards my Phantom whose image was thin and indefinite, as wavering as that of a ghost. I squinted up at surrounding floodlights with their harsh glow that illuminated the night sky. The sky itself was a weeping bank of water-grey mist. Beyond, the conditions made it impossible to make out the Suffolk countryside with its medley of mellow colours and subtle changes towards the coastal areas to the east. In Suffolk there were few hills or valleys that might interfere with flying operations, just a patchwork of flat fields with haphazard villages that poked and prodded their way politely into adjacent countryside.

It was a vivid contrast to my time in the Far East, nonetheless I enjoyed life at Wattisham and I'd been intrigued when briefed on the airfield's history. I'd learned that the airfield, opened in April 1939, had operated initially as a medium bomber station with Bristol Blenheim squadrons based there. In the latter part of World War II, when the airfield had been used by a fighter group of the USAF, the US squadrons had served with distinction during the Normandy invasion of June 1944. Patrolling the Normandy beachhead, the US fighter aircraft had strafed and dive-bombed enemy positions with such effect that later in the year the US Distinguished Unit Citation had been awarded. After World War II, Wattisham was returned to the RAF and was used by squadrons equipped with the RAF's first jet fighter, the Gloster Meteor. In the mid 1950s, with battle-experienced pilots returning from the Korean War, RAF Wattisham, following renovation, became the base for the famous Hawker Hunter Black Arrows display team of 111 Squadron.

Suddenly, to my right, there was a shout from a group of engineers working on a Phantom. I glanced in their direction but the hubbub seemed to subside quite quickly. Ahead, while I walked up to my allocated aircraft, I scrutinised the general vicinity before commencing the detailed external checks. The unusual configuration of three external fuel tanks combined with the aircraft's upturned wing tips and downturned tailplane appeared to reinforce the Phantom's unfortunate reputation of 'double ugly'. The description seemed harsh, especially in view of the limitations imposed by US aircraft carriers where the hangar height dictated the fin height of its aircraft. This had resulted in stability problems for the Phantom. To compensate, the tailplane had been designed with 23 degrees of anhedral and the wing section had been modified too. And the Phantom's arrestor hook was a beefy, clumpy-looking affair, unlike the dainty devices on machines such as Lightnings and Jaguars. The hook was even stronger than those fitted to US aircraft thus allowing our Phantoms to operate from the smaller aircraft carriers of the Royal Navy.

Despite a temptation to hasten in the dismal weather conditions, I ensured that my walk-around checks were thorough. Nearby, a ground crewman placed a fire extinguisher to one side of the Phantom from where he would supervise the start-up procedures. He then stood there, arms folded, looking bored, disgruntled and cold. Meanwhile, I cheerily verified that the air intakes were clear and that the radome, behind which lay the complex AN/AWG-12 radar and fire-control system, was undamaged. Walking back along the starboard side of the aircraft I bent low to inspect the undercarriage mechanism and the wheels before moving to the rear fuselage where I could see that this was one of the few Phantoms currently modified with the tail-mounted radar warning receiver. I glanced up at the box-like structure that housed this device and which was placed just above the squadron emblem of an eagle preying on a falcon. When I walked to the rear of the aircraft, the blackened jet pipes were a stark reminder of the enormous power and scorching temperatures produced by the twin Rolls-Royce Spey engines.

With a sense of awe, I may have lingered there for a second or two, before continuing with the remaining checks and clambering up the front cockpit access ladder. The cockpit itself looked relatively spacious compared to the likes of the Lightning. I used my night-flying torch to check for any loose articles before I climbed into the cockpit and settled into the Martin Baker ejection seat. At this point, while an airman helped me to strap in, he solemnly blinked at me in silence before he ensured that all safety pins were securely stowed.

I completed the cockpit checks quite quickly then raised one finger to make a circling motion to indicate engine start. The ground crewman gave a thumbs up sign and soon, having started the first engine then repeated the process for the other engine, I obtained clearance from air traffic control to taxi to the take-off point. Pressing a small button on the control stick to operate the Phantom's nose-wheel steering system, I moved along the taxiway at a reasonably fast pace. "Clear for take-off…" said the duty controller, a distant figure behind long panes of glass in the Wattisham air traffic control tower. I taxied onto runway 23 then brought the Phantom to a halt before I eased the twin throttles forward. At 80 percent engine revolutions everything looked in order and the Phantom began to lean forward like a greyhound ready for the 'off'. I had a last glance at the cockpit indications. All still looked good. It was time to go.

When I released the brakes, the Phantom sprang forward rather less enthusiastically than usual because of the additional fuel tank. The heavy aircraft continued to feel a little sluggish when I selected reheat; the rate of acceleration, though, was adequate for the runway length available. As normal, I kept the stick fully back until the nose started to rise. It was at this point, just as my navigator cried "one hundred and forty knots", that we heard a loud bang. Simultaneously the aircraft began to swing to the left and a glance at the cockpit instruments revealed that the left engine had failed.

Perhaps I muttered an oath, I don't recall. I do recall, however, the sense of rising horror when I realised how far down the runway the Phantom had travelled. In the remaining runway length I could not be sure that the machine would get airborne on one engine. At once, therefore, I brought back both throttles to idle, deployed the brake parachute, lowered the tail hook, and yelled "Aborting!" on the radio. My voice seemed to trail off into a vacuum as the arrestor barrier at the end of the runway loomed at an alarming rate. I wanted to apply the wheelbrakes but there was no point: the Phantom's brakes were designed to taxi around an aircraft carrier's deck, not stop a 20-ton machine careering along at some two miles a minute.

Before the barrier, the single wire of the rotary hydraulic arrestor gear (RHAG) was designed to catch the tail hook of a runaway aircraft. Suddenly, my navigator, a very experienced Phantom man, shouted: "You've got the wire!" In his rear-view mirror he had managed to spot the movement of tapes attached to the RHAG. The two of us were flung forward onto our seat straps as the aircraft, as if grabbed by a giant hand, decelerated. 1,200ft of cable – the maximum amount – was now stretched to the limits of the device. Like the fault lines of an earthquake, we were taken to the brink but when, at last, the Phantom was halted, the cable began to drag the aircraft backwards.

Immediately, I raised the tail hook and the aircraft was released from the cable. By use of the right-hand engine I was able to taxi clear of the runway and back to the squadron dispersal area. It was not long before I was in the line hut to explain the sequence of events to a glum-looking line chief. Then I walked to join my navigator in the crewroom where we set about the inevitable form filling. As we did so, I could not avoid an intensity of feelings, a curious sense of elation at having coped with such a hazardous situation. I knew, however, that it could not be recorded in my logbook. No part of the Phantom, not even the nose-wheel, had been airborne.

CHAPTER 7

COUP DE GRÂCE

ROGER COLEBROOK'S BAD
WEATHER EXPERIENCES

The January iciness was inescapable. Sea fog, which
reduced local visibility to less than 50 yards, shifted
stealthily across the airfield and the morning pallor of
the fog added an air of grimness to my surroundings.
"Necessity, the mother of invention," I thought as I looked
left and right and listened for sounds of traffic before
attempting to cross the public road at RAF Leuchars. It
would be quite annoying, I reckoned, to be run over by a bus before I reached the
43 Squadron buildings for which I aimed.

Some five months had passed since this squadron, known as 'The Fighting
Cocks', had been reformed at Leuchars in September 1969 following disbandment
in November 1967. Back then the squadron had operated Hawker Hunter aircraft
and even had a small claim to fame having featured in the 1957 film *High Flight*.
Now, though, in its latest reincarnation, the squadron operated the Phantom FG1
in the air defence role. Although most personnel were still fairly new, in my own
case I was even newer as I'd been with the squadron for a mere matter of weeks.
I was especially delighted, therefore, when asked to act as number four in an
unusual five-ship formation due to take place this day, Friday 23 January 1970.
The formation, in honour of the departing station commander, would also include
Lightning aircraft from our fellow units at Leuchars, 11 and 23 Squadrons.

I was a former Lightning pilot myself, a factor, no doubt, that had influenced the
decision to include me in today's formation despite my newness to the Phantom
world. My time in the Lightning force, which had included a tour in Cyprus, had
offered a breadth and depth of experience that was probably unusual for a young
man still in his early twenties. For without doubt I had been through some drastic
situations; even on my first solo flight on Lightnings there had been problems when
my aircraft suffered an in-flight fire. And in Cyprus, where I had been a member of

56 Squadron during the Arab-Israeli Six Day War, I had learned that the realities of life as a fighter pilot did not always match dreamy-headed expectations. Demands could be tough in a belligerent world embroiled in hostilities.

Despite being a non-operational pilot at the time of the Six Day War, I'd had to sleep most nights in the 56 Squadron crewroom where I'd helped to support the operational pilots. Normally, our QRA duty at Akrotiri was restricted to daylight hours but for the duration of this war and for a period afterwards the QRA commitment was extended to a full twenty-four hours. Camp beds were set up in the squadron crewroom and rostered pilots slept in their flying suits. Pilots were briefed to expect possible defectors from Israel's neighbours who might seek safe haven in Akrotiri.

Some time after the Six Day War, when I had been scheduled for a night flight in stormy weather conditions, trouble of another kind had brewed – a hapless, harrowing event, the type that embedded itself within the memory. Even during the pre-flight briefing, which took place in a special, if ramshackle, briefing hut, there were warning signs of trouble when the racket of rain on the structure's flimsy roof had interrupted the briefing officer. The two of us had stared up at the ceiling. "Sod it," said the briefing officer, who was also my flight commander. "We're meant to be an all-weather outfit, are we not?" He'd continued to gaze at the ceiling.

"Yes, sir," I said deferentially.

"In that case," growled the briefing officer, "we should fly in all weather conditions, should we not?"

"That's okay with me." I said, even though it didn't feel particularly okay at all.

The flight commander, though, had seemed unconvinced by his own line of logic. Conscious, perhaps, of my lack of flying experience he'd appeared to struggle with the necessary decision. He'd stepped towards the nearest window and squinted his eyes as he tried to look outside but his attempts were thwarted by rain driven forcefully against the glass. "I think I'll have a word with the engineers," he said eventually. I watched him push past the room's cheap, battered furniture as he headed for the telephone. My thoughts began to churn as I listened to the conversation: "You're joking," he scowled as he spoke, "that seems to be a reasonable theoretical statement on the subject, but…" he made a circling motion with his left hand as if to encourage applause. At length, he concluded: "Fine. All right. Let's do it that way then." He turned to me as he replaced the telephone receiver: "Well, young Roger," he said, "looks like we're going to fill our boots. Or get them filled, more like," he guffawed. "Right-oh," I said.

"The engineers want to adopt special procedures in this weather…" he hesitated. This, I thought, does not sound good. Matters were going crazily from bad to worse, as crazy, I reckoned, as if a dancer were to kick her legs impossibly high then perform a backward somersault during which she'd throw a ball at a spoon that consequently spun up into the air before landing with a clatter in a cup. "The start-up crews," went on the flight commander, "will wear heavy oilskins for protection from the elements. The guys, therefore, won't be able to assist with the strapping-in process. The aircraft canopies will be kept closed for as long as practicable; we'll have to open them ourselves then close them ASAP when we're in the cockpits."

When he had finished speaking, a brief silence ensued; the flight commander seemed uneasy as he gazed at me while we listened to the dull, sullen sound of deluge. "Are you happy with the plan?" he asked. "Ecstatic!" I said. He grinned, looked towards the door then nodded, a signal to don life jackets and headgear before we stood by the door anxiously as if reluctant to take the plunge. At length, he nodded again and we began to dash towards the engineering line hut. As we tried to run, heads down, eyes half-closed, wincing at the sting of driving rain against faces, our progress was hampered by impromptu streams that swirled around the feet. The two of us threaded our way through the torrents until eventually, looking like a couple of drowned rats, we burst into the line hut.

The line chief and his men watched us warily. Too polite to speak their minds, nevertheless their expressions suggested, 'Are you nuts, or something? Are you off your tiny little rockers?' We walked towards a desk to check the aircraft logs. I scrawled a signature, saw that the flight commander had done the same, glanced at the line chiefie and noted his ongoing muteness. The silence remained as we two pilots braced ourselves for another dash.

When, after what felt like a further sea dip, the pair of us finally reached the aircraft, other problems had to be tackled. A fiddly side hatch had to be accessed to operate the Lightning's Perspex canopy. At the press of a switch the canopy could be hydraulically raised, a process, though, that was tricky with wet, slippery hands. By the time I'd completed the briefed procedure and scrambled into the cockpit, the interior, including the Martin Baker ejection seat, had become drenched. There was a puddle of water by my feet; the inside of the canopy had started to mist over; the aircraft instruments, beaded with water, were hard to read. I felt a form of apprehension that started to swell into a tightening of the chest, an increase in the heartbeat.

Attempts to mop up with my handkerchief, gloves, shirt sleeves – anything – were hampered as these items were themselves already sodden. I strived, though, to make the best of things as I carried out the pre-start checks and when I signalled 'engine start' to the attendant ground crewman who, planted there in his stiff oilskins would not have looked out of place on the deck of a square-rigger off

Cape Horn, hastily returned the signal to indicate 'clear to start'.

Luckily, the first, then the second Rolls-Royce Avon engine fired-up without difficulty. The Lightning's powerful demisting system soon cleared the canopy around my head although problems at the other end persisted when pools of water by my feet continued to slosh around. I waited for the leader's radio call to air traffic control for taxi clearance and when this had been granted we made steady progress along the rainswept taxiways. The controller now cleared us for take-off at which the leader moved to the downwind side of the runway to avoid spray and jet-wake blowing across my take-off path. So far, I thought, so good, and as the leader released his aircraft brakes, I pressed the timer on my stopwatch. After thirty seconds, I released my brakes and held the ailerons into wind as the aircraft set off down the runway.

My peripheral vision picked up a spray-filled blur of runway lights on each side as the aircraft accelerated. I peered anxiously ahead. At the appropriate airspeed I pulled back the stick for lift off at which point, quite abruptly, I realised that I had a problem. The main attitude indicator on my flight instrument panel had flopped onto its side. Simultaneously, I needed suddenly to push hard on the stick to retain control of the aircraft. Low cloud at around 300ft was scudding about, nonetheless I decided that my best option was to remain at low level. I therefore pushed the stick forward to level off. However, as I did so the attitude indicator reversed its position and the aircraft pitched violently nose down; my push on the stick had to become an anguished pull. This pull, though, caused the tailplane trim to run fully nose-up and I was faced with another desperate, adrenaline-charged push.

In this see-saw of actions, not to mention emotions, at least a pattern had emerged quite quickly: a climbing attitude induced runaway nose-up trim and vice-versa. Anything other than a straight and level attitude meant trouble. I decided that, come what may, I should not lose sight of the orange glow from station and married quarter lighting which was eerily, but fortuitously, reflected along the base of the low cloud.

Turning the Lightning downwind, I eased the airspeed back to around 185 knots (about 200 mph). As I did so, I noted that, with the flaps down, the aircraft's vertical oscillations seemed to reduce. I double-checked the cockpit 'three greens' indicator to confirm that the undercarriage was down before, still guided by the orange glow of reflected light on the low clouds, I turned onto finals approach. Despite the prodigious, persistent downpour of rain, with air from the twin Avons' mighty compressors blasted directly at the windshield base, I was able to see the runway lights slip into view while I turned. The last part of the approach presented further hazards which caused my pulse to quicken and my brain cells to go into overdrive. However, the thump as the Lightning touched down firmly produced, if not exactly a sense of ecstasy, nonetheless a reaction of sudden relief and a feeling of high satisfaction. I'd made it!

Later, when the engineers examined the aircraft, they discovered that an electrical junction box had ingested water during the night's storms. As the aircraft nose was raised or lowered, water ran to the front or rear of the junction box thus shorting-out terminals connected to the main attitude indicator and to the tailplane trim system.

If meteorological factors were at the root of my difficulties that night, weather conditions of another kind were about to cause altogether different problems at Leuchars some two years later, in January 1970. As, along with aircrew colleagues, I traipsed that day from the 43 Squadron buildings to the main operations set-up to attend the morning meteorological briefing, fog persisted to swirl among a few dimly silhouetted Phantoms lined up outside the squadron hangar. At the briefing itself, the weather man confirmed everyone's worst fears: visibility would remain below the stipulated limits for take-off and landing; the planned formation would be a non-starter. Sure enough, when the weather man had finished, the wing commander operations, who was also acting station commander until the new group captain arrived, stood up to declare that all flying was cancelled with the exception of operational scrambles. At least, I mused, we could gain a certain melancholy satisfaction at the thought of a morning of straightforward ground training while we enjoyed coffee and biscuits.

The briefing over, we trooped back to the 43 Squadron offices. Coffees were brewed, a plan was formulated and we were all set to commence our ground training programme when the squadron commanding officer, a gung-ho type, entered the crewroom. He looked around the room, adopted a wily expression and suggested that it might be a good idea to change into flying kit – "just in case the weather picked up". A few individuals glanced out of the window, some shrugged their shoulders then all, without further ado, began to head for the locker room to don flying gear. A quiet hum of conversation was barely discernible as we changed, after which, suitably attired, we pilots and navigators returned to the crewroom and hot mugs of coffee. Outside, the fog remained as impenetrable as ever. In spite of this, it was not long before the commanding officer appeared once more, this time to announce that he would brief the formation "in case the weather should pick up". More glances outside ensued, along with further shoulder shrugs while the formation members headed for the briefing room.

With suitable use of fingers to point here, hands to indicate there, our contrary commanding officer started his briefing. He was about halfway through when the briefing room door was slid open. Everyone turned in surprise. Standing there, hands on hips, a curious, furious expression on his face, was the acting station commander. "I've heard," he cried, addressing the formation leader, "what you are up to." I'm not sure why, but this comment made me think of little jugs with big ears. "And as the acting station commander," he ranted on, "I absolutely forbid it!" There was an ominous hush. Some in the room gazed up at the ceiling, a few stared outside, one or two looked down at their hands. I pictured squabbling schoolgirls gesticulate and shriek. The embarrassed silence persisted for a moment or two before, without further comment, the acting station commander turned around and stormed off. The outburst, however, seemed to have little impact on the formation leader who carried on with his briefing as if nothing had happened. "Just in case the weather might pick up," he said at the conclusion of his briefing, "we'll go to the line hut and sign for our aircraft."

At the line hut, I began to feel a strange loneliness even though I was not alone. "We'd better man up our aircraft and check out the radios," said the formation leader. He led the way while the rest of us followed dutifully. As we walked to our Phantoms I thought back to the previous night when the moon had been a sharply defined crescent and the sky perfectly clear. The stars had shone with such a fierce, contained brilliance that it seemed wrong to call the night dark. Such conditions, as the weather man had explained, were ideal for the formation of radiation fog which, mixed with local haar (sea fog), produced an unhappy combination. Regretfully, the scientific explanations, no matter how convincing, were little comfort just now as fog continued to linger over the airfield.

At the aircraft, a silvery, glistening coat of dampness covered the airframe surfaces. I shivered when, as part of normal pre-start routines, I walked around to inspect the outside of the Phantom. My sense of trepidation suggested that I was as unclear as everyone else about how far the formation leader intended to pursue whatever plan he had in his mind, but no mind reader was needed to work out the possibilities. Sure enough, when all members of the formation had checked-in on the aircraft radio, the leader called air traffic control for start-up clearance. At this, a familiar voice, that of the acting station commander himself, responded: "Black formation," he cried, "you are not – repeat not – cleared to start engines!"

The formation leader, though, ignored the order. "Black formation," he said, "start engines!" Like a musical concerto, the ding-dong of instructions proved intriguing, if by now predictable and cringeworthy. "Request taxi clearance," said the leader when all members of his formation had started-up. "Negative," said the acting station commander, "you are NOT cleared to taxi." The formation duly taxied out to the runway-in-use. "Request take-off clearance," called the leader. "Negative, you are NOT cleared to take off," came the response. The formation lined up and took off as briefed. If I had thoughts of: 'We shouldn't have done that,' I could console myself only with thoughts that, stuck in the number four position, I was in no place to argue.

We climbed up to discover that the fog layer extended just a few hundred feet above the airfield. Bursting into bright sunlight, we had to squint our eyes against the sun's dazzle. Now the leader ordered us to a new radio frequency which meant that the sort of madness just experienced, as if in some form of parallel universe, was ended at last. A sense of relief was palpable when the new controller, located in a different room inside the air traffic control complex, sounded calm as he directed the formation to fly towards the north and west of Leuchars before turning back to make an approach to the easterly runway.

While we flew back towards the airfield, the leader attempted to follow his briefed plan which was to head in the general direction of the departing station commander's house until known ground features were identified and could be used to navigate visually to the exact spot. Inevitably, though, when the formation descended back into the fog, the plan foundered, the leader floundered; he had to request a GCA (ground controlled approach) and to obey the instructions of the talk-down controller.

During this procedure, the fog was so dense that I needed to alter my position to an exceptionally close one in order to stay in visual contact with the leader's aircraft. The Phantoms on either side did the same but the horizontal visibility was so poor that these aircraft were virtually invisible to me. Perspiration began to run down my face in rivulets – the product, I reckoned, of 80% fear and 20% physical effort.

With the nose of my Phantom now directly underneath the leader's tailplane, I could spot a red glow from each of the twin Rolls-Royce Spey engines, an arc of some sixty degrees at the top of the rear turbines. Through the soles of my flying boots I could feel a trembling effect as the exhaust plume from the leader's aircraft buffeted the tail-fin of my Phantom. In normal circumstances this was a sign that I was too close or too high and would need immediate corrective action. My circumstances, though, were far from normal; I had little choice but to grit my teeth and hang in there as if my life depended on it (which it did).

Despite flying so close to the leader, more than once I lost visual contact with his aircraft. When this happened, I eased back the throttles slightly and told my navigator – that poor soul who had to sit quietly and powerlessly through it all – that I would count to three before commencing a slow pull-up to leave the formation. On each occasion, just as I got to three, the leader's tailpipe re-emerged thanks to a slightly less dense patch of fog. A fortuitous additional aid, I discovered, came from the sooty carbon deposits inside the jet-pipes of the leader's aircraft; these dark deposits stood out against the fog's milky whiteness.

By this stage, as we got closer to the runway, my navigator began to call out our radio altimeter heights. On top of other issues, the 500ft, fog-shrouded presence of Lucklaw Hill provided a further worry while the formation descended ever lower. Suddenly, the leader announced "missed approach – going round" and applied engine power. An air of relief must have swept like a fresh breeze through all of our cockpits. As we commenced a climb, the struggle to hold formation ended abruptly when we burst out from the suffocating blanket of fog to the warm, sunlit brilliance above. "Relax," called the leader, "move out to a loose formation." No further encouragement was needed. Released from a grim and exhausting netherworld, we were delivered to a place of openness and splendour. I glanced at my flying gloves which, soaked with perspiration, had turned from their normal pale grey colour to a ghastly greenish hue.

"Dump fuel," commanded the commanding officer, "we'll reduce weight before attempting another approach to the airfield." Again, he wheeled the formation to the north and west of Leuchars as we prepared for the next attempt. Having dumped fuel, he ordered us back into close formation which we now found easier as the aircraft were lighter. However, when we sank from the sky's blueness to the featureless, opaque haze below, the visual effect was unnerving for the fog proved to be just as dense. I had to apply the same technique of counting to three if I lost sight of the leader but, as before, luckily managed to regain visual contact at the last second.

Soon, even though my focus on the leader was intense, I became aware of uncommon, jerky control inputs – left, right, up, down – and of blurred shadows that started to flash beneath. While he continued to call out radio altimeter heights, the pitch of my navigator's voice seemed to rise with each call as he announced an ever more alarmingly low altitude. Before long, though, we began to climb again and as we burst once more into the clear skies above, the leader ordered everyone to check in on the radio – "Black 2"– "Black 3" – "Black 4"...ominous pause... then: "Black 5". Later, when asked why he had done this, the leader replied that he'd wanted to confirm that number five hadn't been wiped out amongst the trees! It was later, too, when we learnt that the leader's navigator had used his radar's ground-mapping mode as an unconventional, if effective, way to fix the relative position of the group captain's house.

Following the fly-past, the formation split up for mutual training exercises by the end of which the weather had improved sufficiently for all five Phantoms to return to Leuchars without difficulty. After landing, we learnt that the formation had overflown the married quarters just as the group captain was leaving his house and just as the Leuchars' pipe band had begun to play a farewell lament. Observers on the ground were astonished when five Phantoms, as if by the wave of a wizard's wand, appeared suddenly for a few seconds before being swallowed up again by the fog. Those of us in the Phantoms were no less astonished. If we'd expected some form of retribution, none came. It was as if the authorities had decided that the intriguing intrigues involved in our particular, peculiar form of *coup de grâce* should be quietly lost in the mists of time.

CHAPTER 8

AN IMPOSSIBLE DREAM

LES HURST'S DREAM EVENTUALLY CAME TRUE

I'm not ashamed to admit it, tears began to well up. The words that the squadron leader sitting opposite me had just uttered came like a hammer blow. "You're not going to the Phantom but I think you will enjoy where you are going." What, I thought, could have been better than my long-cherished dream of flying the Phantom? Even an overseas tour would have come second best. I was all ears. "You're going to the apprentice school at Halton as a flight commander." I thought, 'what do you mean I'm going to Halton?' Although I didn't say these words, he could see that I was deeply upset and quickly made a second offer, "Would you like to go to the officer training unit at Henlow instead?"

"No, sir," I said, "I will go to Halton." I don't know why I said that, both offers were to me equally unpalatable. But by then, frankly, I was beyond caring. The squadron leader had a job to do but he had shown no real understanding of the depth of my determination to fly the Phantom, an ambition that went back a long way – no ordinary ambition, I might add, but more of a burning desire. I really have no idea why; there was no rational explanation. I can only say that my feelings on the subject ran deep.

*

I was born in Manchester in 1941. My father, a steel worker, was a volunteer with the Home Guard, otherwise none of my family had any connection with the military. My first recollection of anyone showing interest in my wish to fly was a teacher at my grammar school. This man, who had a collection of aircraft pictures and wartime aircraft recognition silhouettes, suggested that I should join the Air Training Corps. It was 1954 and as a thirteen-year-old it seemed to me a brilliant suggestion although my father, when we discussed the matter, would not hear of it. I don't think that he really understood what the Air Training Corps was and I suspect that he thought that I was about to 'join up'. It took about a year but eventually my persistence, plus a little support from my mother, persuaded him that it was not, perhaps, such a bad idea after all. When, at last, I donned my ATC uniform it would be hard to imagine a prouder or more enthusiastic member of that organisation, furthermore my aspiration to fly intensified after a familiarisation flight in an Auster, that venerable light observation aircraft designed in the USA and built by Taylor Aeroplanes (England) Ltd.

At the age of sixteen I was selected for a gliding course at Hawkinge in Kent where I was sent solo in a Slingsby Cadet. My desire to fly grew ever stronger, especially as the experience meant that I was put forward for pre-selection as a member of the Royal Air Force. The pre-selection process took place at RAF Hornchurch and it was here that I received the first of what would prove to be a series of extremely disappointing setbacks. I was told that I'd failed the pre-selection process but that I could try again in two years' time. I was devastated. Through my sixteen-year-old eyes this was as about as bad as it could get. I don't recall my father's reaction — quietly pleased, probably, because he wasted no time in taking me for an interview with the Manchester engineering company of Metropolitan Vickers. At Manchester University my older brother had gained a PhD in polymer chemistry and I think that my father wanted me to follow a similar path. I don't recollect the outcome of that interview but I do remember that I stayed on at school with one aim in mind: to gain the five O level examinations needed to apply for the Royal Air Force.

So it was that, after the required two-year interval, I went back to Hornchurch for re-assessment. To this day I recall vividly the moment when the greatly-anticipated letter containing the RAF's decision was delivered. The suspense was unbearable. With shaking hands I tore open the letter, but was almost afraid to read the contents. Slowly, an enormous wave of relief flooded through my system: I had been accepted; this time I had made it! I literally jumped for joy and could not wait to tell someone, anyone!

It was not long before I received a further letter with details of my joining instructions. I was nineteen years old when my mother walked me to the bus stop near our home to send me on my way to RAF South Cerney in Gloucestershire for officer training. The four months spent there (which I did not enjoy particularly) ended in a passing-out parade followed by a move to Number 2 Flying Training School at RAF Syerston where I commenced pilot training. My target in life, so it seemed, was coming to fruition. On 17 March 1961 this was verified when I was sent solo by my instructor on the Hunting (later British Aircraft Corporation) Jet Provost Mark 3, that legendary training aircraft powered by a single Viper 102 engine. At this stage, little did I know of the problems ahead. Two months went by after which I was summoned to the commanding officer's office. My progress, it appeared, was not up to standard. I was to be suspended from the course with immediate effect. With considerable effort I managed to retain a measure of composure even though something was telling me that, this time, it really was the end of the road.

Despite the feelings of guilt at having let down my parents, of exasperation at having failed to achieve a long-held ambition, the selection officers at Hornchurch managed to divert my thoughts in a rather more positive direction. Would I like, they asked, to consider becoming an air electronics officer? Or a navigator? On the basis that I had no idea what an air electronics officer did, I decided to opt for navigator training. It soon began. In June of that – for me – fateful year of 1961 I went for basic navigator training at RAF Thorney Island. This was on Vickers Valetta and Vickers Varsity aircraft, and was followed by advanced training at RAF Stradishall in Suffolk

At about this juncture a new thought occurred to me. If I couldn't be a pilot then perhaps the next best thing would be to become a navigator on a two-seat aircraft. At the time this meant, in effect, a posting to the English Electric Canberra fleet which I duly requested. It was with a sense of dismay, therefore, when I received instructions, not to train for a Canberra squadron, but instead to join the V Force as a nav/rad (navigator/radar). My ambitions, it appeared, had been thwarted yet again.

After a period of training at the Bomber Command Bombing School at RAF Lindholme and the Victor Operational Conversion Unit at RAF Gaydon I was eventually posted to 55 Squadron at RAF Honington to start my first operational tour flying the Handley Page Victor B1 bomber. As a free-fall nuclear bomber unit, this squadron's aircraft carried a single, rather large, weapon in the bomb bay and it was my task as the nav/rad to find the target by use of H2S radar which would lead to automatic weapon release. Looking back, the concept makes me shudder. I am amazed to reflect that we had regular practise scrambles which involved taxiing to the runway, accelerating to one hundred knots before the pilot throttled back to taxi the bomber back to the dispersal area. All of this was with a nuclear bomb on board.

Designed in early post-war years, the three V bombers, Valiant, Vulcan and Victor were, for their day, 'state of the art'. That is to say: analogue state of the art. There were no inertial navigation systems (INS) or global positioning systems (GPS) in those days, just basic navigational systems which included the use of astro-navigation and computers, known as calculators, the size of small dustbins. Although the crews' composition was the same and using the same equipment, the cockpit environment for the Victor rear crew was greatly superior to that of the other two V bombers. The Valiant and Vulcan rear crew sat in the dark unable to see out whereas in the Victor we sat higher than the pilots and were able to look forward through the windscreen.

A good aspect of life in the V Force was the opportunity for plenty of overseas detachments, especially to North America and the Far East. After my tour on 55 Squadron I was posted to 57 Squadron when, not long after the move, I was scheduled for a crew pre-positioning flight to the Far East by civil airliner. I have an abiding memory of this trip. It took 25 hours in a piston-engined Douglas DC-7C and for one leg the captain, who seemed to us youngsters to be at least eighty years old, joined us for a chat shortly after take-off. The chat lasted for the entire ten-hour stretch, the captain returning to his cockpit only for the landing. I even remember his name; the eighty-year-old Captain Hermes.

When in the Far East, I would take every opportunity to turn up on the doorstep of the resident Javelin, Hunter and Canberra squadrons to try to cadge flights. The squadrons on the whole were very accommodating and I found that these flights reinforced my ongoing aspirations to join a two-seat squadron.

Further hurdles, however, had yet to be tackled. From 57 Squadron I was posted to the staff navigator course where I would learn instructional techniques before qualifying as a navigator instructor. On my last night as a member of the V Force, by which stage I was at RAF Marham temporarily attached to the Tanker Training Flight, I was scheduled for a sortie designed for the benefit of a new co-pilot. As the nav/rad member of the crew, I was not really needed for this sortie so I decided not to fly. It was a fateful decision. Soon after take-off from Marham, while the Victor was in the climb and positioned over the north Norfolk coast, the aircraft collided with a Canberra. All on board both aircraft were killed.

With this tragedy at the forefront of my mind I left Marham and the V Force with a heavy heart. The captain of the Victor and I had started life together in the V Force. I could hardly believe what had happened. Recovery from my profound sense of loss would take some time because of the close friendship and high regard I had for this man.

On completion of the staff navigator course I was posted to the RAF College at Cranwell, a tour which turned out to be one of the most enjoyable during my service career. I found great satisfaction from instructing at the navigation school, furthermore there was plenty of opportunity for Jet Provost flying. At the end of the tour an unwritten rule stated that I could have the posting of my choice and I had announced in the loudest and clearest terms that a posting to Phantoms was my unequivocal preference. When I travelled to visit my 'desk officer' at the Ministry of Defence in London to discuss my students' postings as well as my own, I was full of the joys of spring, happy and confident that, finally, at the age of thirty-one, nearly twenty years on from when I had first donned that Air Training

Corps uniform with such pride, my impossible dream was surely about to become possible.

I was still in a cheerful and relaxed frame of mind when I walked towards the desk officer's office. Fixed in my head was an image of the Phantom picture pinned to my office door at Cranwell. I entered the desk officer's office and shook hands with him. He invited me to sit down. Hardly had I done so before he started to deliver his news. What he was saying sounded barely believable. The fellow had begun to talk about a ground tour at Halton. A ground tour! Where did that come from? What about the promised Phantom posting? He could not have been aware that he had just delivered the cruellest and most painful blow that it could have been possible to deliver in the long journey to achieving my ambition. I can't even remember discussing my students' postings. The fickle finger of fate had struck again and, thoroughly downhearted, I left the office and the Ministry of Defence to return to Cranwell.

With my posting to Halton confirmed, I moved to that place with a fair amount of reluctance to take up my new job of looking after thirty or so apprentices as their mentor and 'house master'. Unsurprisingly, I did not really settle into this line of work even though it was made more bearable by activities such as the Ten Tors weekend hike held annually on Dartmoor. My sense of frustration at Halton was compounded by my squadron leader who was less than sympathetic to my plight. With my home at Billinghay, close to Coningsby, I commuted to Halton and it was a very determined Les Hurst who now set about organising his next move – that posting to Coningsby.

It was a radical idea which seemed, in the end, to clinch the matter. I wrote a formal letter to the Ministry of Defence to explain the reasons why I should be at Coningsby and not at Halton. To this letter I attached a picture from *Flight* magazine of a Royal Navy Phantom and said that, if it would help my cause, I was prepared to volunteer for a tour with the navy. The reply was predictable and rapid and said something like: 'wind your neck in, you will be looked at in three years time along with everyone else'. If, on receipt of this letter, I lapsed into a further state of the blues this was not for too long because, out of the blue, just three weeks later, I received a further letter. This time the writer explained that a navigator on a Phantom course at Coningsby had dropped out and that I had been nominated as his replacement. My impossible dream was, at long last, about to become a reality.

My combined air defence/ground-attack course on the Phantom FGR2 at Coningsby, when it got underway, was a revelation. Needless to say that I enjoyed it enormously, apart from the practice ground-attack strafes at Cowden Range; these involved going round and round in a routine which made me feel queasy. At the end of the course I was offered the opportunity to join a squadron in

Germany but decided that, no, I'd stay with the plan to volunteer for a tour with the navy. This turned out to be one of the best decisions of my life.

In June 1973 I drove up to RAF Leuchars, the base for the Fleet Air Arm Phantom Training Flight where, in addition to receiving indoctrination into the ways of naval aviation, I would be converted to the FG1 (F4K) version of the Phantom (an aircraft which was surprisingly different to the Phantom FGR2). The course, which lasted for three weeks, involved twenty hours of flying designed to reflect the Fleet Air Arm's dual duties of air defence and ground attack. I recall a particular flight when I made the mistake of glancing away from my radar screen to look outside for a moment. The sortie involved a low-level run but I was taken aback by quite how low. I had no idea of our actual height but it seemed to me as if the water was about to lap our wings.

My first catapult launch from an aircraft carrier took place on 10 July 1973. Just the day before I'd been flown by helicopter to HMS *Ark Royal* which was positioned in the Moray Firth to the east of Inverness in Scotland. My head seemed to buzz with excitement and anticipation, not to mention a great deal of information following my naval indoctrination.

On the big day itself I was flown by the commanding officer of 892 Squadron. I'd already been extensively lectured on the take-off procedures but when he briefed the sortie the CO went through them again. He described how, when the Phantom had been strapped into position on the catapult, water-cooled jet blast deflectors would be raised behind the aircraft. The pilot would advance his throttles to cold power, pause, and then select reheat. (At night, incidentally, this was an awesome spectacle.) When satisfied, the pilot would place the back of his right hand against the cockpit canopy as a sign that he was ready. The flight deck officer now made a final check before he lowered his green flag (wand at night) to signal that the launch could proceed. At this point, the pilot and navigator adopted a brace position with the head pressed back hard into the headrest. After about three to four seconds, in a cloud of steam, the Phantom literally leapt down the deck achieving 4'g' and 120 knots in some one-and-a-half seconds. This phenomenal rate of acceleration was faster, more dramatic and more mind-boggling than I could ever have imagined. On that first launch I doubt if I could have reacted in time if anything had gone wrong, and during my time with the navy the thrill of a catapult launch never diminished.

As I began to settle into naval life as a member of 892 Squadron, it worked out that I spent around half of my time on board HMS *Ark Royal* and the other half based at RAF Leuchars when the ship went in for a re-fit. No flying took place on long passages to the Mediterranean Sea or when crossing the Atlantic Ocean which meant periods of boredom for the aircrew. To make up for this, therefore, I volunteered as night crew to gain extra flying time. One problem which was exacerbated at night was that of finding the ship after a training sortie or an operational mission. This may sound strange but on many occasions the ship would be under emission control restrictions which meant that on-board navigation aids had to be switched off. While, before launch, the crew would be given a so-called position and intended movement of the ship (PIM) it was not always accurate.

One night, at the end of a training sortie, I was, as usual, making use of the Phantom's versatile radar to locate and home onto HMS *Ark Royal* – 'Mother' – which had deployed a towed target behind the ship. Part of our routine on approaching the towed target was to deploy Lepus flares. Delivered by a special toss manoeuvre, once released these flares descended slowly by parachute to light up an area in a brilliant yellowish-coloured glow. Before flight, the flares could be manually adjusted for time of flight so that, for instance, if three Lepus flares were released at, say, thirty, thirty-five and forty degrees of pitch, they could descend together to provide broad illumination of a target area. On the night in question we released the Lepus flares only to discover as we dived down to 'attack' the towed target that, to our horror and astonishment, we had a cruise liner in our sights. Passengers and crew, eyes with pupils the size of pinpricks, would have stared at the blinding centres of light that drifted down by parachute. Perhaps they thought that they were about to be treated to an impromptu fireworks display; hopefully they never realised the truth. We, of course, aborted the attack profile at once and climbed up to initiate a further search for the correct ship.

Another occasion when the Lepus flare system worked with remarkable, if unconventional, success was when an 892 Squadron Phantom on exercise in the Mediterranean Sea had problems trying to land on HMS *Ark Royal*. By then late at night and very short of fuel, the crew had no option but to divert to a land airfield, the nearest of which was Naples. They reached Naples only to find that the airfield was closed although an Italian air traffic controller was on duty and informed them that the runway was clear although no airfield lightning would be available. The crew said: "not to worry we have brought our own" and in a masterful piece of quick thinking they 'tossed' a Lepus flare which they just happened to be carrying. The flare was tossed at high speed at a height of 500ft before the Phantom landed in a blaze of light, if not exactly a blaze of glory.

My experiences with the navy included a number of such close shaves, including an incident I witnessed when, during a catapult launch from HMS *Ark Royal,* one of the Phantom's engines failed. Unable to achieve flying speed, the aircraft crashed into the sea some seven seconds later. Fortunately the crew members both ejected successfully to be picked up shortly afterwards.

One time, a curious incident occurred when I had been detailed to fly to the Royal

Naval Air Station at Yeovilton for an open day. My pilot decided that, as he had a medical appointment at the Institute of Aviation Medicine, it would be a good opportunity to fly via Farnborough where the institute was based. Having landed and parked the Phantom, my pilot set off for his doctor's appointment. Meanwhile, as I waited by the aircraft, a car drove up and several smartly-suited gentlemen got out 'to admire' the Phantom which, at that time, was an unfamiliar sight at Farnborough. One of them sniffily inspected the aircraft tyres before he came up to me to announce that the tyre wear was out of limits and that as superintendent of flying he could not allow the Phantom to leave.

"But the tyres are within naval limits," I protested.

"Naval limits?"

"Yes. They're good for at least one more landing."

"Are you serious?"

"Absolutely." I tried to look earnest but he had a strange air of seriousness about him. "Furthermore," he went on, "there are so many panel fasteners missing on this aircraft that if it was a Royal Air Force machine it would not be permitted to fly." The end result, in any case, was that a de Havilland Devon aircraft was despatched with ground crew and new wheels so that, finally, we could get underway to Yeovilton.

Towards the end of May 1974, during a shore-based period at Leuchars, I was programmed for a rocket attack practise sortie in Phantom XT872 at Rosehearty Range near Fraserburgh in Scotland. The flight went as briefed but as we flew back to Leuchars my pilot said that we had a problem – a utility hydraulics failure was indicated on the warning panel. At once, I reached for the Phantom's emergency check list and read out the relevant procedures. These included the requirement to lower the aircraft's arrestor hook which was designed to catch a cable stretched across the approach end of the runway. With all the checks completed, we declared an emergency and continued on towards Leuchars.

My pilot made a good approach to Leuchars: the angle of approach was fine, the airspeed was correct, and he touched down in the right place just before the cable. However, when the Phantom passed the cable we felt no retardation; the hook must have bounced. At this point I expected to hear the Rolls-Royce Spey engines 'spool up' as the pilot applied power for an overshoot and a second attempt. But no, this did not happen: the Phantom stayed down and within seconds I heard a loud bang followed by another bang which I took to be the sound of the main tyres bursting.

A mass of different thoughts now began to rush through my mind. The Phantom was still travelling quite fast and I had the distinct impression that the aircraft was about to veer off the runway. I was conscious of other incidents when this had happened, in particular the case of a Lightning which, having left the runway, struck some airfield infrastructure which forced the nose-wheel upwards; the displacement of the nose-wheel in turn dislodged the ejection seat thereby making the seat unusable. I quickly decided that my best option under the circumstances was to eject.

XT872 on the grass with its rear cockpit ejection gun clearly showing.

Without further ado I used both hands to grasp the ejection seat handle between my legs. As confidently as if I had done it a thousand times I snatched the handle firmly upwards. There was a faint mechanical thud through the seat. A dreadful pause followed which appeared to last forever but which was actually less than half-a-second. Suddenly, as if pushed skywards by an enormous fist, I felt myself thrust from the Phantom's cockpit. Events now passed in a blur. I was vaguely aware of a violent wind-rush, a sensation of tumbling over and over, then an abrupt pull as the main parachute deployed. I glanced down to see the ground rushing towards me. I could see the Phantom I'd just abandoned as it was still charging down the runway.

Real life hit me abruptly when, within seconds, I landed. There was no opportunity to prepare for the tidy parachutists' roll that I'd practised many times on my parachuting course. Instead, I landed on my backside like a sack of potatoes: the parachuting instructor might have been less than proud. I'd had no time to release my dinghy pack but luckily I landed on grass just a few feet from the runway – unlike the ejection seat which had been cut free by Martin Baker's automatic systems and which was subsequently deposited on the runway. I stood up and checked myself for injuries. Despite the shock it seemed that I was not physically wounded to any significant degree so I lay down again. I looked for the Phantom but I couldn't see it properly. Later, I learnt that the aircraft hook had caught the runway over-run wire and XT872 had slewed off to the right before coming to a halt on the airfield grass. There was a stroke of good fortune in this for had the aircraft gone left and not right it would have hit a fully-fuelled Victor tanker parked immediately opposite on the ORP (operational readiness platform).

Aerial view of XT872's crash – a fully-fuelled Victor tanker can be seen on the left.

Soon, having been carried into the back of a military ambulance, the vehicle roared off to take me, accompanied by the station medical officer, to Ninewells Hospital in Dundee for a check-up. Although still very sore, I was declared uninjured and 'fit' to leave. On the return journey to Leuchars it was decided to collect my wife, Linda, from Dundee College where she was a student on a course. Summoned from her class by the college principal, she was told that there was someone downstairs to see her. Her heart pounding, she ran along the corridor to the top of the stairs to see the familiar face of the station doctor down below. With her mind already full of dread she gazed down at the doctor who looked up and shouted:

"He's okay!"
"What?" her voice must have echoed through those cold corridors of academia.
"Les - he's okay, he's okay."
"Why...what's happened?"
"He's been involved in a flying accident but he's okay. Now he's waiting in the ambulance outside."

It was only later that it struck me that the whole shocking experience had been worse, in a way, for her than for me. Although the Dundee doctors had declared me fit it transpired, in fact, that I had a compression fracture of the spine as a result of the ejection but this was not discovered until three months later when I was summoned to Farnborough for a medical examination. By then I had been flying routinely – indeed I went back to flying five days after the accident. Other ramifications of the affair were remarkably straightforward. No formal enquiry was held by the Royal Navy; they appeared to take the view that the ship was fine and that was the important thing; the loss of an aircraft was something of a detail. The aircraft, in any case, was not lost but patched up, flown to a maintenance unit then put back into service.

Not long after my own incident I witnessed another ejection. As number two in a pair, we were returning to base after a training sortie and duly followed the leader as he broke left into the circuit for Leuchars' easterly runway. The turn had barely started when the leader abruptly rolled off bank and started to head due north towards Dundee. We wondered what was going on so followed to observe. Suddenly, without any radio call or other warning, both crew members ejected. At once we began to circle the area, put out a Mayday relay call and watched the pilot and navigator while their parachutes floated earthwards. Their Phantom created a ball of fire followed by a pall of black smoke as the machine crashed. Luckily the two crew members, one of whom was a United States Navy exchange officer, landed safely. We heard later that the pilot, as he broke into the circuit, had pulled back both throttles too hard, the throttles consequently had passed through the 'gate' and shut down the engines. The FG1 version of the Phantom had limited battery back-up which did not include a facility to re-light the engines. Amazingly, this was that US Navy officer's fourth ejection using a Martin Baker seat. Tragically, when he returned to the USA, he was involved in a mid-air collision when flying a Grumman F14 Tomcat and was killed.

Towards the end of 1974, when I was told that the RAF wanted me back, I was not particularly happy about it. I asked for an extension of my time with the navy but this was turned down. The following February, therefore, during missile-firing trials at the US Navy Atlantic Fleet Weapons Range in Puerto Rico, I left 892 Squadron and the navy with a paradoxical sense that this tour had been the best during my many years as a member of the RAF. I was flown back to the United Kingdom to join 29 Squadron at RAF Coningsby, a posting which lasted for just nine months before I moved to Coningsby's 228 Operational Conversion Unit as a navigator instructor. It was in the latter role that I spent the last four years of my service career.

At the age of 37, when told of my selection for promotion to the rank of squadron leader, I was informed that I'd be posted to 56 Squadron at RAF Wattisham as navigator leader. I'd be required, however, to serve to the age of forty which, from a civilian employer's point of view, was a difficult age if I decided to leave the service at that point. In a quandary about what to do, one day I spotted in *Flight* magazine an advertisement for navigators in the Royal New Zealand Air Force. I filled in the application form after which, having been summoned to New Zealand House for interview and medical examination, I was offered a job. At about the same time I visited the British Aerospace Company at Warton to look round the air combat simulator there. This simulator was a novel concept at the time and I decided that, when back at Coningsby, I should telephone Warton to ask about the prospects of a job. I spoke to the chief navigator at Warton and to the chief test pilot who said: "Get yourself a flight navigator's licence and you'll have a job in our Tornado test programme."

Les Hurst with pilot Simon Tomkins (on the left), celebrating the completion of flying 1,000 hours on the F-4 in 1978.

I turned down the promotion to squadron leader and told the Ministry of Defence of my decision to leave the service at the age of thirty-eight. I also turned down the job in New Zealand. So it was that I joined British Aerospace (later BAE Systems) a month before my thirty-eighth birthday and test flew the multi-role, variable sweep wing Panavia Tornado for the next fourteen years. In 1993 I retired from the company as their chief test navigator with 899 test flights totalling some 1,200 hours of Panavia Tornado flying.

When, on looking back, I ponder my thirteen-year-old self and how desperately keen I was to join the RAF, I recall the bitter emotions of hope raised and dashed on so many occasions. Perhaps, because of the fierce determination inside me, the setbacks themselves provided, perversely, a catalyst to drive me on. I like to think that, despite all the setbacks and even though they were not alive to see it, my parents would have been proud that in the end I managed to achieve my impossible dream.

CHAPTER 9

TOUGH OLD BIRD

RICK PEACOCK-EDWARDS'
RED HOT OVERSHOOT

If the McDonnell Douglas Phantom was a tough old bird then the pilots and navigators who flew the aircraft had to be tough too. Of course, the same should be said about our predecessors, the Hurricane and Spitfire pilots who flew in World War II, and as the son of a Battle of Britain pilot I was well aware of this. It was especially the case, I suppose, for someone like me who was brought up in South Africa. Pilots from South Africa had gained a reputation for fearless flying and in the Battle of Britain they had suffered high losses relative to their numbers.

If, for me, flying was in the blood, maybe this was further encouraged when I attended Michaelhouse College, a South African boarding school for boys in the midlands of KwaZulu-Natal. From there I went to Johannesburg's University of the Witwatersrand, commonly known as Wits, before I joined the Royal Air Force. After pilot training in the RAF I was fortunate to be posted to the English Electric Lightning world where I gained experience as an operational fighter pilot before converting to the Phantom. My tour on the Phantom began in August 1977 as an executive officer with 111 Squadron, otherwise known as 'Tremblers', based at RAF Leuchars, a tour that would last for just over three years.

One night in February 1978 I was programmed for a pairs sortie for which I was detailed by the Tremblers operations officer to act as leader. It was a dark and rather dirty night and the hour was late when, together with my navigator and the other two aircrew members, I left the operations room to walk out to the aircraft. I had, as usual, to go via the engineering set-up to sign for our allocated aircraft (XV403). When, along with the other pilot, I entered the engineering line-hut the atmosphere seemed tense. "How did he know?" I heard a corporal ask someone at the back of the room. "I went to his office and told him." These words seemed to intrude the corporal's thought processes slowly. He looked up after some seconds.

"You did what?" he demanded shrilly and jumped to his feet in apparent rage. "You went over my head without even asking?"

All in the room froze with embarrassment. As if I'd committed some misdemeanour I looked around guiltily like a criminal caught in the act. "Everything okay, chief?" I asked the chief technician in charge. He coughed and moved across to the desk where I stood. "Yes, sir," he glanced behind him. "A spot of trouble over there but I'll sort it, don't worry." Perhaps I thought, 'lost the plot, full stop'. But I knew that in reality it was fatigue brought on by the lateness of the hour that had probably stirred up feelings. There was no doubt that the Phantom with its complex technical systems placed high demands on our ground crews. As I left the engineers to their tête-à-tête, I stepped outside into the chill of night. All around, the brilliance of sodium lighting contrasted strongly with the dull blackness beyond. The two Phantoms, lined up ready for the start procedures, looked business-like in their 111 Squadron colouring of yellow and black. The squadron motto of *Adstantes* ('Standing by') seemed, I thought, rather apposite just now.

As I walked towards the Phantoms, I reflected on my good fortune to be a member of such a legendary squadron. This had been politely pointed out to me when I first arrived at Leuchars. Formed in 1917 in the Middle East, it was in the 1950s that 111 Squadron, under the leadership of Squadron Leader R L Topp, introduced the Black Arrows aerobatic demonstration team with the Hawker Hunter. At the Society of British Aircraft Constructors' airshow at Farnborough in 1958 twenty-two Hunters had performed a loop – a world record for the greatest number of aircraft looped in formation. In the 1960s the squadron re-equipped with the English Electric Lightning and continued its secondary role as an aerobatic demonstration team, famously barrel-rolling twelve Lightnings. After almost eighteen years based at RAF Wattisham, the squadron moved to RAF Coningsby where it operated the Phantom FGR2. In November 1975 the squadron moved again, that time heading north to RAF Leuchars to take up duties there.

When I had joined 111 Squadron, I'd soon learned other, less formal, aspects of life with the squadron including a song in bar room vernacular which was sung to the tune of the Beatles' *When I'm Sixty-Four* and for which it would be best, perhaps, not to repeat the words here. Not all such songs, incidentally, were limited to bar room patois. I was reminded of this some years in the future when involved in the lead-up to the first Gulf War as the RAF commander at Dhahran, Saudi Arabia. At the start of Operation Desert Storm on 17 January 1991, by which stage I was commander of the front-line Panavia Tornado base at RAF Leeming, we heard how the XV Squadron (the 'MacRobert's Reply' squadron) going to war song, made up by the army ground liaison officer, had been sung just before the squadron aircrew got airborne in their Tornados for the briefed mission. Some of the aircrew reported how they suddenly felt lump in the throat reactions as they sang. Reciting such a song on exercise, they said, was one thing and they could have a good laugh about it. But just before flying into heavily defended territory with the very real prospect of not coming back was something entirely different. They realised that some of the men singing in that room may not return and it was with a rousing chorus that XV Squadron went to war.

"Evening, sir," said one of the members of the ground crew as I walked up to XV403. He busied himself with a check of the ground power unit and the positioning of a fire extinguisher. "Evening," I replied. For this evening's flight I had briefed a sortie which would include the two Phantoms alternating as fighter and target for a series of practise interceptions before we carried out a rendezvous procedure with a Handley Page Victor tanker. The tanker would top-up our fuel after which the Phantoms would break away for further mutual interceptions. As an ex-Lightning pilot I was well acquainted with this type of sortie profile although I was conscious, along with other ex-Lightning pilots, that during my five-month operational conversion course at Coningsby the notion of 'crew co-operation' with a navigator was challenging. Having been drilled for years in the Lightning pilots' necessary art of self-sufficiency, an entirely different approach was needed to make the most of the Phantom's versatility with two members of crew and the aircraft's novel radar and weapons systems. Tonight I was unaware at this stage, of course, of the urgency with which I'd need to apply such versatility in rapidly changing and difficult circumstances.

The Phantom's angular, no-nonsense lines, bathed in the glow of sodium lighting, were familiar to me by now as I carried out the ritual of external checks. For this sortie, with three external fuel tanks fitted, I would have the capability to fly for some two to three hours even without the planned in-flight refuelling. Such a concept was indeed novel for an ex-Lightning pilot. All seemed sound as I looked around the Phantom so, having completed my external look-around which finished with a check of the port side of the aircraft, I climbed the access steps to enter the front cockpit.

The Phantom cockpit always struck me as reasonably roomy, especially after the confines of the Lightning cockpit which, like many aircraft of that generation, seemed surrounded by a cramped, claustrophobic confusion of wires and pipes carelessly threaded together before the days of ergonomics. Immediately in front of the Phantom pilot the flight instruments were logically laid-out and clear; to the left, the large undercarriage operating lever appeared functional and well-placed compared to the fiddly buttons in the likes of Lightnings and Hunters; to the right, the engine instruments were in neat, easy-to-interpret rows. Later, this facet would help me with the swift decision making which would become necessary.

The start-up procedures went as planned and before long I was leading the other Phantom as we taxied towards the current runway-in-use. "You're clear to line up and take off," said the duty air traffic controller at which both Phantoms moved onto the runway to take up pre-briefed positions. When there, I re-applied the Phantom's brakes, ensured that my number two was in position, then with my left hand advanced the Rolls-Royce Spey engines to around eighty percent revolutions. At this point, the engine indications were normal and gave no hint of the trouble to come. I therefore released the brakes, advanced the throttles to full cold power, allowed the engines to settle, and then selected reheat. The appliance of science was thrilling; I felt a momentary tingle through the nerves while the engines paused before responding to deliver a prompt and punchy kick-in-the-back.

As we climbed through layers of cloud, my number two maintained a thirty-second trail. When we broke clear of the cloud tops, the radar controller gave separate headings to each Phantom for our first 'split' and the interception exercises soon got underway. On a moonless night such as this one, when my only guide was the voice in my ear, accurate responses to the navigator's instructions were key. While he stared at his radar screen and worked away to calculate the intercept geometry, his instructions flowed and my reactions had to follow as if pilot, navigator and Phantom were one unit. Life could become more than a little interesting during the last phase of an interception when we drew near to the target. In the final stages, as the interceptor closed for a visual identification, or Visident, to determine the type and details of an 'intruder', good crew co-operation could make the difference between success or failure.

After an hour or so of interceptions, the ground radar controller gave instructions for our rendezvous with the Victor tanker. I was used to the art of air-to-air refuelling, nonetheless it could be daunting to think of approaching, in the dark and at several hundred miles per hour, a circular drogue ('basket') that dangled in the sky and which was virtually invisible until you were nearly on top of it. As with the interception techniques we had just practised, I had to rely on my navigator's patter while he used his airborne radar. That night, conditions remained dark and, as before, the only guide was his voice in my ear. The navigation lights on the Victor tanker itself showed up well enough but the pinpoint circles of fluorescent light around the drogue's rim were hard to make out until the last moment.

Our technique was different to that used by some other air forces and navies, including the USA. In the latter case, the US 'receiver' aircraft would hold a steady formation position on a Boeing KC-135 Stratotanker while a member of the tanker crew, a boom operator, manoeuvred a refuelling drogue onto the receiver's probe. In the Royal Navy and the Royal Air Force, however, it was the pilot's task to manoeuvre his aircraft onto the refueller's drogue.

As I applied the required skills on that dark night, it occurred to me that our basic techniques amounted to an art more than a science. I found it best not to stare directly at the drogue but to look at, and formate on, the tanker itself. This, of course, was easier said than done and inevitably different shades of dark and grey, blind spots and patterns, could confuse a pilot's night vision. To avoid tunnel vision, it was necessary to keep the eyes moving; an awareness of the 'big picture' was important. While a pilot needed intense concentration, he had at the same time to remain relaxed. It was a trying paradox; an individual's capacity could easily become overloaded, and the hazards of night-time refuelling could become mind-boggling in conditions of heavy turbulence. Sod's Law, of course, stated that a pilot's success rate was inversely proportional to the degree of urgency dictated by the need for fuel.

That night, however, all went well and having topped up to full tanks, both Phantoms bade farewell to the friendly Victor crew before peeling off to set up for further interception practises. It was at this point that the other Phantom crew announced that there was a problem with their aircraft and that they would have to return to Leuchars at once. "That's copied," I said on the aircraft radio.

My navigator then asked, "What the hell are we supposed to do now with all of this fuel we've just taken?"

"We could carry out a practise diversion, I suppose," he said.

"Okay," I said. "Where do you fancy going to, Pete?"

"Lossiemouth will be open. I'm sure they'll be delighted to see us at this time of night."

"And the noise we make when overshooting?"

"It'll be appreciated, I'm sure."

"As much as a blast of Arctic air in the face." With a chuckle at our own good percipience, I declared our plan to the ground controller. "Understood," she said, "I'll arrange it with Lossiemouth."

On the southern shore of the Moray Firth, RAF Lossiemouth's weather factor was favourably influenced by the Gulf Stream's milder waters. The airfield, therefore, was used regularly as a diversion airfield by other units (it was used also, incidentally, by 617 [Dambuster] Squadron to launch against the German ship *Tirpitz* in November 1944) and a practise diversion there seemed a logical way to use excess fuel as well as to re-familiarise ourselves with local procedures.

The ground controller told us to change radio frequency to Lossiemouth's radar controller and soon the Phantom was settled on the glidepath for an instrument approach. In the distance, the airfield lights, ringed with night-time haze, stood out from the blackness of the Moray Firth. I told the controller that, in view of the aircraft weight, we'd plan to overshoot rather than perform a touchdown and 'roller' procedure. "Okay," he said. "You're clear to proceed."

It was just as the runway approach lights began to flash beneath that I pushed the Phantom's throttles forward to their full cold power position to commence overshoot. I expected to hear the normal wind-up sound of the Rolls-Royce Speys. Instead, I heard something very different – an almighty bang – a noise so loud that it seemed to shake the whole structure of the aircraft. I nearly jumped out of my skin. "You're on fire!" yelled the controller. I glanced at the neat rows of engine instruments; in an instant I could spot the cause of the problem. The gauge for the left-hand Spey's engine revolutions showed a big, fat zero. There were no residual revolutions; the engine had seized solid. 'Shit!' I thought. "Mayday!" I cried.

The damage caused by the engine explosion.

In view of the Phantom's weight, an immediate landing would not have been a good idea. I needed instead to overshoot and dump fuel before making a single-engine approach and landing. With fingers firmly crossed I selected reheat on the good engine to initiate the overshoot. I say with fingers firmly crossed because, at that current aircraft weight and position, we'd probably have had to eject if the reheat had failed. Luckily, the reheat did not fail and the Phantom climbed away slowly. I explained to my poor navigator what had been going on and, as we made for a suitable height and position to dump fuel, it was not long before I was able to downgrade the emergency status from 'Mayday' to 'Pan' and to head back for Lossiemouth.

Despite my anxiety, the subsequent recovery went as planned. When the Phantom finally touched down on terra firma, my first emotion was one of satisfaction; I experienced a considerable sense of relief as the runway lights rushed past in pairs. I streamed the tail parachute then, as speed reduced, touched the brakes. Using the good engine, I was able to taxi to the visiting aircraft dispersal area before closing down and climbing out of the cockpit.

When I spoke to the air traffic controller he told me that his men had driven along the runway to check for debris while we had been away from the area to dump fuel. They had collected a bag-and-a-half of engine blades scattered along the runway. The fire that he'd reported had been red hot blades ejected from the engine tailpipe. He said that we'd been fortunate that the blades hadn't caused airframe or other damage as they flew around within the engine. I thought about this for a moment then nodded and said:

"True enough, but the Phantom is a rugged machine."

"Rugged?"

"Oh, yes," I said. "There's no doubt about that. She's a tough old bird."

CHAPTER 10

NAVAL WHAT-KNOTS

ALAN WINKLES' LIFE ON THE OCEAN WAVES

The news, I noticed, caused a fleeting grimace to fall across his face. "There's nothing we can do about it," said my observer with a shrug. I gazed at the observer, the naval equivalent of a RAF navigator, as the two of us, anxious to proceed, hovered by the operations room door. "As they say, time to spare, go by air," he concluded for this was already our third delay and, until our Phantom could be fixed and bearing in mind the occasion with its potentially hazardous prospects, my nerves were becoming distinctly nervier. The aircraft, though, was still unserviceable and we had no choice but to wait for better news from the engineers.

We decided to return to the 892 Squadron aircrew crewroom. "Coffee?" he asked. "Thanks," I said. "Standard NATO please." This meant white coffee with plenty of sugar. As he dealt with the makings, I glanced around the crewroom. Models of aircraft carriers, ship-related artefacts, pictures on walls, left the casual onlooker in no doubt that this was a naval establishment with long-established naval traditions. The very air seemed to exude naval niceties, and heaven help anyone who should show even the mildest lack of concern for scrupulous nautical terminology. The ceiling, for example, was not a ceiling but a deck-head. The floor was not a floor but the deck. Furthermore, 'companionways' were not to do with friendship but were concerned with – well I wasn't altogether certain at this early stage of my naval induction but understood that they were to do with access hatches and ladders. And to 'fish' was unconnected with the hobby of sticking a line and bait into water but involved securing an anchor to the ship's side.

On the aviation front, the term MADDL, (mirror-assisted dummy deck landings), was far from meaning to get in a muddle. I had practised quite a few of these at RAF Leuchars. On the easterly runway there, a simulation of the flight deck of the aircraft carrier HMS *Ark Royal* had been painted along with imitation cables to represent those on a real flight deck. To one side of the runway, an optical landing system (part of which was nicknamed 'meatball' or just 'ball') had been set up to guide the pilot as he came in to land. Special techniques were required and, having flown five sessions of twenty minutes each, I'd been declared ready

892 Naval Air Squadron photograph, 1976. Note the 11 RAF aircrew.
Alan Winkles is third from right in the front row.

for the real thing. And the real thing was about to happen if it were not for these irksome delays.

In addition to MADDL and other specialised aspects, as an air force man ('crab' in navy parlance) newly-appointed to take command of the Royal Navy's Phantom Training Flight based at Leuchars, I was keen to learn about broader features of life on the ocean waves. I glanced at HMS *Ark Royal's* photograph which had been placed on an adjacent wall. The aircraft carrier's profile was distinctive and her hull carved tidy trenches in the sea before the waters collapsed in a chaos of froth. Amassed astern, great waves were churned up by her propulsion system. To one side of the *Ark Royal's* picture were photographs of lined-up members of 892 Squadron, the unit to which I had been detached before commencing my new job. Eyes large and fine, chins strong and determined, these were individuals who looked tied up in positively ideal naval knots. I mused, however, that despite superficial jollity, life in the navy could prove to be an introspective one where someone from a non-naval background might not feel particularly happy. In my own case, I was fairly familiar with the set-up having just completed a tour as a newly-promoted squadron leader and flight commander on 43 Squadron, another Leuchars-based unit. I already knew a number of the 892 Squadron aircrew, nonetheless I was aware of tales, for instance, of walking up to an old sea salt to engage him in striking conversation only to find that the latter seemed bored and would turn his back.

I was aware of something else, too, an issue which tended to foster an undercurrent of ill-feeling. In an environment of endless defence cuts, 892 Squadron personnel had convinced themselves that theirs would be the Royal Navy's last fixed-wing squadron (an unjustified prediction, as it turned out, for in 1980 the Fleet Air Arm would start to be equipped with Sea Harriers). As a result, the squadron had adopted a symbolic inverted omega, 'the end of everything' according to one bleak interpretation of this, the last letter of the Greek alphabet (and the very antithesis, incidentally, of the symbol Pi – 3.14 – that simple shack with a slanted roof which, so went one theory, represented the entrance to civilisation). On the tail of 892 Squadron's Phantoms, an inverted omega was painted boldly and poignantly on a white diamond placed on a red fin flash. Some held the view that the Pi symbol might have portrayed a more constructive attitude. Regretfully, the squadron's pessimistic outlook, if inclined to colour feelings, also cast an unfortunate shadow over an impressive past. For it was seven years earlier, in May 1969, that 892 Squadron had gained a claim to fame when one of their Phantoms had won *The Daily Mail* Trans-Atlantic Air Race with a record time from New York to London of 4 hours 46 minutes and 57 seconds.

During induction briefings, I'd had to read, mark, learn and inwardly digest other general information about the senior service. I'd learned, for example, how the *Ark Royal*, launched in May 1950 from the Cammell Laird shipyard, held 'first and last' records; when commissioned in 1955, she was the world's first angled flight deck carrier. Now, though, she was the Royal Navy's last remaining conventional catapult and arrested-landing carrier. The ship's motto (*Desire Does Not Rest*) and her nickname (*The Mighty Ark*) had appeared rather apposite in the context of a NATO exercise in the Mediterranean Sea six years earlier, in November 1970. *The Mighty Ark* had collided with a Soviet Kotlin class destroyer which had been shadowing the aircraft carrier and which, without warning, had turned across her bows. Both ships sustained minor damage and the Soviets lost two crew members. On another notable occasion, the conventional catapult system was used in an unconventional way – to shoot a piano into the sea for the 1960s TV series *Not Only, But Also* (which starred Peter Cook and Dudley Moore).

2-inch rocket salvo.

At present, another television series, the documentary programme *Sailor*, was the cause of a buzz of excitement within naval circles. In the month of February 1976, the *Ark Royal* would commence a Western Atlantic deployment during which life on board would be filmed. Before the deployment, *Ark Royal's* aircraft, including Blackburn Buccaneers from RAF Honington and twelve 892 Squadron Phantoms from RAF Leuchars, were due to rendezvous with the carrier which was currently steaming off the approaches to the Bristol Channel. Today, 6 February 1976, I was scheduled to fly in the number four position for the first wave of four Phantoms. The leader's aircraft, however, had developed technical problems, he'd therefore taken my Phantom and consequently I'd slipped to the second wave. I was about to walk out for the second wave when the senior engineering officer had hurried up to me to say that my aircraft had been reallocated and that I would now be on the third wave. When the third wave was cleared to start up, the left engine of my aircraft had failed to start, the other three Phantoms had proceeded as planned and now my observer and I were stuck until the machine could be fixed.

This situation, perhaps, had predisposed me to think many thoughts and while my observer and I continued to wait in the crewroom, I began to speculate about life on board an aircraft carrier. When, eventually, we'd begin to set sail across the Atlantic, even the near 55,000-ton displacement of the mighty *Ark Royal* would not be immune to the effects of wind and wave. I could picture the clouds that might stumble along before the freshening wind that signalled stormy weather ahead. The sea would take its cue, no doubt, and as the rise and fall of the swell developed, as mere hillocks gradually grew into mountains with valleys so steep that the ship would seem to slide down them, the hearts of crews might sink correspondingly. Observers in the carrier's bridge might train binoculars on the snow-white crests of waves which would burst into a frenzy of foam and phosphorescence until the ship, in a most stomach-sickening way, would commence its descent into the next giant valley. While the ship tackled the fearsome gradient, the sea would crash against the hull as if Poseidon himself had decided to pummel the vessel with a great fist. At length, though, the storm would pass, perhaps during the night, and I would glimpse the night sky, starry and cloudless, as the sea started to settle.

I wondered about members of the ship's crew, especially the more senior ones, and how they might take to the presence of an air force 'crab' on board. If I was a 'crab', then presumably I'd have to adopt anthropomorphic habits. In my fertile imagination I could picture meeting the ship's captain ('Big Wilf' Graham) or maybe one of the senior commanders. I'd expect a large, fat individual with a red face and a booming voice to burst into the room, but instead a slight, not very tall, man with a hint of ready humour in his eyes might greet me. From the so-called 'goofers' gallery beside the ship's bridge I might spot wildlife – whales, even, or pods of dolphins that would plunge, turn and race near the ship for no purpose other than to have fun. There's been recent talk that the United States Navy trained dolphins to kill enemy divers in the Vietnamese War, although the rumours have been denied. I might catch sight of an albatross, though nowadays these are rarely seen in the North Atlantic which, as in Samuel Taylor Coleridge's *The Rime of the Ancient Mariner*, may help to explain one of the reasons behind this seabird's aura of myth – something almost supernatural and incomprehensible. Certainly, I was aware that many sailors would regard it as disastrous to shoot or harm an albatross.

The voice of the duty operations officer abruptly interrupted my reverie. "Okay!" he yelled from the open door of the ops room. "The engineers have just rung through. Your aircraft is serviceable." At once, my observer and I leapt into action. We grabbed our bone domes, Mae West lifejackets and other paraphernalia before hastening towards the engineering line hut where I'd sign for our Phantom. By now it was 15:00, the daylight already showed signs of wanting to creep away from the dank, wet, wintry conditions but at least the engineering chiefie appeared upbeat when we entered the line hut. "The aircraft should be fine now, sir," he said, "I'm sure you'll have no more bother, like." I wasn't entirely certain whether this was said in a spirit of 'nudge, nudge, wink, wink' but I took his remark at face value as I hastened towards the lone Phantom with its inverted omega-painted tail.

If I had doubts, these were unjustified because this time both engines started satisfactorily and before long we had taken off to head south across Wales and towards *The Mighty Ark*. As we drew near to the ship I had to dump fuel to lighten our aircraft to the level required for landing on a carrier. The flying control officer ('Flyco') cleared me to make an approach and soon I could determine the ship's outline on the horizon. As briefed, I set up at an altitude of 600ft in a downwind position. But it was not, I recall, until the finals turn that suddenly, as the carrier's deck began to loom faster and faster, that the full significance of the task dawned on me. My grip on the flight controls might have become ever firmer, like that of an over-anxious rookie pilot. No amount of MADDL training, I realised, could prepare me for this. The shock was profound; the idea of pressing on and on to land in an area so small that it looked more like a dinky toy than anything else seemed risible – impossible. I tried to gaze fixedly at the 'meatball', but it was no use; the miniscule nature of the landing spot became a fixation. My first approach missed the flight deck altogether.

When I overshot for another attempt, the deck landing officer (Little 'F') instructed me to try a couple of approaches – "practise bolters," he said, "to get the feel of things". To add to the pressure, daylight was now beginning to fade fast. At least the optical landing system's lights showed up well – the horizontal row of green datum lights, the vertical meatball light which revealed my position relative to the correct glideslope, and the red flashing wave-off lights which, when lit, ordered a mandatory go-around. On the next attempt, the Phantom's wheels actually touched the carrier's deck but well beyond the fourth and last arrestor wire. On the subsequent attempt the same thing happened. Then, to my astonishment, Little 'F' said: "Lower your hook and try it for real!"

By now an intensity of feelings had started to well up inside me, an unstoppable wave. 'Once more unto the breach, dear friends,' I thought bizarrely as if I was Henry the Fifth himself. 'Hold hard the breath and bend up every spirit,' seemed an equally apposite part of that kingly, if theatrical, discourse. My mind snapped into overdrive; hell-bent on success (or perhaps on avoiding failure), I tried to fly the required datums as accurately as possible. I recall muttering instructions to myself like some do-it-yourself fiend: Watch that airspeed... don't over-control... the wind's down the centre line, but be wary of the black hole of sink before crossing the stern... anticipate a neck-snapping retardation if the hook catches – 145 knots to zero in just 150ft of deck... close your mouth and keep your teeth clamped together... watch that meatball... up a bit... now down a bit... left... right... down... down... THUMP... shit! Hit the deck... missed the wire... full power... go round, Alan...

As I pushed the throttles forward to select full reheat I glimpsed a sea of faces lined up in the 'goofers' gallery high up on the carrier's island. Bad news travels fast, I thought; word must have spread that the chief 'crab' was having problems. When I turned downwind, a glance at the fuel gauges showed the lowest fuel state that I'd ever seen in a Phantom. At once, I raised the undercarriage and began a turn towards the diversion airfield of St Mawgan in Cornwall. It was at this juncture that my poor observer, who had remained silent up to now, spoke: "We're not allowed to divert yet," he said. "Little 'F' will decide when we head for the 'beach'. That's why we call out our fuel state on finals." This was one of many things that the navy had failed to tell me until the issue arose.

Swiftly, I reduced power, lowered the wheels again and manoeuvred back down to 600ft. I could hear a few unusual crackles on the aircraft radio, otherwise a poignant silence dominated the airwaves. I wanted to wipe the cold sweat from my brow but there was no time. In the closed confines of my immediate world a sense of apprehension assaulted my senses in a way that made the head reel, the stomach churn and the legs feel weak. At a height of 300ft astern the ship, everything seemed to be going wrong. I approached the carrier's stern in a blur of moving ailerons, tailplane and throttles. The deck's round-out point loomed: 'this cannot work...I'm too low...now too high...it looks horrendous – an absolute fiasco – an impossibility.' Suddenly, with a whopping great wallop, the Phantom struck the deck. My head snapped forward; the control stick flew out of my right hand; my left hand inadvertently pushed both throttles fully forward. The landing felt so hard that I could almost feel my eyes drop through my neck.

However, despite the whirl of flight controls, the incredible, erratic and thoroughly dangerous approach path, not to mention the generally and altogether not-so-whizz actions of the new whizz-kid on the block, the Phantom's hook had caught cable number four. It was, as they say, a case of by hook or by crook. With full reheat unwittingly selected, the engines persisted to blast flames, fumes and fury across *The Mighty Ark*'s flight deck. The cable, though, managed to hold on to twenty-or-so tons of as out-of-control machinery as anyone could possibly envisage. For a moment, I remained in a state of icy, paralysed stillness as time and motion appeared to stop. My breathing, too, seemed to stop until, in an abrupt, almighty gush of relief, I exhaled air from my lungs. I slumped down in my seat while, in a robotic movement, pulling back the throttles.

But now the Phantom started to roll backwards. I was on the verge of applying the brakes – but that would have tipped the aircraft onto its tail. I realised that the cable was de-tensioning; this, fortunately, was one thing that the navy had told me. Quickly, I carried out the after-landing checks: hook up – flaps up – operate the wings-fold mechanism. Ahead, I spotted a marshaller who waved his arms frantically; I applied engine power to follow his directions to a parking slot. On the aircraft radio I heard Little 'F's' voice: "Well done, Alan!" Above, in the 'goofers' gallery, I glimpsed the row of onlookers execute a slow handclap.

When I'd parked the Phantom in the 'Fly 1' area and closed down the engines, I was aware of sea rushing past on my right side, some 60ft below. While the deck crew fastened the Phantom to the carrier with sixteen chains, I opened the canopy and stood up to survey my new 'airfield'. This was not a good move: I nearly fell out of the cockpit as the ship was heaved round in a steep turn out of wind. I glanced at the seafaring objects around me; the lifebelts, the painted deck, the chains, ropes and assorted equipment, all of it weather-beaten, sun-bleached, rain-drenched. The subjugating, salty environment wanted to eat away with a million hungry mouths to bleach all in its path to a faded whitish hue. In the background, the steady throb of machinery, the distant hum of the ship's four Parsons turbines, left me in little doubt of the need to acquire sea-legs as rapidly as possible.

FIVE MONTHS LATER

My first attempt at landing on an aircraft carrier's flight deck may have been the cause of furrowed brows and pursed lips, but eventually, after several more practise 'traps' (cable engagements), I was reasonably happy with my deck landing skills. By June 1976, my six-week planned deployment on HMS *Ark Royal* to 'learn the ropes' had already stretched to nearly five months. However, the flying schedule had been intense and I was confident that I'd learnt a rope or two; indeed, having achieved fifty 'traps' I felt like an old hand.

Operationally, I'd had opportunities to fire live air-to-air Sparrow and Sidewinder missiles against head-on, high-level targets. On the Vieques firing range located on the island of Vieques adjacent to the main island of Puerto Rico, I had practised live bombing runs. A dramatic sequence of the documentary *Sailor* featured footage of Phantom aircraft at the Vieques range with *Shine on You Crazy Diamond* by Pink Floyd playing in the background.

Heavyweight launch. 13x 500lb live bombs
bound for Vieques range, Puerto Rico.

In the wardroom, even though I was acutely scrutinised at first, after a while I seemed to be accepted as acceptable and I began to settle into naval ways. To reach my miniscule cabin in the ship's bowels I had to negotiate a series of labyrinthine passageways and it took a while before I could find my way without getting lost. Entertainment on board was restricted, more or less, to an intermittent supply of old newspapers and occasional film shows although, as ever, the navy's social scene was energetic. *The Mighty Ark*'s personnel, never averse to shore runs, appeared to enjoy a greater number of such runs than usual, but this was probably thanks to the USA's 200th anniversary celebrations. Next month the Queen and Prince Philip would visit the United States as part of the bicentennial events and on 4 July 1976 the Queen presented a bicentennial bell bearing the inscription: 'For the people of the United States of America from the people of Britain – 4 July 1976 – let freedom ring.' On the same date, a large international fleet of tall-masted sailing

'Duskers' catapult launch.

ships gathered in New York City.

A fortnight or so before these events, when HMS *Ark Royal* was positioned in the Caribbean area, I was programmed for so-called 'duskers' sorties. Such sorties entailed a launch for radar training exercises and were timed to arrive back at the carrier shortly before darkness set in. Night flying from a carrier involved particular hazards so the Royal Navy applied strict criteria; crews selected to join the limited number of 'night team' members had to be specially trained and qualified. One requirement, for example, was that a pilot should have flown at least one hundred 'traps' by day before he could start 'duskers' flights prior to full night flying. In my own case, therefore, the fifty 'traps' I had acquired to date were inadequate although 892 Squadron's commanding officer, an observer in the rank of commander, had called me to his cabin to say that 'they' had decided that it would be beneficial for me to experience carrier night flying before commencing my new job. "We know that you've logged only fifty 'traps'," he said, "but we think you should get a feel for night flying. It'll help you to gain an understanding of the problems." I believe that I swallowed hard, said nothing, and thought about my family who, in a week or two, I was due to rejoin at Leuchars.

That evening, my 'duskers' sortie worked out well enough. The following night, a similar sortie also went well except for a brief delay before landing which meant that, with the rapid nature of tropical sunsets, the light had almost vanished by the time I landed. The next day I was programmed for an afternoon flight then an early night sortie. For the latter, the carrier-controlled approach at the end of the sortie went swimmingly with a smooth transition onto the glidepath. At a range of half-a-mile from the carrier I looked up to see the meatball to the left of the deck with all of the lights perfectly aligned; the Phantom was positioned on the ideal glidepath and centre line. I applied a touch of engine power just before crossing the stern to avoid the black hole of sink caused by the ship's 26 knots of forward speed and we took the number two wire. Perfect, I reckoned, and definitely worth a small pat on the back if not a large celebratory drink in the bar.

It was later in the wardroom bar when I was surrounded by the lesser types, those excluded from the elite 'night team', that I was able to recall my success with a certain amount of swagger. "All this fuss that goes with carrier night flying seems rather overstated," I announced in what was probably an unduly loud voice. I hadn't noticed that standing nearby with his back to me was the 892 Squadron commanding officer. He turned and his eyes flicked up. I felt suddenly hot. I stared at my drink, surely the cause of immediate misfortune. Officers in the vicinity fell silent; the banter quietly fizzled out and in the ensuing hush I could almost hear the metallic clatter of a mistimed clanger.

"Is that right, Alan?" said the commanding officer. He spoke softly, with a barely perceptible smile, his tone one of silky fluidity. "In that case you'd better have another go tomorrow evening." How vainly I must have endeavoured to appear assured and eager.

So it was that the next evening, as my observer and I headed for our Phantom, we had to be wary in the dark of stepping over the ship's side into the watery abyss. As I stumbled around checking the aircraft, the observer, who had spent all day shaking his head at me as he interjected the odd comment about 'the walls have ears' and 'careless talk costs lives' and 'how many times must I tell you what you already know?', clambered into his cockpit. Before long I had started the engines, all was well in both cockpits and we were cleared to manoeuvre to the carrier's catapult. When the deck crew gave the appropriate 'wind-up' signal, I eased the twin throttles forward. Soon, the massive might of the twin Rolls-Royce Spey engines' reheats lit up a sea of little white faces looking up as the deck crew monitored every move. Now, with a right-hand salute, I committed to the launch. My flying helmet was pressed back against the ejection seat's head rest; I tensed my arm muscles for the launch from zero to 145 knots in 2.7 seconds. Suddenly, as the well-rehearsed chain of events reached its climax, a violent acceleration of 5.7 times the force of gravity propelled the Phantom into abrupt and absolute blackness. The situation was not helped as, foolishly, I had impeded my night vision by staring at bright lights on the carrier's surrounds. For a short period I could not see the horizon but as we climbed, the twilight gradually emerged. That night, the Caribbean darkness was complete apart from the brilliance of the stars. The sun, which beat so mercilessly during the day, had set and there was no moon. All colour had disappeared; miles of blackness stretched to infinity – dark cloud, dark surroundings, dark shadows, pure darkness.

After an hour or so of radar-controlled practise intercepts we began our descent to low level where the cloak of night seemed even darker than at high altitude. There was little wind and the ship, to minimise the landing speed of its aircraft, had to hunt for whatever headwind it could find. At a range of five miles from the carrier I turned right through thirty degrees. The controller then ordered me to turn fifty degrees to the left to regain the all-important centre line for the approach. This large amount of turning, though, meant that I flew through the centre line in a zig-zag pattern. By the time I reached a range of just half-a-mile or so from the carrier, the aircraft was still not quite on the centre line and the meatball lights showed white: the Phantom was above the required glidepath. With the aircraft closing rapidly towards the touchdown point, I reduced power. Now the approach lights appeared to indicate that I was way off to the left, though I found out later that it was, in fact, a matter of a few yards. Applying bank, I over-corrected to the right. Meanwhile, having reduced power, I forgot about the 'black hole' effect, the Phantom started to sink and suddenly I became convinced that I was about to crash into the ship's stern. At once, I selected full reheat to initiate wave-off action.

The Rolls-Royce Spey engines fitted to Royal Navy Phantoms had been modified with a fast reheat facility; when reheat was selected, just 1.25 seconds would elapse before the effects were felt. That night, at that moment in time, one-point-two seconds felt like an eternity. The spectre of storms, slippery slopes and uncontrolled spirals began to dance before my eyes; I wasn't myself and couldn't work out why; I wanted to hold up my hand, shout "Stop!" and rewind the tape. Instead, I perpetrated my final and worst error of the night, I pulled back the stick.

As the reheats lit, the Phantom started to react but at 145 knots the aircraft was behind the lift/drag curve – that dreaded diagram of aerodynamics so carefully explained to students of the subject. By pulling back the stick, the angle of attack of the wings increased but I gained no extra lift; the Phantom merely rotated around its lateral axis thereby lowering the hook towards the deck. The hook now attached itself to the deck's fourth wire even though the aircraft wheels were still airborne. It was with a savage thud, therefore, that the aircraft, as if grasped by a huge hand, slammed onto the deck. Meantime, the Rolls-Royce Speys remained in full reheat. When I looked to my right the carrier's island was lit up like Trafalgar Square's Christmas tree in the festive season. There were few signs of festivity, however, shown by the members of the deck crew who, in spontaneous acts of self-preservation, had thrown themselves down. The prostrate bodies remained illuminated until I cancelled the Phantom's reheats, carried out the post-landing checks and, as surreptitiously as possible, steered the Phantom to the 'Fly 1' parking area.

Having closed down both engines, I believe that I remained still for some moments as if unable or unwilling to move but aware that I seemed to be shaking badly. Perhaps I spoke to my observer, I don't recall, though I do recall how he admitted later that the episode had nearly caused him to operate his ejection seat. I recall, too, the voice of 892 Squadron's commanding officer who, from the 'Flyco' position on the carrier's bridge, had watched the whole shameful sequence of events. Just before I'd closed down the Phantom's engines I'd heard his voice on the aircraft radio, "Well, well, well, Alan," he'd said dryly. "Not quite so easy tonight was it?"

CHAPTER 11
SOBERING MOMENTS

IAN HARTLEY IN THE FALKLANDS

I suppose it's happened to everyone: there'd be sunlight and shade, spots and patterns, the mind was elsewhere and you'd fail to make out what was right beside you. I'm not trying to invent excuses for that pilot, but I retain an enduring image as he bumbled along in his British Aerospace jump-jet Harrier aircraft while he admired the spectacle of a Falkland's early evening. Admittedly, as the sun's descent in a near-cloudless sky created a soothing scene, he may have had valid reasons for his evident state of reverie. For the vault of the world appeared in magnificently tinted colours that evening in 1984, and below his aircraft the bleak landscape looked benign as it was ruffled by gentle breezes. The splendour of the surrounds, the glory of the light, the sense of solitude all added up to an atmosphere of tranquillity and security. Perhaps, after the hard lessons of the day, this was a good opportunity for him to relax at last.

Meanwhile, in my 23(F) Squadron FGR2 Phantom, an alternative plot was developing. "There's a Harrier in the vicinity," said the radar controller, "would you like to intercept it?" This, of course, was tantamount to waving a red rag at a bull. "Affirmative," I said, "but I thought we were the only one airborne?" "So does he," he said, a trace of glee in his tone. I pictured the controller by his radar screen on Mount Byron in West Falkland as he now gave us vectors onto our unsuspecting target. It was not long before I spotted the Harrier visually. "He seems to be enjoying the view," I said to my navigator. Cautiously, I closed up to a loose echelon starboard position expecting the Harrier pilot to react at any second. He did not react, however, but continued to stooge along as if in some form of meditative state that a Buddist monk might envy.

"Let's move into close formation," I said to my navigator, "maybe that'll wake him up." Carefully, I eased into a close echelon starboard position thinking as I

Top: 43 Squadron F4-K on approach to RAF Leuchars, 1971. (*Roger Colebrook*)
Above: 43 Squadron F4-K. (*Roger Colebrook*)

Opposite clockwise from top: 43 Squadron
Phantom FG1. (*Roger Colebrook*);
43 Squadron FG1s in 'line abreast' formation.
Roger Colebrook is at the far end in 'C', 22
June 1970. (*Roger Colebrook*);
43 Squadron. (*Richard Pike*);
A Phantom FGR2 of 6 Squadron carrying a
selection of its varied armaments.
(*The Aviation Bookshop*)

Top: 92 Squadron Phantom flying over
Mount Etna, Sicily. (*Ian Hartley*)
Above: 111 Squadron on the last Aramament
Practice Camp at RAF Luqa in May 1978.
In the background are two Phantom GR2s.
(*Phil Owen*)

Opposite top: Crewroom photo of 92 Squadron aircrew, October 1981. (*Ian Hartley*)
Opposite below: F4-C of the 58th Tactical Training Wing from Luke AFB over the Arizona desert in 1978. (*John Walmsley*)

Top: Chris Stone starts engines for an air gunnery exercise in Malta, 1977. (*Chris Stone*)
Above: 'Goose' Ganse and 'Holgi' Radmann in the cockpit of a Phantom F-4 following the official decommission, Wittmund 2013. (*Ian Sykes*)

Opposite top: In-flight shot of Soviet Badger taken by QRA Phantom. (*Richard Pike*)
Opposite below: Luftwaffe Phantom F-4 37+18 refuelling. (*Peter Becker*)
Above: Luftwaffe F-4 38+28 in the hardened aircraft shelter at Wittmund 2013. (*Ian Sykes*)
Left: In-flight shots of 43 Squadron FG1, 1975. (*Richard Pike*)

Top: Luftwaffe Phantom F-4
38+34. (*Peter Becker*)
Above: No 20 Course
photograph, March 1973. Author
Richard Pike is first from left on
the front row. (*Richard Pike*)
Right: Phantom F-4K with one
second to hook on.
(*Alan Winkles*)

did so that surely he would do something now. I waited patiently but, no, there was still no reaction and I knew that I'd have to think of something else. With the sun behind me I realised that by easing the Phantom upwards its shadow would begin to darken the Harrier's cockpit. So it was then, as I manoeuvred judiciously, the Harrier pilot suddenly seemed to realise that all was not well. He looked round to be met by the sight of the muzzle of our Phantom's SUU gunpod a mere matter of feet above his head. He appeared physically to jump as far as his seat harness would allow. This was followed by the Harrier executing a brief series of wild gyrations before returning to a semblance of controlled flight. Fortunately for that Harrier pilot, however, we were in a training environment, the situation wasn't for real and it was not long before he was able to continue to wend his merry way back to Stanley airfield while we, too, flew the Phantom back towards that airfield which was our temporary home.

It was home, too, for some 2,000 detached military personnel although the airfield would be replaced as a base the following year when Prince Andrew opened RAF Mount Pleasant, the newest airfield in the Royal Air Force. With the motto 'Defend the right' (the Falkland Island's motto was 'Desire the right') Mount Pleasant would become renowned, amongst other things, for the longest corridor in the world – a half-mile passage that linked barracks, messes, recreational facilities and welfare areas. In the interim, after the surrender of Argentine troops on 14 June 1982 following seventy-four days of conflict, the runway at Stanley airfield, which had been bombed by Avro Vulcan aircraft with moderate success in a series of 'Black Buck' missions, had been fully repaired by British military engineers. Additionally, the runway had been extended by means of aluminium planking, and arrester equipment had been installed to allow Phantoms from 29(F) Squadron to operate as an air defence unit. 23(F) Squadron had taken over in late 1983 and the following year I'd been posted to the Falklands as a member of that squadron.

While, that evening, we flew above the peaty Falklands terrain I was conscious of Mount Usborne which, at 2,313ft in the central part of East Falkland, presented a potential hazard to aircraft. Below us, the naturally treeless nature of the islands stretched into the distance although wind-resistant vegetation in the form of dwarf shrubs stood out in the rugged landscape. This was no place, I reckoned, for the faint-hearted. There was a notable absence of roads although, in their place, rough peat tracks joined scattered communities such as Goose Green, San Carlos and Bluff Cove – places with names delivered from obscurity by the war of a couple of years ago. The tracks were used by locals on horseback and military vehicles although the latter, despite their all-terrain design, still tended to bog down in the swampy surfaces.

As we continued to fly towards Stanley, the recency of the war with Argentina was emphasised by the sight of occasional military dumping grounds. These made sad scenes, pictures which depicted the evident state of panic that afflicted the Argentinian conscripts as the war drew to a close. The many difficulties confronting the young men were reflected by a rag-bag collection of discarded oil drums, cooking utensils, fragments of vehicles, odd assortments of furniture and camping equipment, discernible aircraft parts. The latter consisted mainly of bits of FMA 1A 58 Pucará aircraft and Bell Huey helicopters. Over the coming months, Captain Mark Harrisson, a member of Bristow Helicopters Limited, the company currently contracted to provide two Sikorsky S61N helicopters to fly personnel and equipment to remote military sites across the Falklands, will extract from far-flung corners of the islands oddments of Pucarás and Hueys in order to reconstruct them into complete aircraft.

Pucará A-529 before its restoration,   *Pucará A-529 after its restoration,*
8 November 1985.   *23 March 1986.*

The Pucará, in particular, interested Mark Harrisson for it was an unusual aircraft manufactured by the *Fábrica Militar de Aviones*. A low-wing, twin-turboprop machine, the aircraft was capable of flying from unprepared strips. During April 1982 a dozen Pucarás were deployed to the Falklands by the Argentine air force (*Fuerza Aérea Argentina* or FAA). These aircraft, in addition to operating from Stanley airfield – which, incidentally, had a runway which was too short for Skyhawks and Mirages of the FAA – flew from small grass airstrips improvised at Goose Green and Pebble Island. Their role was one of reconnaissance and ground attack.

At the beginning of May 1982, three Pucarás at Goose Green were destroyed, and one of their pilots killed, by cluster bombs dropped by Harriers. Two weeks later, six more Pucarás were destroyed in a raid on Pebble Island by members of the Special Air Service. A number of other Pucarás were lost during the war and it was the remnants of these which Captain Harrisson sought out.

He had negotiated a deal with the Falkland Islands government whereby two

Pucarás and two Hueys would be reconstructed, one of each type for the Falkland Islands museum, the others he could keep to transport back to the United Kingdom. It was a complex task, but he was a determined individual helped by willing colleagues (including Captain Richard Pike) and by RAF engineers interested in the project. In an unfortunate conclusion, however, both of the aircraft donated to the Falkland Islands government were ploughed into the ground some years later, by then evidently unwanted.

AE-410 & A-529 on display at RAF Stanley,
30 March 1986.

"Ten miles to Stanley," my navigator prompted me. Soon, as the east-west runway of Stanley airfield loomed, I flew above the craggy peaks of Mount Tumbledown, scene of the war's final engagement in mid June 1982 when ten British and thirty Argentine lives were lost. The airfield, a mile or two beyond Port Stanley and situated on a remote site between Yorke Bay and Surf Bay, was renowned for fickle winds on the approach to landing. Indeed, fickle winds were a feature of the Falklands generally and I was reminded of an impromptu instance of this when I'd been flying in the vicinity of Falkland Sound. I'd spotted a Zodiac-type inflatable craft struggling against the winds and I'd been relieved to see the single occupant wave cheerily as I flew the Phantom in a low pass above him. It soon became clear that he was not in difficulty when, in a series of weaves, he set up a spectacular pattern of waves while Phantom and Zodiac followed each other as if in a mock dog-fight. Now, as I flew the Phantom into a 'break' manoeuvre at Stanley airfield, I called on the aircraft radio, "Downwind to land". "Clear to land," responded the air traffic controller.

After landing, when I conjured up images of the half-asleep Harrier pilot, my feelings were a mix of mirth, satisfaction and unease. For I had thoughts about how a fighter pilot can be likened to the duellist – how he must stalk, follow, act using techniques which are at once controlled, accurate, dispassionate. If our interception had been in a war environment, if it had been a case of kill or be killed, then that Harrier pilot would have been shot down, of that I had no doubt. And with the Falklands War still fresh in minds, the incident, though minor under the circumstances, nonetheless seemed to assume a certain significance, especially as some post-war commentators had credited Argentine air units with bearing the brunt of the battle.

Despite disadvantages, the FAA had inflicted serious damage and caused severe losses to British resources. Argentine low-flying jet aircraft attacking British ships had provided some of the grimmest and most dramatic images of the war. By the end of the conflict, the FAA's spirited conduct in the face of an effective air defence network had been admired by British commanders, including Admiral Sandy Woodward who had said, "The Argentine air force fought extremely well and we felt great admiration for what they did."

When, that evening, I'd parked the Phantom and shut down the aircraft, I walked together with my navigator to the 23 Squadron operations Portakabin to sign in the aircraft. We then made for the aircrew crewroom where we'd debrief the sortie over post-flight mugs of coffee. When my navigator made some comment about the Harrier pilot and his lack of lookout, I smiled and said: "How true. How very true." Then I thought – to judge or not to judge, that's the question. I glanced outside and noticed that the sun was sinking fast. Maybe, I mused, those FAA fighter pilots, exhausted by the relentless combat requirements, had struggled sometimes to recognise themselves or to make sense of their surroundings. In which case it was not so very different for that Harrier pilot. It had been a sobering moment but we all had lessons to learn.

CHAPTER 12

STERLING SERVICE

JOHN WALMSLEY'S LONG EXPERIENCE ON THE PHANTOM

Sardinia revealed many skies. Sometimes, when I watched from the Italian air force base at Decimomannu, I would observe a density of dark and blustery rain clouds which would pass overhead. At other times the sky would be dominated by a heavy, suffocating blanket of grey-ish cloud. Sometimes I'd gaze up at a sky dappled with white, fleecy clouds or a sky invaded by a mass of different clouds at many levels, some thick and opaque, others that looked like cotton-wool stretched apart. On some days, though, the sky was cloudless and a brilliant blue, stunning to the senses, would deprive the Italian military authorities of an excuse to close the practise firing range at Capo Frasca on Sardinia's west coast.

There were other excuses, too, especially at night when the lure of Chianti appeared to outweigh the need to keep the range open for use by our 54 Squadron detachment. It was the early 1970s and even though we needed the range for an intense period of weapons training and our timetable was tight, "the-range-she-is-a-closed" became a common cry.

The diversity of excuses was intriguing: the rescue helicopter, she's-a-broken...the sea state's too rough ("but we don't intend to go on the sea". "No? But the rescue boat does – anyway, the rescue boat, she's-also-a-broken")...the cross-winds are too high...the clouds are too low... the air traffic controllers are at lunch...Mamma, she has a headache (no, I made that one up). Oh, yes – another good one: the bloody Germans have fired at the wrong target. At least the latter was true, if unusual. Evidently, a Luftwaffe F-104 Starfighter, instead of firing, as briefed, at the right-hand set of strafe panels had fired instead at the left-hand panels while they were being checked by Italian conscripts.

If the challenge to complete our concentrated weapons training schedule was matched by the challenge to persuade the Italians to keep the range open, perhaps our informal scoring system helped to ease frustrations. When we were successful, the score would be marked as: Italians – zero, Brits – one. As the squadron weapons instructor, it was my task to maintain a tally. Another of my tasks, to analyse post-flight gun-sight film, was foiled one time when I noticed that our pilots, as they opened fire, were flying much too close to the strafe panels. These were attached to poles which I could use as datums to assess the gun-sight films.

The distance between the poles was stated accurately in the Italian range order book and I used this information to create a suitable 'gizmo' to measure pilots' firing ranges. I knew that the pilots could be relied on in the UK to fire at safe distances but my 'gizmo' indicated that this was not happening here. Eventually I asked the RAF range safety officer to measure the interval between the poles and, sure enough, they were further apart than stated in the book, thereby ruining my 'gizmo' and making me feel a little foolish. The result? Italians – one, Brits – zero. If, at times, I felt like a drowning man who struggled to swim fast against the rush of debris that followed a flood, it was surely understandable.

It was a year or two after this episode, by which time I had left 54 Squadron to become a weapons instructor at the Phantom Operational Conversion Unit at RAF Coningsby, that events sometimes came together to remind me of Sardinia. For despite operational challenges, in truth I retained fond memories of the island with its particular atmosphere and singular skies. Crews had to be wary, of course, of the mountainous terrain, especially the Sulcis range with Monte Linas rising to some 3,500ft which had to be negotiated when we flew to the range.

But we enjoyed good flying there and I could recall, too, the unique ambience marked by aromas – a confusion of orange blossom, smoke, silage – that seemed to complement the friendly attitude of local folk from nearby villages. Occasionally, when not required for flying, some of us would explore the area on foot. The rocky landscape was punctuated by cork trees, olive trees, scrub, roamed by a variety of animals, notably mountain goats with bells strung around their necks. Often a light sea breeze would wander in and out to rustle olive leaves which flashed a tangled semaphore of dark green and silver.

The flat Lincolnshire terrain around RAF Coningsby provided a stark contrast to this Sardinian scene. One hot summer's day at Coningsby, I took off with a student for a practise bombing sortie on the Wainfleet range in the Wash. I was in the Phantom's rear cockpit in my capacity as instructor. On the range, while the student flew round and round in a tight bombing pattern, the combination of a torrid, horrid immersion flying suit and the Phantom's ineffectual cooling system reminded me of the hot days we sometimes experienced on the range at Capo Frasca. I think that this, in turn, must have stimulated memories of the Luftwaffe F-104 pilot's blunder especially when, at about this time, I heard from one of my fellow instructors of another German gaffe. "You realise," the Luftwaffe pilot had said as he manoeuvred his Phantom to attack a target on the Wainfleet range, "that this is probably the first German bomb to be dropped on your country since the war?" At this, the instructor, aware of an unofficial five-second rule that, following a ludicrous comment, a suitable response should come within five seconds, elected to remain silent. However, when the Phantom was positioned downwind ready for the next pass, the range controller announced that the last pass had been 'unscorable at six o'clock'. Evidently the bomb had dropped well short of the intended target:

"Unscorable?" said the German.
"So it seems," said the instructor.
"Wozu ist das gut? ...what's the use of that?"
"No wonder you bloody lost the war," growled the instructor.

During my service career I would spend quite a few years at Coningsby. The first time was in 1969 as a member of No 2 Ground Attack/ Air Defence course. I was one of over two dozen students – a relatively large number following the build-up, which began the year before, of 228 (Phantom) Operational Conversion Unit (OCU) for the aircraft's introduction into squadron service. On graduation from the OCU, members of my course went on to form 54 Squadron (motto: '*Audax Omnia Perpeti*' – 'Boldness endures anything') at Coningsby.

Twenty-two years later, by which time I was the commanding officer of the OCU (at that point based at RAF Leuchars), our courses were rather smaller, sometimes with just one or two members. By then, however, the Phantom had had its day although it struck me as ironic that the aircraft was being taken out of service just as the first Gulf War (Operation Desert Storm) was in the process of storming away. Nonetheless, like it or not, the so-called 'Options for Change' had been announced by the Conservative Secretary of State for Defence Tom King and the following year, in October 1992, the last United Kingdom Phantoms were retired when 74 Squadron disbanded.

But it was before that contentious conclusion that I was posted, in the late 1970s, as an instructor pilot with the United States Air Force (USAF) at Luke Air Force Base in Arizona. Luke Air Force Base was a remarkable set-up. In introductory briefings I learned that the base was named after Second Lieutenant Frank Luke, a World War I fighter pilot with eighteen aerial victories to his credit. In September 1918 Luke's Spad S.X111 biplane was shot down at Murvaux in France after he had destroyed three enemy balloons. He survived the crash, scrambled out of the wreckage, drew his Colt model 1911 pistol and fired a few rounds at his attackers before he was killed. He was awarded a posthumous Medal of Honor, and Luke field in Hawaii was named after him until the name was transferred to the Arizona site. I was told that during World War II Luke field was the largest fighter training base in the US Army Air Forces, graduating more than 12,000 fighter pilots and earning the sobriquet 'Home of the Fighter Pilot'.

In further briefings about Luke Air Force Base I was astonished by the statistics. The base population consisted of some 7,000 personnel with double that number of family dependents. It was estimated that with many retired military members living in nearby Phoenix, the base served a total population of some 100,000 people – approximately the same number of personnel serving in the entire RAF at that point (and about three times the current number). An integral part of fighter pilot training at Luke was the Barry M Goldwater Air Force Range – nearly two million acres of relatively undisturbed desert to the south-west of the base. The range, which bordered Mexico, contained two airfield mock-ups as well as arrays of targets including vehicle convoys, aircraft, armour and various building structures. Overhead, I was told, there were about 57,000 cubic miles of airspace for us to practise air-to-air combat and to engage simulated ground targets. The size of the complex allowed simultaneous training activity on nine air-to-ground ranges and two air-to-air ranges.

Perhaps, having absorbed some of these numbers, I might have taken a deep breath and wanted to lie down in a darkened room. There was no time for histrionics, though, and I was soon drawn into the required training regime before I could qualify as an instructor pilot with the USAF. I flew the venerable Phantom F-4C, an early 1960s variant many of which had seen service in Vietnam; some even had red stars still painted on the engine intakes as symbols of a 'MiG-kill'.

I learnt that in July 1965 it was Phantom F-4Cs, firing AIM-9 Sidewinder air-to-air missiles, that scored the first USAF victories against North Vietnamese MiG-17s. Later that month, the first US aircraft to be lost in the war was a Phantom shot down by a surface-to-air missile. It was over a year later before a US jet was shot down by an enemy fighter, a MiG-21 firing an air-to-air missile. I was told that by the war's end in April 1975 an astonishing number of over 500 USAF Phantoms had been lost to enemy action.

During my training at Luke, a curious incident occurred which had far-reaching implications, although none of us realised it at the time. I was relaxing at home in our allocated temporary officers' quarter (TOQ) when I heard a muffled explosion not far away. My wife called out: "Look at this," and at once I went to where she stood. Both of us stared through a window.

"My God, what's going on?" A mains electric power cable had started to glow red and simultaneously we heard more explosions. It was not long before sirens started to wail and emergency vehicles began to dash about. We spotted military police rushing around with drawn weapons. Still uncertain what was going on, our concerns were hardly eased by several more explosions. Eventually, an especially large explosion seemed to signify the conclusion of the affair for the electricity cable stopped glowing red and, having earlier lowered itself mysteriously to the ground, sprang back up to its original position.

Later, I heard about the cause of the commotion. A technician who had been briefed to ground-run an engine in a McDonnell Douglas F-15 Eagle had started both of the powerful Pratt and Whitney F-100 engines instead of just one. To compound the problem, Phantom wheel-chocks had been used, not the much larger variety needed by the F-15. The technician had been briefed on how to start the engines but not on how to operate the wheel brakes. As the aircraft leapt forward over the inadequate wheel chocks, he was unable to control the machine. Within seconds, the F-15 had collided with another F-15 causing a loud explosion and a fire which destroyed both aircraft.

The technician, leaping clear of the carnage, lost an ear although fortunately he survived. Now, from this remarkable incident, came something even more remarkable. From the heat of the conflagration, strands of carbon fibre, a new material at the time, were released into the atmosphere and began to drift with the wind. Before long the recalcitrant strands became entangled with nearby electrical transformers causing them to short circuit and blow up. Intriguingly, the lessons learnt from this unplanned experiment were applied a dozen years later in the first Gulf War when cruise missiles delivered carbon fibre to Saddam Hussein's power stations.

At the height of an Arizona summer, when the sun shone with a fierce, contained intensity, the temperatures could soar to the high-forties centigrade. When I flew to the Goldwater range across the Sonoran Desert (which, incidentally, was the only area in the United States inhabited by 'big cat' Jaguars), the desert scrub, which included the famous saguaro cactus, was usually bathed in a relentless play of sunlit splendour. The scale was confounding – the volume of air above, the vast expanse of scrub beneath my Phantom, the interminable desert stretches that reached to the horizon. It could seem as if, in the grand setting on all sides, I beheld the entire universe; significant activities could appear suddenly finite and less consequential. Perhaps the ambient heat distorted perspectives and, certainly, the Phantom's pitiful cockpit cooling system hardly helped to assuage the oppressive temperatures.

If someone touched a parked aircraft without gloves, the scorching surfaces would cause a nasty burn. Before flight, I learnt the need to drink plenty of liquid from the water fountain in the squadron building. After the ritual of pre-flight external checks, and having strapped into the Martin Baker ejection seat which had been basking happily in the sun, heat seemed to radiate into one's body core. I carried a small bottle of cool water to drink at this juncture.

With engines running, a formation would be cleared to taxi to the inside runway (there were two runways at Luke Air Force Base, the inside one for takeoffs and landings, the outer one for 'touch-and go' procedures). Before entering the runway, the formation would stop at the 'last chance' area for a visual inspection for leaks or loose panels, and the weapons' safety pins would be removed. Now was the time for a last bottle of water. Once cleared onto the runway, the formation would line up for take-off, normally in pairs. Canopies would be closed at which point the insufferable heat would be concentrated with a vengeance as the Phantom cockpit turned into a suffocating greenhouse. Once airborne, at the first opportunity I would pull positive 'g' to encourage the mass of perspiration on my face and head to pour down over the eyes ready to be mopped up by a handy handkerchief.

One time, after I had qualified as an instructor, I was demonstrating to my student a so-called 'guns jink-out' manoeuvre. In this situation, an enemy fighter would be on your tail and in-range to fire its guns. It was a scenario that went back to the earliest days of fighter combat; a 'last chance saloon' situation – a case of kill or be killed. The sky was cloudless that day and below us the Sonoran Desert reflected its usual mix of greens, browns and yellows. I glanced at my altimeter. "Standby," I warned my student for this last-ditch manoeuvre involved savage flying. "Rolling now," I cried, and moved my control stick sharply. Then I hauled back the stick to pull the maximum allowable 'g' – in this case plus 6 'g' with external fuel tanks fitted. Now I reversed the direction of roll and pushed the stick forward to achieve the maximum allowable negative 'g' – minus 3 'g'. Within seconds, the process was repeated until, in a whirl of flying controls and violent movement, the attacker was thrown off.

The aim was to move from the initial position of disadvantage, progress towards a power vacuum before finally turning the situation into one of advantage. Throughout the process, it could feel as if I was tackling crocodile-infested waters with torrents that hissed and frothed and tossed about. After a drawn-out, exhausting tussle that would employ copious amounts of effort and energy the other Phantom should end up in my firing sights. By that stage, feeling very tired and very hot, perspiration would be running down my face in rivulets.

However, on that day, as the manoeuvres persisted, I suddenly sensed a control restriction: the control column would not move fully back. Thankfully the aircraft's roll function was normal. At once I called on the aircraft radio to halt the combat session, and simultaneously rolled the Phantom inverted. Now I pushed to the allowable limit of negative 'g', paused, then rolled in the opposite direction. This seemed to do the trick. The controls felt more-or-less normal again and I was able to maintain straight-and-level flight. Without delay, therefore, I turned gingerly for Luke Air Force Base and declared an emergency. A slow-speed handling check en route revealed no particular problems and a visual check by the other Phantom suggested nothing unusual. I opted, therefore, for a straight-in approach and landing which, fortunately, went without further mishap.

After landing, having recovered a measure of equilibrium, I talked through the incident with my student. The next day I wanted to speak with the technicians who were working to rectify the fault. This proved to be more problematic than I'd anticipated. With the large number of Phantoms based at Luke, engineering tasks were carried out centrally, unlike a RAF set-up where I could have gone directly to the squadron hangar to speak with engineers. At Luke, frankly, it took me most of the day to locate the correct hangar with the relevant aircraft. When, at length, I succeeded in this, I found the Phantom with its so-called third cockpit (an area behind the rear cockpit) opened up to allow access to the aircraft's control runs. "What's up?" I asked the technician in charge.

"It's this wiring loom, sir," said the technician, "look!" I could see clearly that the loom was able to move around loosely and thus interfere with the control runs.
"The combat manoeuvres must have shaken the wiring out of position."
"I guess so."
"Those looms are pretty close to the control runs."
"Sure are, sir."
"I never realised that before."
The technician grinned. "Sometimes it's best not to know," he said.

By the end of my tour at Luke, even though I'd grown to accept the scale of operations there, on occasions I still found that the sheer size of their organisation seemed overwhelming. I'd discovered that the Americans tended to do things very much their own way – a way which did not necessarily coincide with the methods I'd learnt as a member of the RAF. The American 'can-do' attitude was refreshing and widespread; woe betide the organisation or individual who was accused of being 'a day late and a dollar short'. Perhaps Winston Churchill's words were an apposite summary of my own experiences when he apparently said that the Americans could always be trusted to do the right thing, but only after they had exhausted every other possibility.

In the mid 1980s, by which stage I had left the USA and was a member of 43 Squadron based at RAF Leuchars, the squadron was scheduled for an armament practise camp (APC) in Cyprus. As preparations began, an air of expectancy and exuberance infused the squadron atmosphere. A detachment to sunny Cyprus was always a popular event. Sometimes in Cyprus I would stand by our squadron set-up at Akrotiri on the island's southernmost tip and listen to the faint pounding of the sea upon the nearby beaches.
The air would be heavy with a strange coalescence of sweet orange blossom

and not-so-sweet aviation fuel. The black surface of the east-west runway was a dark scar set between sandy-coloured grasses. As the day progressed the runway would begin to shimmer in the noon sun and sometimes near the squadron buildings the heat would soften the tar so that personnel had to step carefully. A heat haze would hang like a vapour over the airfield and we learned that on really hot days it could feel, as in Arizona, as if the heat was touching the inside of lungs. It could be helpful to take short, quick breaths with half-closed lips.

When the APC got underway, the programme was centred around concentrated sessions of air-to-air gun firing against a banner towed at a nominated height above the sea by brave souls flying an English Electric Canberra of 100 Squadron (whose motto 'Sarang tebuan jangen dijolok' – 'Never stir up a hornet's nest' – seemed, under the circumstances, somewhat optimistic). Our technique was to fly the Phantom at an airspeed of 400 knots (twice that of the Canberra), perform a series of manoeuvres, fire a half-second burst of 20mm cannon at the banner (about fifty rounds), then pull away to reposition while another Phantom repeated the process. At the end of a session, the Canberra crew would drop the banner over a designated area at Akrotiri so that individual Phantom pilots' scores, identified by different coloured shell holes, could be counted up. During the APC's early stages a pilot would fire only on the best passes. Later, when fully qualified and in good practise, he would fire on each pass.

One day, having enjoyed a good session of four passes, I flew back to Akrotiri with a sense of satisfaction. Approaching the airfield circuit at the usual airspeed of 400 knots, I broke hard left and pulled 4 'g' for the downwind position. Simultaneously, I eased back both throttles to the idle stop – this was standard procedure so that by the time I rolled out downwind the Phantom's airspeed would be just below 250 knots ready for operation of the flaps and undercarriage. However, when I lowered the undercarriage on that day, the indicator revealed that the Phantom's main wheels were locked down but that the nose-wheel was unlocked and therefore unsafe for landing. I felt a sudden dread. Potential hazards began to play through my mind and I was conscious that the squadron's tight schedule might be interrupted. I imagined the detachment commander pacing up and down as he muttered to himself and looked impatiently at his watch.

A fly-past at slow airspeed adjacent to the air traffic control tower proved less than illuminating: the controller said that the wheels looked down as normal, but regretfully she was in no position to confirm that the nose-wheel mechanism was locked. My navigator double-checked the actions stipulated in the emergency flight reference cards and I carried out the recommended procedures. The indicator, though, remained stubbornly unmoved. We had, therefore, to assume the worst – that the nose-wheel might collapse on landing.

The flight reference card's next prescribed procedure made my heart sink even further than it had sunk already. The Phantom's centre-line station needed to be obstruction-free. Any fuel tanks, external stores or weapons had to be jettisoned. In our case, this meant that our carefully nurtured and harmonised (and expensive) SUU23a gun-pod with its valuable Gatling gun had to be handed over to Davy Jones' locker in deep water off the southern Cypriot coast. When I did this, the heavy thump felt when the gun-pod was explosively ejected was accompanied – yes – by a final frustration: a nose-wheel locked indication.

After landing, the subsequent engineering inspection failed to determine whether the indicator or the nose-wheel system itself was defective. Some components were changed, the fault did not recur and, to sighs of considerable relief all round, the squadron training schedule could continue apace.

It was after my tour with 43 Squadron that, in 1989, I received my final posting in the Phantom force, that of officer commanding 228 Operational Conversion Unit which by then had moved from RAF Coningsby to RAF Leuchars. By the time of the OCU's closure in early 1991, a number of our aircraft had logged over 5,000 flying hours and it seemed paradoxical that many of them were in better structural and modification states than ever before. On looking back, I was conscious that the performance and potential of this magnificent multi-role combat aircraft had combined with another increasingly important aspect, that of cost-effectiveness. Such a capability involved qualities that ran rather more than skin-deep. I felt proud to have been part of the Phantom force, and privileged to have been involved with an aircraft that had provided our country with so many years of sterling service.

CHAPTER 13

HATCH CATCH

ROGER COLEBROOK'S
UNSCHEDULED
INTERCEPTION

"Incredible!" said my navigator
as we drew near to the Soviet
machine. The sheer size took
us by surprise. Undaunted,
I continued to fly our 43
Squadron Phantom FG1 ever
closer to this, the most potent
of potential foes. For the
Myasishchev 3M machine,
NATO code-named Bison B,
with its length of over 154ft was some 90ft longer than our Phantom. The disparity
in wingspans, at around 127ft, was even greater. Britain's Avro Vulcan bomber was
designed to carry a weapons load of up to 21,000lbs of conventional bombs, but
this was dwarfed by the Bison's capacity to carry weapons up to a weight of nearly
53,000lbs.

It was perhaps natural, therefore, that the profundity of the implications
should cause a sense of apprehension as well as awe while, in our lone Phantom,
we approached this mega brute. Furthermore, the bomber was not alone for, at
a distance of about half-a-mile, another Bison flew in a loose formation with its
Soviet colleague as the pair headed due north over the North Sea. While I closed
up so that my navigator and I could inspect the first of these machines, we were
intrigued to observe at first hand the aircraft type which had featured so regularly
but hypothetically in our intelligence briefings. We'd learnt, for instance, that the
bomber's four engines, which were placed close to the fuselage at the root of
slender, highly swept wings, were more powerful than those fitted to the original
Myasishchev M-4 (Bison A). The latter aircraft had first been displayed in public
on May Day in 1954, an event which had sent shock waves around the world

110

especially in the United States of America where, apparently, the emergence of such a machine had come as a complete surprise.

Intelligence sources revealed, however, that the bomber had insufficient range to attack the United States and still return to the Soviet Union. A new model, the 3M (Bison B), was therefore produced, a variant which first flew in 1955. In July that year Western observers at a Soviet air show were alarmed to watch a fly-past of 28 Bisons in two separate groups. It was not realised at the time that the display was a trick: some of the first group had gone round again to join up with the second group thus creating the impression of a greater number of aircraft.

The ruse, though, worked; the US government believed that the bomber was in mass production and the CIA predicted that 800 of the machines would be constructed within five years. American politicians warned of a 'bomber gap' and, from the Soviet perspective, the plan of misinformation was successful. When production of the Bison ceased in 1963, the truth eventually emerged: less than one hundred had been built.

At the time of my interception in the early part of 1970, some years had elapsed since these Myasishchev machinations. Nonetheless, I had been briefed on the background and I was well aware that the Bisons still posed a substantial threat. Stealthily, therefore, I continued to creep up towards the two bombers. Behind them, contrails drifted back sublimely into the sky. Inside each Bison I could picture the eight members of crew as they observed our Phantom; a total of sixteen Soviet crewmen versus the two of us. Despite the disparity in numbers, perhaps the Russians felt as anxious as we did, although I imagined that a good crew would enjoy plenty of repartee on such flights.

The crew's spirit of camaraderie, however, could be dampened if there was a political observer on board. We'd been briefed about such characters. The political observer would doubtless be a shrewd negotiator with the necessary lack of penetration to the human heart, someone interested only in the professional aspects of his job. On long, dreary flights, he might try to engage members of the crew in political dialogue, offer less-than-convincing arguments that might cause individuals, in their minds, to develop a conclusive refutation of Communism. "Do you not agree, comrade?" the political observer may press his point at which a crewman might sigh and adopt a weary, path-of-least-resistance look on his face. "Good grief," the political observer could insist, "if you resist bright ideas you condemn yourself to dinosaur-hood."

No doubt supplied with a meagre diet of Soviet sandwiches, flasks of coffee, maybe even the odd tipple of vodka, each member of the Bison crew would sit at his allocated station with his specific role, his particular concerns, his own take on the state of affairs. I speculated on what they would be like, these men who were supposed to be our official enemies, men who, in extreme circumstances, could end up in a situation where it was our duty to shoot them down. Cocooned inside a warm environment, maybe they preferred not to dwell on such issues or on the hostile conditions immediately outside, the freezing temperatures, the potentially grim scene if a technical fault developed; Soviet technology was hardly world-famous for its fault-free features.

There were other concerns, too. For one thing, our radio communication with the Bisons was non-existent and there was little doubt that dark clouds of possible misunderstanding could lead to trouble. This seemed especially pertinent just now because, as newcomers to 43 Squadron, my navigator and I had yet to complete our training programme; it would be some time before we were declared operational. In any case, such a task should normally be assigned to an aircraft on QRA duty, a Phantom or a Lightning equipped with armed missiles, cameras and a fully operational crew.

Despite these limitations, when the controller had asked: "Have you sufficient fuel to investigate a pair of strangers?" my reply had been in the affirmative. Without further ado he'd cancelled the remainder of our training sortie and given us a heading to steer towards the 'strangers'.

It had not been long before my navigator had reported two large blips on his radar screen. "They're big'uns," he'd said which was confirmed when we spotted the aircraft visually. Now, as we manoeuvred into a close formation position on one of the Bisons, I was aware that my mouth felt dry and that my heartbeat seemed to have increased. Presumably the controller had received the go-ahead from 43 Squadron for us to carry out this interception, even so I could not avoid an uncomfortable feeling. I tried not to remind myself of the lack of qualifications or proper authorisation to conduct the task. At least, I reckoned, my previous experience as a Lightning pilot should help. Another positive aspect was the weather – it was a fresh winter's day with good visibility and just a few big puffballs of cloud that rolled across the sky from the west.

We concentrated initially on an inspection of the Bison's enormous wings that spanned an amazing 165ft and 7 inches (by comparison, the Avro Vulcan B1 bomber's wingspan was just shy of 100ft). We noticed, however, that there were no underwing stores on this particular Bison although my navigator, in the absence of a camera, made a swift sketch to note markings and other details which might be useful to intelligence specialists. Now I reduced power so as to position the Phantom aft of the Bison's wings from where we could look up at the forward fuselage and bomb bay area. At this juncture some might ponder images of being cast alive into a lake of fire burning with brimstone, but as a professional crew my navigator and I remained calm and systematic while we focused on the task. Immediately above his head my navigator noticed some Cyrillic script written on a panel. "Can you close up a bit?" he asked. "I'll try to copy it for the intelligence chaps." "Okay," I said, "but it'll mean flying very near to this mighty beast."

Our sense of tension gradually rose as I eased closer to the Bison. I trusted that at least one member of the Soviet crew was watching us through some form of periscope device. If the Bison turned suddenly or performed any sharp manoeuvre I'd have to move rapidly. As events turned out, it was not a sharp manoeuvre but a large panel directly ahead of my cockpit which started to slide open and which, in an instant, caused me to jink hard left like a scalded cat. My navigator complained that his writing had been spoilt but I was worried that the Bison's crew might be about to eject something unpleasant.

After a while, when nothing undesirable – no strips of aluminium 'chaff', no Soviet sandwiches, no cold coffee or worse – appeared, I returned cautiously to our previous position until the Phantom was adjacent to the now fully-open panel. Suddenly I spotted a large camera lens of pinkish colour. Now it was obvious that the Bisons were here to photograph vessels involved in a NATO naval exercise; in our pre-flight briefing we'd been warned about the exercise. This explained the unusual position of the Soviet aircraft; normally these machines would route to the north of Scotland through the Iceland/Faroes gap en route to Castro's Communist Cuba. Their position today, some 20 miles off the east coast of England, was exceptional. "We'd better put a stop to this, Tim," I said to my navigator. "Righto," he said. "Do you propose to ram 'em?"

"We'll position ourselves directly beneath the camera lens to block the view." At this, as I manoeuvred the Phantom even closer to the Bison, my navigator said that he'd undo his seat straps and turn around to kneel on his ejection seat. It was a courageous thing to do, especially under the circumstances, but from his new position he was able to guide me as I held very close formation underneath the Soviet machine.

"Move forward one foot," he instructed, "steady...hold it there...now go back slightly...good position..." He kept this up for some time until, at length, he said that the camera port was closing. "They must have stopped taking piccies," he went on, "so can you ease back again? I'll try to finish my sketch of the Cyrillic script." "Standby," I said as I manoeuvred judiciously.

However, just as we reached the required spot, my navigator yelled: "The camera port's opening!" We can't keep this up all day, I thought, but as a dog shakes a rabbit, members of this Soviet crew appeared to be playing games with us. It's like a process of steady strangulation, I mused, and sure enough, when we'd moved forward to cover the lens once more, the camera port began to close. "They're playing silly buggers," said my navigator. "Sod 'em – try to move back again and I should be able to finish the sketch next time." True to his word, my navigator was soon able to announce: "Okay, I've got it all down."

"What's it say?"

A slight pause ensued until he replied: "*Jnoxta Bixok*."

"You want a biscuit?"

"No...*Jnoxta Bixok*...that's what the characters seem to spell out in English."

"But what's it mean?"

"No idea!"

Inside the Bison – I could picture it all – eight members of aircrew would be smiling at each other conspiratorially as they rolled their eyes in mock horror at our ignorance. It was poignant, I reckoned, to know so much and yet so little. I began to move away from our position close to the Bison and glanced to the left where, huddled together as they drifted over the sea, I could spot the clouds below.

By now the Phantom's fuel state dictated the need to return to base quite soon. There was still sufficient daylight at present but dusk came early at this time of the year and, before long, streaks of red would spread across the sky as the sun went down behind the clouds. Before this happened, I wanted to bid some form of farewell to the Bison's crew, men who, in this paradoxical environment, were at once our colleagues and our foes – the serendipity of circumstances would decide which. Both sides, it seemed, were influenced by some strange, mythical bond, an ichor in the veins that, despite the lack of verbal contact and the potential for misinterpretation, held qualities which were intrinsic even if grudgingly recognised. My fertile imagination could conjure bizarre images of our prospective enemies with their capacity to create a terrible darkness across the world.

The Bison's captain, for instance, might be an eccentric fellow with a slow smile that revealed a gold tooth or two and the aura of someone who God should have made with sunglasses on. I surmised that the mission specialists, on the other hand, would be scrawny creatures, evasive and quick to reveal obsessive traits. The gunners, though, would be altogether different characters. These were men who'd been trained to operate the Bison's potent 23 millimetre cannon placed tactically in dorsal, ventral and tail barbettes so as to achieve optimum reach around the bomber. These men, I reckoned, would be likely to assume lazy, contemptuous gaits; mavericks who would walk around with their eyes half-closed for much of the time. To these individuals would fall the task, if ordered, to obliterate the presence of our Phantom by firing a few short bursts of cannon.

"What's cookin'?" asked my navigator who by this stage had re-strapped into his ejection seat. "Before we return to Leuchars," I said, "perhaps, as one does, we should bid this big, bad Bison a bonny bye-bye." "Okay. Why not? Fallen leaves will find the way back to their roots," he concluded philosophically if a little obscurely.

At this, I advanced the Phantom's throttles slightly and manoeuvred forward until I was level with, and well to the left of, the Bison's cockpit. Now, gingerly, I eased rightwards to place myself eye-to-eye with the Soviet pilot. Perhaps I wanted to identify those conjectured gold teeth – which, of course, I failed to do – when suddenly the Soviet pilot held up his hands as if to say: "Take it easy, man...that's close enough!" My navigator then called:

"Watch out! The other Bison's sneaking up on our left."

I glanced left but saw nothing. Returning my focus to the close formation position, I said: "Check well behind for the other Bison, Tim."

After a moment he said: "Oh, yes...I can make it out now...an outrigger pod on this 'ere Bison...I mistook it for the other aircraft creeping up on us. Sorry about that."

"A trick of the light, perhaps."

My last impression of the Bison was of the way the Soviet pilot, as he sat in his pokey, riveted-aluminium, very Soviet-looking cockpit, returned my friendly final wave. If only, I pondered, the circumstances were different. However, they were not – indeed, the circumstances were highly tenuous – and the reality for the Soviets as well as for us meant that we had to carry out duties as ordered and that was that.

I turned hard left to ensure a clean break-away, then set heading for home base. The Bisons, meantime, continued on their northerly course – a route that would take some considerable time before they reached their base at, perhaps, Engels airfield situated between Moscow and the Caspian Sea. At this wintry season with typical surface temperatures below minus ten degrees centigrade, no doubt the airfield would be covered with snowdrifts. When the Bisons eventually landed, I supposed that the crews would face a desolate military scene with airfield lights infiltrating the pitch black night to cast a yellowish glow on the bleak surroundings. I could picture rows of military huts with ice on the windowpanes, white cobwebs of hoarfrost, personnel in heavy wadded jackets and thick gloves. With winds that could penetrate to the very bones, there might be a hint of wood-smoke in the air as folk struggled with the conditions. I could visualise the airfield perimeter, marked by tall posts and barbed wire, patrolled by hard-bitten guards. The thought made me shiver.

While we flew back to Leuchars, I discussed with my navigator the issue of the Soviet's disregard for air traffic control procedures, civil airways, notified areas and other internationally agreed systems designed to ensure aeronautical safety. Fortunately, under the watchful eye of controllers relying on radar screens, safety had been maintained because civil airliners had taken avoiding action. But the lumbering Bisons, as if under some kind of special charm, had blundered on regardless of others.

After we'd landed at Leuchars, and as my navigator and I set about completing the required mission report (MISREP) to send off to headquarters, a number of squadron members gathered round to ask about our experience. One of the squadron navigators, a Russian linguist, was stumped by the *Jnoxta Bixok* script so he decided to hurry home to search for his Russian-English dictionary. On return, he announced with an amused look: "You'll never believe this."

"We're all ears."

He grinned and went on: "It means 'entrance hatch'." At this, everyone present burst out laughing.

"Entrance hatch?" someone said eventually. "But that's surely balderdash. What lunatic would design an entrance hatch next to the bomb bay?"

"A Russian lunatic, presumably."

The MISREP was duly despatched and it was not long before the squadron received a signal from HQ: 'Congratulations to your crew for their ability to read two-inch grey-on-silver letters from the minimum permitted closing distance of two hundred yards.' I had to concede that our efforts may have proved a little over-enthusiastic. After all, there should surely be a limit to the commotion stirred up for the sake of an entrance hatch.

CHAPTER 14

RUSH!

ALAN WINKLES AND THE HAZARDS OF HASTE

It had been a long day. The sun had started to sink and now, as my observer and I moved past the salt-covered, weather-beaten structures of the aircraft carrier HMS *Ark Royal*, we hastened towards our allotted Phantom. If I felt a little jaded it was because this was my third flight and sixth cockpit-manning of that late spring day in 1976. However, I was becoming accustomed to the early starts and long days which seemed to be part and parcel of naval routines. I'd found this difficult at first and perhaps, as we hurried along, I remembered back to the time that I'd first joined the aircraft carrier when all was new and bewildering. Back then I'd felt like some oceanic hitch-hiker who struggled to adapt to naval ways but now, a few months later, my learning experiences with the 'dark blue' service had helped considerably. I'd even grown to appreciate some of the advantages of a life on the ocean waves. It was a highly specialised life, of course, a self-contained one with around two-and-a-half thousand people who, as if living in a small town, had to provide a multitude of services. Within the ship's grey, sombre outlines could be found aircrew, engineers, armourers, administrators, stewards, medics, caterers and a profusion of other disciplines – including, bizarrely, a contingent of Chinese folk, stateless individuals who lived in the ship's bowels and who provided laundry, tailoring and shoe-making facilities. (Even today I have a pair of black leather boots made by them and still going strong after forty or so years!)

Sometimes, when not required for flying, I would like to observe proceedings from the so-called 'goofers gallery' placed within the island on the ship's starboard side. With a sense of fascination, I'd watch the great waves stirred up astern and listen to the deep rumble within the ship's bowels as four sets of Parsons' geared turbines stormed the carrier through the sea at over thirty knots. On occasions, when conditions were too rough for flying, I'd observe with trepidation as waters snatched from wave crests were hurled against the carrier's island. The crests would tower out of the sea to windward before a high wall of water struck the ship. On such days, the wind's howl, as if afflicted by some demoniac hysteria, would rise to a shriek. The storm's onslaught could seem interminable but eventually the blackness of ragged clouds driven by the wind would lighten and the vexation of crew members would ease. While I gazed at the sea's effervescence, the waters could appear to chatter as if in conversation with gulls. The gulls, I had learnt at an early stage, should not be referred to as seagulls. That was the kind of terminology used by ignorant landlubbers. There were Black-headed gulls, Great black-backed gulls, Franklin's gulls, Herring gulls – but not seagulls.

Amongst the carrier's crew, I was struck by the spirit of camaraderie. Discipline was strict, and as a member of the RAF I was well acquainted with rigorous standards, nonetheless I noted how the carrier appeared to benefit from a particular coalescence of camaraderie and discipline. This was evident just now as I spotted the foreign object damage (FOD) crew at work. Just before the start of flying, dozens of men would walk slowly from the ship's bow to stern as they scrutinised the deck for loose objects which could create a hazard to aircraft. Meanwhile, as my observer and I approached the lined-up Phantoms in the 'Fly 4' parking area on the port stern of the carrier, I noted the state of *Ark Royal's* other aircraft parking areas: the 'Fly 1' position at the bows was unoccupied as was normal when aircraft were about to be launched, 'Fly 2' under the bridge was reserved for an in-flight refuelling Blackburn Buccaneer at five minutes' notice in case it was needed, and 'Fly 3' on the starboard stern was occupied by other Buccaneers. If Westland Sea Kings were due to launch then, with onboard space so severely limited, these helicopters would be held below deck. Since the carrier's refit nine years ago in 1967, a total of thirty-eight aircraft could be accommodated on *Ark Royal*.

While my observer climbed into the Phantom's rear cockpit, I carried out a walk-round inspection of the aircraft. This was a fairly rapid procedure on that day – I was, as usual, in a hurry, and additionally the rear section of the Phantom, suspended over the ship's side, was unreachable. It was not long, therefore, before I'd confirmed that the engine intake protection 'blanks' had been removed, the fuselage looked undamaged, and the undercarriage and nose-wheel assemblies were ship-shape. I clambered up the front cockpit's access steps, strapped into my ejection seat, swiftly went through the pre-start checks then, fingers drumming impatiently on the cockpit coaming, waited for engine start orders from 'Flyco'.

By now the FOD team had finished and I imagined the banter within the group as the men resumed other duties. As I waited, I recalled a conversation with a naval colleague one time when we'd discussed the qualities needed to maintain good morale onboard. We'd talked about the way in which poor leadership could result in things going very wrong very quickly – alarmingly so, as had happened at Invergordon in the early 1930s. The implications had been profound. I'd learnt that trouble had been brewing for a while but was overtly evident when the prime minister of the time, Ramsay MacDonald, had visited the Atlantic Fleet's aircraft carrier HMS *Courageous*. MacDonald had enjoyed a laudatory welcoming speech from the ship's captain at the conclusion of which, as was customary, the captain had called for three cheers. "Hip, hip, hip…" cried the captain as he raised his hat high. There was no response. The carrier's crew, congregated in the carrier's hangar, remained silent apart from one man who blew a raspberry. The captain's face reddened. He tried again: "Hip, hip, hip…" but the silence persisted apart from more raspberries.

On another ship in the Atlantic Fleet, HMS *York*, the captain had read out details of the proposed pay cut then said: "I'm sorry about this, but if you cannot manage, your wives could be asked to take in washing to augment your pay." At this an angry voice from the ranks had shouted: "You fat bastard! How would you like your old woman to crash out the dirties?" The shaken captain had immediately issued orders for the quarterdeck to be cleared and for the ship's company to resume their duties. These, though, were undertaken with dissension and amid heated discussions. It seemed that the Royal Navy's captains and admirals were still rooted in the times of Nelson when ordinary sailors had to sign their names with a cross. Their Lordships of the Admiralty had failed to appreciate that modern ratings were educated individuals and that an entirely different style of leadership was required. Maybe the admirals' focus had been diluted by distractions, but whatever the root reasons, like the paradox of an unstoppable force against an immovable object, a tidal wave of pressure had eventually…

"Start engines…" my pulse quickened at the sudden sound of Flyco's voice. Now, as I initiated the start cycle for the Rolls-Royce Speys, the air behind the Phantom began to shake visibly, like the shimmer above a road on a sunny day. In practically no time, the Speys were 'turning and burning' quite happily but a glance at my cockpit instruments revealed a separate problem: hydraulic pressure was low on the number one primary controls system. At once I reported this to the starter crew who came back with the news that they'd spotted a leaking hydraulic pipe. A shiver of angst went through me. I had no option but to close down the aircraft before rushing to the reserve Phantom.

So it was that, in an explosion of unwelcome activity, I sent seat straps flying, re-inserted the ejection seat safety pins, collected maps and other gear, then scrambled down the cockpit access ladder. With my observer and three members of starter crew in tow, I scampered in a series of zigzags towards the spare Phantom. As rapid as racing cars, as urgent as an ambulance, we sprinted for all our worth but had to duck down to dodge other aircraft and various obstacles while we weaved this way and that. Our mad dash was hardly helped as the *Ark Royal* began to heel over to the port side while the carrier turned into wind for aircraft operations. Despite the sound proofing of my bone dome, I thought that I heard structural groans while the ship manoeuvred. We had to contend with a wind of some thirty to forty knots over the deck and at one point, when I hopped over two of the deck's arrestor cables, I stumbled and almost fell. No harm done; I steadied myself and pressed on. Below us, when I glimpsed the sea, the waters appeared to surge and rage like a riotous crowd. We ran past the duty engineering officer and the duty pilot whose facial expressions disclosed what we knew already: that, if late, we'd hold up all of the Buccaneers and Gannets.

Soon, though, when we reached the reserve Phantom, I realised that we could still meet our planned launch time – but only just. We'd have to continue to hurry. A thumbs up sign from the duty pilot suggested that the external checks had been done already; no need to waste time on that business. This appeared to be confirmed by an encouraging nod from the duty engineering officer who, having followed me for the last part of the dash, held the Form 700 technical log for me to sign. I scribbled a signature, turned round and stepped up the ladder into the Phantom's front cockpit. A crewman, out-of-breath after our dash, helped me to strap in before he shinned down the ladder. I glanced behind to check that my observer was ready, then looked ahead at a row of expectant faces. There were five in all: the duty pilot, the duty engineer and the three members of the start crew. They stared at me intently as if willing me to get a move on. In all there were ten eyes and yet, as I was about to discover, not one of them could see.

Perhaps I felt vulnerable; maybe, under the pressures of the moment, I'd missed the unmissable, lost sight of the obvious, allowed the mosaic of the mind to become entangled in a web of confused haste. Whatever the cause, the scene was set, I was absorbed in my task; nothing could stop me now. I breathed deeply and sighed. The only way was up. I gave the standard signal for a scramble start procedure, glanced inside the cockpit, selected both start master switches on and eased both throttles forward to the idle position. The whine of the starter motors commenced. The revolutions gauge for the starboard Rolls-Royce Spey, usually the first engine to react, began to increase. I checked my watch. We might just make the planned launch slot. Then I noticed something unusual: the starboard engine revolutions had stopped increasing; the gauge had stuck at a reading of around eight percent. Now the engine began to make peculiar muffled sounds, as if in the act of choking. I glanced outside.

A mere matter of feet from my head I noticed a red object, a flag of some sort. The flag appeared to be waving a message. I shrugged my shoulders. It was probably nothing. I blinked my eyes. A voice inside me cried: 'Oh, no. For God's sake, no.' I gaped in horrified disbelief as, prompted by instinct, I closed down both engines. But it still seemed too incredulous to take in. It was true, though: the red flag was fastened to the top part of the starboard engine's intake 'blank' – a wooden device that measured approximately four feet by two feet. Printed in bold letters on the attached warning flag were the crucial if painfully obvious instructions: 'REMOVE BEFORE FLIGHT'.

Still in a state of denial, I switched my gaze to the port engine. Fortunately, there were no signs of trouble on that side. I therefore looked again at the starboard side's red flag which continued to display the dreaded words: 'REMOVE BEFORE FLIGHT'. I yearned to poke at the thing with a forefinger, push it away as if it had never existed. I wanted to act swiftly before anyone noticed. But people **had** noticed. The expressions on the faces of the five individuals near the cockpit had suddenly changed. Now they stared at me, eyes wide, mouths open, shoulders sloped. How pitiful they look, I thought. Perhaps, at this stage, in an intuitive, if weird, protective measure, my eyes began to glaze over. Maybe I tried to sink lower in my Martin Baker ejection seat. If only I could have waved a magician's wand to make myself vanish altogether. How pleasant it would be if I could forget about immediate calamities, enter a contented state of mind, just watch the reddening sun as its crimson light softened the surrounding scene. It was not to be, though. Indeed, the reactions of the famous five beside the cockpit suggested that worse was yet to come: wide eyes were becoming ever wider, the bottom jaws of open mouths seemed about to strike the *Ark Royal*'s deck, and sloped shoulders sloped further than could be imagined possible. 'What's the matter now?' cried the small voice inside my head.

The answer came quite quickly. Even though I'd closed down the engines, residual revolutions had caused the top of the starboard intake blank to begin to sway. The cautionary words 'REMOVE BEFORE FLIGHT' appeared to wave at me as if in an act of polite farewell. Now the flag, still affixed to the intake blank, began to recede into the intake itself, drawn by invisible forces of mighty suction towards the rotating blades of a Rolls-Royce Spey. For a microsecond I held in my head a picture of the poor blank, wrenched from its place of security to be thrust down a tunnel of destruction. Meanwhile, in a flutter of indignation, the cautionary flag waved its important advice to the last.

By this stage feeling like a deflated balloon, I remained in my Martin Baker ejection seat for some moments. I sat quite still. My breathing slowed down. My heart eased its thumping about in my chest. My senses seemed gradually to return. I appeared to hear an inner voice say: 'Everything is lousy. I can't stand it anymore.' Stand it I did, though, and having eventually climbed out of the Phantom's cockpit, the next port of call was my cabin where I changed into my best Number 6 uniform (officers-for-the-use-of, warm weather regions, stone coloured) ready for the inevitable tannoy message. It took about thirty minutes before the tannoy voice said sternly: "Squadron Leader Winkles to report to commander 892 Squadron immediately."

As I walked along the labyrinthine corridors of HMS *Ark Royal*, a dozen different emotions seemed to race through my mind. Here I was, the most experienced Phantom pilot on board, the senior RAF officer to boot, and now I was about to be given a dressing down for the type of mistake that even the newest of new student pilot would be unlikely to make. It was shameful. It was disgraceful. Shame and disgrace appeared to fall around my head in bucketloads.

When, at length, I reached the cabin door of commander 892 Squadron, I hesitated for a second or so before entering. I ensured that my hat was straight. I glanced at my service shoes to check that they were highly polished and unscuffed. I tried to make my best Number 6 uniform look wrinkle-free. The time, though, had come; the music, as they say, had to be faced. I swallowed hard and knocked on the cabin door. A voice from within commanded: "Come!"

As I entered the cabin and saluted, I noticed that the commander raised an eyebrow. He gazed at me for a moment or two, then frowned before he spoke. The rebuke, when it came, was, I felt, the very model of how a rebuke should be delivered. I offered no excuses and he expected none. Eventually he said: "There'll probably be a Ship's Inquiry."

"Yes, sir."

"But nothing will be put in writing on your records."

"Nothing?"

"No." He paused. "Luckily," he went on, "from what I've just heard from the engineers, the Spey is okay – undamaged."

"No damage at all?"

"They'll have to run more tests but an initial inspection suggests that, no – there was no damage apart from a bent pressure probe which can be replaced quite readily."

After this, a few further comments followed at the end of which I saluted and turned around to leave. Just before I reached the cabin door he said: "At least one good thing's come out of it, Alan."

"Sir?"

"There must be a fair few others who've learned a valuable lesson today."

He was right, of course, although, even years later, I still look back on the event with a sense of mortification and embarrassment. It had been a classic case of 'more haste, less speed'. Many eyes had been staring at that intake blank, nonetheless I was the captain of the aircraft, it was my responsibility to ensure that the thing had been removed.

On my desk today stands a model of a Phantom's starboard engine intake blank – a memento of the whole sorry affair. The model blank, just fifteen centimetres high, is mounted on a piece of black-painted wood. A brass plate states: 892

SQUADRON FOD PRIZE 1976. The model-maker, one of the squadron's superb team of ground crew, had paid careful attention to detail: two black metal handles with cloth edges replicate the real thing; the numbers '011' have been painted to represent the side number of the aircraft I'd attempted to fly that evening. As a final touch, the following words have been inscribed: 'REMOVE BEFORE FLIGHT'.

The model of the F-4 intake blank.

CHAPTER 15

BIG ISSUES

IAN HARTLEY RECALLS THE GOOD, THE BAD
AND THE DOWNRIGHT UGLY

"Heads or tails – you choose!" the illusionist held up a coin to show to onlookers. The atmosphere was tense as he turned the coin carefully to reveal both sides. He continued to hold the coin up in the air as he turned a full, slow circle. "You call," he said to his colleague, "and I'll throw." His colleague nodded. The illusionist then spun the coin upwards and there was a slight gasp from the crowds as they heard a loud, resonant voice declare: "Tails!" "It's heads!" said the illusionist when the coin had dropped to the ground. "In that case," he went on, "the dummy airfield should go there." With outstretched hand he pointed due west.

This account may have been closer to myth than reality, nonetheless it was said that the famous stage magician and illusionist Jasper Maskelyne had been employed in World War II to apply his skills at RAF St Athan in South Wales. In successful attempts to conceal the real airfield from enemy bombers, a dummy airfield was constructed a few miles due west of the genuine site. Wood and cardboard were used to replicate aircraft and buildings; old tractors were driven around the site to deceive enemy reconnaissance. As a result of the ruse, the Luftwaffe attacked the dummy airfield a number of times after which it was rebuilt each time.

When, in 1986, I was posted to St Athan, I learnt how the station was used in the early stages of World War II as a training unit for ground crew and aircrew. Later in the war, when the station's role was broadened to include a fighter group pool and a maintenance unit, the number of personnel on the base swelled to a total of some 14,000. After the war, the station's multi-role status changed and by the time I arrived there St Athan had become the RAF's major maintenance base. As officer commanding flying, my main tasks were to conduct post-maintenance flight tests, the collection and delivery of aircraft and the running of the airfield. I spent six years in this capacity, a period which covered another war, the 1991 Gulf War – Operation Desert Storm. Over this period, the behind-the-scenes activities at St Athan became ever more significant and our efforts to support front-line squadrons proved key to the country's war effort.

As part of my responsibilities, I had to become qualified and current to fly a number of different aircraft types, including Phantom FG1s, FGR2s and Js. Other types included Panavia Tornados, BAE Hawks, BAC Jet Provosts, Scottish Aviation Bulldogs, and de Havilland Canada Chipmunks. If some regarded my place of posting as something of a backwater, I found this to be far from the case. I was always very busy and I relished the unusual opportunity to fly so many different aircraft types. For liaison visits across the United Kingdom as well as overseas I was allocated a personal, private Jet Provost Mk3. This was an aircraft which I knew well from my days as a flight cadet at RAF Cranwell, although in my new capacity I had to learn different aspects.

After several tours in the fighter world, a return to flying the Jet Provost seemed to stir up a sense of nostalgia as well as some curiously deep-rooted memories. For one thing I could recollect how, as flight cadets, my colleagues and I would talk about the need to make every effort to get along well with our flying instructors. If a point of difficulty or contention arose, we agreed that it could be best, as they say, to go with the flow – a necessary part, we assumed, of building up one's moral fibre. On looking back, I realised that this somewhat simplistic approach had its limitations – in particular when I was faced one time with an unexpected and most disagreeable dilemma. My instructor back then was an ex-Gloster Meteor pilot, an old-school type – intimidating, aggressive and not disinclined to lean across the cockpit to swipe at his student in the event of a foolish mistake. The punishment may have been deserved, nevertheless I found it disconcerting and counter-productive. One day, I was chatting with a fellow student who shared the same instructor when we began to talk about the swiping issue. "It's a problem," I said, "and I'm not sure how to deal with it."

"Don't worry," he said, "I've had the same problem myself."

"Did you just ignore it when he hit you?"

"Hell, no."

"What did you do, then?"

"I hit him back, of course!"

It was not long before I had an opportunity to put this theory to the test. Having made some crass error which duly brought forth the instructor's fist, at once I cuffed him back, told him to lay off and to let me get on with the flying. The reaction was immediate. The instructor began to laugh out loud, clapped me on the shoulder and said that from now on we'd get along just fine – which, indeed, was how it worked out for the rest of my time with that instructor.

For the second part of my flying course at Cranwell, however, I was allocated a different instructor, a young ex-Vickers Valiant co-pilot who, it appeared to me, suffered from a chip-on-the-shoulder approach to life. Before too long I discovered that this character, as with my previous instructor, was not averse to lashing out in the cockpit. I found it hard to fathom the psychology. Perhaps it was a hangover from the war, or maybe it was a generational thing, but whatever the reason, the tactic of some instructors seemed to be – if in doubt, hit. Anyway, when I made a foolish mistake one time, this new man leant across the cockpit and thumped me. Without so much as a second thought, I turned towards him and cheerfully thumped him back. This time, the response was quite shocking. The instructor immediately took control of the aircraft before, in silence, he flew us directly back to Cranwell. After landing, the silence persisted and very soon afterwards I was summonsed to the commanding officer's presence for a formal interview. In fear and trembling at the possibility of instant suspension, I explained how my previous instructor's reaction had influenced my actions this time. Fortunately, my previous instructor backed me up, I was duly absolved, all subsequently became sweetness and light with the new instructor – so much so that I passed the course and still recall the day of my graduation from Cranwell as one of particular pride.

My keenness to go to Cranwell and an ambition to fly probably stemmed from my father, although he didn't try to push me into this career path. As a World War II Supermarine Spitfire and Republic P-47 Thunderbolt fighter pilot, my father had flown with the RAF Third Tactical Air Force (Third TAF) in the Burma campaign. I had learnt from military history lectures at Cranwell how the Third TAF, formed in late 1943, was established at a time when it was decided that British forces should at last go on the offensive against the Japanese. I'd learnt, too, how the pilots of Third TAF had bombed and strafed, often at very low level, as they engaged the Japanese in drawn-out and vicious fighting. I did not, though, discuss this with my father; as with many of his generation, he would not talk about his wartime experiences, even when I became a fighter pilot myself on the Lightning force.

I spent five years in the Lightning force on two separate squadrons – starting, in 1970, with 23 Squadron at RAF Leuchars followed by a tour with 56 Squadron at RAF Akrotiri. A ground tour ensued after which I was posted in 1977 to the Tactical Weapons Unit at RAF Brawdy. In 1981, I joined the Phantom force for a three-year spell. I remember a less than auspicious start in the Phantom world. Like other experienced single-seat fighter pilots, I found it hard to adjust to sharing a cockpit with a navigator. Furthermore, difficulties were compounded by the poor standard of leadership at the Phantom Operation Conversion Unit at RAF Coningsby. Never before or since have I come across a more unfriendly unit.

Matters, however, improved with my posting to 92 Squadron based at RAF Wildenrath in Germany. I was crewed with an experienced navigator, the two of us got on well and I enjoyed the challenge of low-level flying across Germany and elsewhere. Squadron exchanges with other NATO countries featured regularly in our training schedule. I recall one of special note which involved a visit to the Royal Netherlands Air Force station at Leeuwarden, the base for two Dutch squadrons equipped with General Dynamics F-16 Fighting Falcons. During this detachment, our pair of 92 Squadron Phantom FGR2s were joined by two USAF McDonnell Douglas F-15 Eagle aircraft from the nearby base at Soesterberg, as well as two Phantom F-4Fs from the Luftwaffe base at Hopsten.

The international character of the exchange appeared to stimulate a competitive spirit in more than one sense, including off-duty activities. Our Dutch hosts, ever exuberant and game for a bit of fun, had organised an assortment of events which included, one night, a striptease artiste laid-on for the entertainment of one and all. To spice up the proceedings, clandestine arrangements were made for one of our 92 Squadron pilots, the junior pilot on the detachment, to join the artiste on stage before, at a predetermined moment critique, thunder-flash fireworks would be set off as, simultaneously, the lights were turned off.

On the night itself, clutching beer tankards filled with copious quantities of Dutch courage, we were ushered into a dingy, beige-painted room with a make-shift stage in the centre. A short period of waiting ensued until, to rapturous applause, the artiste appeared through parted curtains which had been rigged-up at the back of the stage. The light was subdued but I could still see that, despite a slight air of world-weariness, undeniably she had beauty. To the recorded notes of mood music, including David Rose's *Stripper* song, her act began. A new eagerness touched the audience whose rowdy interjections gradually dissolved into an expectant hush. All eyes focused on the small stage; imaginations intensified; attention was absolute. The room – warm, smoky, airless – developed an atmosphere filled with the stickiness of aroused desire; fantasy, unreason and lust grew best in such conditions. She moved slowly yet nimbly across the stage, arched her body backwards and allowed her blond tresses to tumble down the top part of her back. Mouths agape, members of the audience watched the precision of her slender, erect shape as she side-stepped in time to the music.

When our junior pilot suddenly crept up to join her on the stage, I spotted her look of icy puzzlement although this eased as, fingers crooked above her head and in sensually controlled motion, she gyrated her hips to the deliberate, rhythmic beat of the music. Meanwhile, in attempts to make his spark grow to a flame, our protagonist flung himself energetically this way and that. The efforts were, perhaps, a little too vigorous for, before too long, we were startled to pick up mumbled comments from the artiste. Evidently she was becoming irritated by the impromptu intervention. "Hah!" she seemed to be saying. "Erectile dysfunction!" "Says who?" said the junior pilot. "Squishy, squashy!" said the artiste. This appeared to unsettle the junior pilot who moved intimidatingly close to her. She pushed him away but stumbled in the process. "Look what you've done!" she cried. "Flippy, floppy!"

It was at about this point that several thunder-flashes exploded, the dim lights flickered then went out altogether. With the abrupt interruption, and resisting any temptation to join in the 'squishy, squashy' business, I considered two possibilities. The first was hazardous and uncertain. I therefore opted for the second even though it, too, was hazardous and uncertain. There was just sufficient residual light for me to see my way to the stage, jump up and grab the artiste by her wrist. "I blame myself," I breathed in her ear as I pulled her towards the nearest fire exit, "but nobody could have predicted…" "Don't tell me," she muttered as we moved across the stage. "I come from a very practical background," I assured her. I wrenched open the fire door and dragged her outside thereby saving my colleague from further embarrassment. From across the Dutch flatlands we felt the blast of a wind that must have nipped the buds off tulips from Amsterdam. When the artiste started to shiver (she was hardly equipped with woollen hat and gloves against the cold), a number of aircrew volunteered to help warm her up when we were inside again. By now the lights had been switched back on so all of us decided to head back inside including the artiste herself who, as if drawn by some strange homing instinct to the place where she had started, returned to the stage. When there, amidst cheers and general commotion she waited for the uproar to die down before, in the grey shimmer of the dimly-lit room, she carried on with her act as if nothing much had happened. With practised proficiency she managed to navigate the delicate division between the salacious and the sensuous. This, I thought, was clearly the stuff of a true professional.

Professional, too, was my approach to flying on the diverse tasks we were given the next morning and on subsequent days as part of the squadron exchange programme. The primary role of the resident Dutch F-16 squadrons was that of air defence, nonetheless the crews were expected to maintain a level of expertise in the art of fighter ground attack. For the week of the squadron exchange, therefore, the F-16 crews would fly to a firing range to loose off a variety of ordnance. En route to the range, they might employ a 'hi-lo' profile – flying at high altitude initially before a descent to low level – sometimes 'hi-lo-hi', or maybe the whole sortie would be 'lo-lo'. Our job, and that of the USAF and Luftwaffe squadrons, was to intercept the F-16s and to disrupt their procedures before they reached the firing range. The scenarios were testing, lessons were learned and debriefs at the end of each sortie stimulated unusual and thought-provoking ideas. When, at the end of the week, the crews dispersed to return to home bases, all of us, I believed, felt that our common competence had improved as had our understanding of the need for flexible mentalities in our fast-changing environment.

Top: Phantom F-4M XV420 of 56 Squadron. (*The Aviation Bookshop*)
Above: Phantom FG1s in 'box 4', June 1970. (*Roger Colebrook*)

Opposite top: Phantom FGR2 with centre-line gunpod and 4 x SNEB anti-tank rocket launchers. (*John Walmsley*)
Opposite middle: Phantom FGR2 XV408 of 92 Squadron. This aircraft can be seen today at Tangmere Military Aviation Museum. (*The Aviation Bookshop*)
Opposite bottom: Phantom FGR2 XV467 with 19 Squadron markings. (*The Aviation Bookshop*)

Top: Phantom XT597 was used as a laboratory aircraft by the A&AEE from 1974 and was fitted with a long nose probe.
(*The Aviation Bookshop*)
Middle: Phantom XV581 of 43 Squadron.
(*The Aviation Bookshop*)
Above left: Phantom flying at sunset. (*Peter Becker*)
Above right: Phantoms in formation during an event to celebrate their decommissioning from Luftwaffe service. (*Ian Sykes*)

Top: Photograph of Soviet Bear from the side taken by the author on QRA duty, February 1975. (*Richard Pike*)

Above: Roger Colebrook shadowing a Tu95 Bear D, 1972. (*Roger Colebrook*)

Right: Photograph of Soviet Bear taken by the author on QRA duty, February 1975. (*Richard Pike*)

Top left: The crowded deck of HMS *Ark Royal.* (*Alan Winkles*)

Top right: XT872 on the grass having taken the over-run arrester wire. (*Les Hurst*)

Below: The two RAF St Athan crews with fleet of aircraft (Phantom in the centre), September 1991. (*Ian Hartley*)

Opposite top: XT874 of 111 Squadron at RAF Wattisham. (*The Aviation Bookshop*)
Opposite Middle: XT899 with 19 Squadron markings and blue colour scheme to celebrate the 75th anniversary of the RAF. (*The Aviation Bookshop*)
Opposite bottom: XT902 of 19 Squadron in a line-up with other Phantom F-4s from 92 Squadron. (*The Aviation Bookshop*)
Above: XV582 involved in a scramble, 18 February 1975. (*Richard Pike*)
Left: XV571 departed the runway fully laden at high speed sliding to starboard as can be seen by the undercarriage track. (*Steve Gyles*)
Below: Oberstleutenant Alexander Berk and Oberst Roubal in Phantom 37+01 decorated in blue for the official decommissioning of the Phantom F-4 from Luftwaffe service in Wittmund, 2013. (*Ian Sykes*)

Top: Phantom F4-F 37+01 in flight during the 'Phantom Pharewell' event in Wittmund, 2013. (*Ian Sykes*)
Right: Phantom F4-F 38+28 in the 'Phantom Pharewell' event in Wittmund, 2013. (*Ian Sykes*)
Below: Phantom F4-F 38+37 outside a HAS in Wittmund 2013. (*Ian Sykes*)

*

It was no surprise when this need for a flexible approach followed me as I left the Phantom force for my new job at St Athan. With such a diversity of aircraft types, I had to adapt rapidly in order to cope with the detailed technical data, check lists and emergency procedures. The training aircraft were relatively straightforward and I was familiar with the Phantom, but the complexities of the Panavia Tornado, a machine developed from the multi-national multi-role-combat aircraft (MRCA) project, could prove more than a little challenging. All modern aircraft could be described as complex, and the Phantom was certainly no exception. In the case of the Tornado, however, complex high-tech systems appeared to be taken to a whole new level.

For one thing, the wings' variable sweep facility, which allowed the pilot to adjust the angle of sweep from anything between 25 degrees and 67 degrees, did not prove trouble-free. Fortunately, I never had to deal with the most hazardous case, that of the wings stuck fully back, but I did experience situations where the wings were stuck in a partly-swept position. Furthermore, I found that the Tornado's primary flight control system (for its time a novel, so-called fly-by-wire hybrid with analogue quadruplex command and stability augmentation linked to a digital autopilot and flight director system) could cause problems. To enhance pilot awareness, artificial feel had been built into the flight controls, and there was a level of mechanical reversion in case of failure of the primary system. It seemed that all of these elaborate systems were more-or-less bound to give trouble at one time or another.

The Tornado's Rolls-Royce RB.199 engine was no exception to the designers' apparent fondness for complexity. As with some versions of the Phantom, variable air intake ramps were fitted to control the RB.199's airflow across a wide range of conditions and airspeeds up to Mach 2.0. Unlike the Phantom, however, in the event of a Tornado suffering a double engine or a double generator failure, a single-use battery could operate the fuel pumps and aircraft hydraulics for a limited period. Additionally, and as a rare feature on fighter aircraft, the Tornado's RB.199 had thrust reversers to reduce the aircraft's landing run. For greater stability when the thrust reversers were activated, a yaw damper was fitted to the nose-wheel steering system. Although the connection was never proved, it was a synthesis of engine and nose-wheel trouble that one day led to dire consequences when I was due to fly a Tornado GR1 from RAF Laarbruch to St Athan.

Positioned on German territory but adjacent to the border with The Netherlands, RAF Laarbruch was hastily developed by the British army as the Allied forces prepared in early 1945 for a final push across the River Rhine. Nine years later, the airfield was rebuilt when the Cold War started to freeze up east/west relations. At the time of my visit, Laarbruch was the home base for a squadron of Jaguars and two squadrons of Tornadoes. It was one of the latter that was scheduled for deep maintenance at St Athan.

That day, having filed a flight plan and inspected necessary paperwork, my navigator and I could have had no inkling of the trouble ahead as we walked out to the Tornado which had been suitably prepared for the transit flight across international boundaries. While my navigator climbed into the Tornado's rear cockpit, I carried out external checks. As I walked around the aircraft, I looked for signs of hydraulic leaks, examined movable surfaces including the full-span flaps and the leading-edge slats, scrutinised the fuselage and the undercarriage assembly before, when satisfied, I climbed into the front cockpit and strapped-in. The ejection seat pins were removed and stowed, after which I went carefully through the cockpit initial checks. All appeared fine so, by means of the intercommunications system, I spoke with the start-up crew: "Clear to start APU?" The APU (auxiliary power unit) was a mini-jet engine within the aircraft starter system which was designed to wind-up the main engines.

"You're clear to start APU, sir," said a voice over my headset. At this, I pressed the relevant button. As the familiar sound of engine wind-up crescendoed, I monitored the cockpit instruments. Soon, with both engines happily settled and all checks completed, I called air traffic control for taxi clearance. Blissfully unaware of the peril about to strike, I taxied the Tornado at a good pace towards the take-off point. When my navigator read out the pre-take-off checks, I acknowledged routinely. However, as we approached the runway, from force of habit I had a last look around the cockpit: fuel and oxygen sufficient; engine temperatures and pressures normal; flaps set; maps secure. The controller cleared us to move directly onto the runway. As I lined-up the aircraft, I noted that the runway's slick, black ribbon of tarmac was obstruction-free. I re-applied the aircraft brakes and waited for the controller's 'clear take-off' call. On both sides, the tapestry of farmland, a blend of greens, browns, yellows, was on German territory; beyond the end of the runway was a similar mix on Dutch soil. A line of trees marked the airfield perimeter and further away I could see low barns and fields with livestock. The weather conditions were good with reasonable visibility, if a little misty. "Standby for take-off clearance," said the controller. "There's conflicting traffic ahead."

"Copied," I said, then asked my navigator: "All set?"

"All set," he confirmed.

After a moment or two the controller said: "You're clear to take off now." None of us could have realised the drama that was just seconds away.

With brakes still applied, I eased the Tornado's twin throttles forward. I glanced at the cockpit instruments. Everything was present and correct. Like an Olympic sprinter eager for the 'off', the aircraft began to lean ahead. At the appropriate engine revolutions I looked in front, released the brakes and applied full power. The Tornado leapt into action as the noise from twin Rolls-Royce RB.199 engines began to soar. I continued to focus on the visual picture ahead with an occasional check of the airspeed indicator. The rate of acceleration was normal. I began to ease back the control stick and now, as the nose-wheel left terra firma shortly followed by the main wheels, I was ready to raise the undercarriage. It was at this point that our troubles began. When I selected undercarriage 'up' the indicator showed that the nose-wheel had failed to retract.

At once, I brought back the twin throttles to keep our airspeed within stipulated undercarriage limits. Unplanned events now started to happen fast. While discussing the nose-wheel issue with my navigator, I eased the throttles forward for a minor airspeed adjustment. The engines, though, failed to react. "Standby," I said to my navigator, "we've got another problem." I advanced the throttles again but, as before, the engines refused to accelerate.

"Our airspeed's low," said the navigator.

"The engine's aren't responding to throttle input!"

"The airspeed's still reducing."

"Standby."

"We're approaching stall speed."

"Standby. Standby." Frantically, in last-ditch attempts, I moved the throttles repeatedly to try to coax a response from the engines. "It's no good," I cried, "the bloody engines just aren't responding." Pulse racing, I yelled: "Prepare to eject, prepare to eject!"

I don't remember if my navigator acknowledged this, but I do recall that, following a hurried Mayday call to air traffic control, my next order came very swiftly: "Eject! Eject!" I shouted. Now, in a whirl of white-knuckle activity, I hauled up my own ejection seat handle placed between the legs. At once, the canopy disappeared; seat straps whipped around me; my limbs were drawn roughly against the seat frame. The fractional pause that ensued seemed like an eternity until, in a violent upwards thrust, I was propelled clear of the doomed Tornado.

Even though I'd closed my eyes tightly, I was aware of a bright flash followed by a roaring sound – a combination of wind-rush and noise from the seat's rocket motors – and a sensation of tumbling over and over. This ended promptly when a savage jerk confirmed that the parachute canopy had snapped open.

I hardly had time to catch my breath before, within seconds, I landed with a thump, unceremoniously deposited in a Dutch field. I released the parachute harness and removed my bone dome. Then I reached for my yellow fibreglass dinghy pack and sat on it grimly, hardly able to take in what had just occurred.

My limbs felt numb; my mind felt numb; in fact, everything felt numb: the entire incredible experience was totally mind-numbing. About 50 yards away I spotted my navigator; we called out to each other to make sure that we were okay. He then walked over to where I was sitting and offered me a cigarette.

In contrast to recent anguish and clamour within the cockpit, all around was eerily quiet although I heard a dog yelp in the distance. In an adjacent field, cows observed nonchalantly as they continued to munch at grass. Stupid creatures! Did they not realise that something was wrong? What had to be done to arouse them from their infernal, eternal munching? I pondered the transformation from ultra high-tech to mega low-tech. It seemed barely believable. Behind me, a pillar of black smoke rose up into the sky to mark where the Tornado had crashed.

For a while, the surreal nature of the situation appeared to swamp my thoughts. Gradually, though, a sobering realisation of the implications began to sweep through my mind. Perhaps I wished that time could be reversed, that what had happened hadn't really happened – but this line of reasoning was, of course, absurd; such ideas should be driven from the head. I began to ask myself questions: why hadn't the engines reacted? Had I done anything wrong? Could I have done more? Had I failed in some way? The fear of failure can be the greatest fear of all.

Later, when engineers combed through the wreckage to try to find answers, I hoped to receive some form of explanation. But it was not to be; despite the stalwart efforts of specialists, the cause of the problem was never established. Less than 60 seconds had elapsed between the start of the take-off run and the destruction of a multi-million-pound aircraft, yet the root reasons remained a mystery. They still do.

*

It was not long after the ejection before my navigator and I were picked up by helicopter to be taken for medical checks. Having been declared fit to travel by Laarbruch's doctors, we were taken by ambulance to the RAF Hospital at Wegberg where I was diagnosed with a broken ankle and a compression fracture to my back. After a week, I was flown by a RAF Hawker Siddeley Andover aircraft to the RAF Hospital at Wroughton were I spent six weeks waiting for my back to heal. My navigator, who was fifteen years younger than me, was uninjured.

Meanwhile, back at St Athan work continued apace. Following medical clearance and discharge from Wroughton, it became almost routine for me to fly three different sorties daily in three different aircraft types. One day I logged six flights on three different types with four air tests on BAE Hawks, one on a Tornado F3 and one on a Phantom FGR2. By the early 1990s, by which stage I was getting towards the end of my tour at St Athan, the Phantom, too, was

*Dramatic photo taken after Tornado ZA468 had crashed
on take-off, July 1989.*

approaching retirement (the last British Phantoms retired in October 1992 when 74 Squadron was disbanded). If we'd hoped that by then all of the Phantom's original faults had been ironed out, our hopes proved optimistic. The aircraft kept us engaged to the last.

In fact, the very last Phantom to pass through St Athan's major servicing programme was a 56 Squadron FGR2 – XT896. Remarkably, in order to rectify various snags before the machine could be returned to squadron service, my colleagues and I had to conduct no less than fourteen separate air tests on XT896 over a period of two-and-a-half months. One particular problem concerned the pilot's angle-of-attack indicator which, try as they may, the engineers could not re-jig to correlate correctly with the airspeed indicator. At length, after much head-scratching and convoluted discussion, it was discovered that the mounting plate for the angle-of-attack probe had been incorrectly fitted during manufacture by McDonnell Douglas. The aircraft had been in service for a quarter of a century yet, in all of that time, the fault had not been found.

Another persistent problem with XT896 concerned the Rolls-Royce engines. One day, when I was asked by St Athan's specialist engineers to conduct an engine air test, they explained that they'd had difficulty setting up the engines to meet the correct criteria. My navigator and I duly started-up and took off in XT896 for the air test. Initially all seemed in order. We climbed up in weather conditions which were reasonable with, as I recollect, a few patches of broken cloud at medium level.

As the air test progressed, my navigator read out instructions from the technical schedule while I carried out the required actions. These involved various tests at different altitudes. Eventually, he said: "The next item is a controlled slam check." By this point we had reached an altitude of 45,000ft. The check involved a rapid movement of one throttle from the idle position to full cold power, followed by a test of that engine's reheat system. The procedure would then be repeated for the other engine.

To give my navigator due warning, I counted down from five seconds before I said, "Slamming now," and moved one throttle as briefed. However, when I did so we heard a peculiar noise, symptomatic of a compressor surge or axisymmetric stall caused by a breakdown in compression within the engine. From the cockpit instruments I could see at once that the engine had indeed flamed-out (i.e. the flame inside the engine's combustion chamber had extinguished). No problem, I thought, I'll just increase power on the other engine and head for base. But when I tried to advance the second engine's throttle, this engine, too, immediately surged and flamed out. We were now effectively in a flying toboggan. Perhaps at this juncture my brain struggled to come to terms with reality, nevertheless out of instinct I lowered the Phantom's nose. Simultaneously, I put out a Mayday distress call on the aircraft radio. My aim was to glide at a sufficiently steep angle to maintain a degree of windmilling engine revolutions for the hydraulic pumps to operate – they were needed to power the aircraft's flight controls.

I was conscious that, as we descended, our flying toboggan would reach the key height of 25,000ft quite rapidly; above that height the chances of an engine re-light were minimal. Meantime, it crossed my mind that, having ejected fairly recently from one of Her Majesty's aircraft, a second opportunity was now looking distinctly possible. When I glanced below, I could make out the landscape of the southern part of Wales. It was strangely comforting for the area felt like home to me now, even so I had no desire to visit it by parachute. Furthermore, my cockpit was cosy and familiar; I had no wish to abandon it. Nonetheless, I realised that, unlike at Laarbruch, there was now time to tighten my ejection seat straps as much as possible and to consider other aspects. If we were forced to bale out, I'd aim to point the Phantom away from populated areas. And if we got to the stage where I needed to pull the ejection seat handle, I would pull it as hard as on my last adrenaline-charged effort.

"Approaching 25,000ft," the navigator's voice cut through my thought processes. "Standby for re-light," I said. The air of suspense, already high, rose even more as we neared the critical height. The implications for our immediate future had not escaped our attention. "Standby…" I gazed fixedly at the altimeter and the eye-watering rate at which it was winding down. "Standby…" I repeated. Then, as our flying toboggan passed through 25,000ft, I pressed the engine re-light button. I monitored the cockpit gauges anxiously; time and perspective seemed to become distorted. Suddenly, though, I felt a great surge of relief: the engine gauges were reacting; our procedures had worked. "We've had a successful re-light!" I said to my navigator. I could picture his look of relief. "Standby," I went on, "I'll try the second engine now." When this engine, too, had relit without difficulty, our tension began to ease although not completely – not until we had landed safely at St Athan and XT896 was back in the hands of the engineers.

So it was that, after further head-scratching and technical debate, the Rolls-Royce engines were tweaked in a Rolls-Royce way, the Phantom was declared serviceable once more, and my navigator and I were ready to try again. Any hopes of a straightforward solution, though, were swiftly dashed; the test proved to be a carbon-copy of the last one. Having climbed to 45,000ft for the slam checks, both engines flamed out as before. Yet again, we found ourselves tobogganing downwards. However, also as before, luckily both engines relit in time for a safe return to St Athan. It took a fair amount of additional tinkering, but eventually this did the trick and in the end we carried out a satisfactory air test.

On completion of this, the last Phantom air test at St Athan, I suggested to my navigator that some form of demonstration to mark a final Phantom farewell would be appropriate. Indeed, we decided that not to do so might be regarded by some as a dereliction of duty. It was a sunny Friday in November 1991, the time was late afternoon, officers were gathering in the officers' mess for end-of-week 'happy hour'. The time and the place, we reckoned, were ideal; now for the action.

It was unfortunate that our line of approach took the Phantom directly above the station commander's house. It was even more unfortunate that information about the station commander's absence on holiday had proved incorrect, and that we were ignorant of the news that he had decided to host a cocktail party attended at that very moment by numerous dignitaries.

Our first pass at a height of 100 feet and an airspeed of 500 knots with full reheat engaged was appreciated, we felt certain, by onlookers. We therefore tried to ensure that the second pass was no less impressive. Considerably less impressive, however, was my summons after landing to the station commander's presence. I was made to feel more than a little uncomfortable when, in no uncertain terms, he explained a thing or two about aspects of the incident that had slipped my attention. "Were you not aware?...The way you thundered by!...There'll be hell to pay!...Do you not remember?...Of course you do!..." he seemed to make quite a big issue of it. By this stage in my career, however, I suppose that I'd become rather adept at coping with big issues.

CHAPTER 16

HIT OR MYTH

ROGER COLEBROOK'S IN-FLIGHT REFUELLING DILEMMA

There was no moon to rise from the far, shadowy horizon and even the stars were faint. As we climbed up in our Phantom, perhaps I had images of a coal fire, of how, piece by piece, it would be wonderful to place great lumps of coal to build the flames and warm the world. For beyond my cockpit the freezing temperatures and black expanse suggested a fearfully hostile place. Below me, the grim, restless stretches of the North Sea seemed equally uninviting and I looked forward to our rendezvous with the Handley Page Victor tanker when the friendly sound of the crew's voices could encourage us to hone our skills in the particular art of night-time in-flight refuelling. However, if I'd only known, matters that night would prove to be less straightforward than anticipated.

As a newly-arrived member of 43(F) Squadron based at RAF Leuchars I was in the process of squadron conversion training. My navigator, a USAF officer on an exchange tour, was experienced in night in-flight refuelling, although not with 43 Squadron. In my own case, having returned recently from Cyprus where I flew English Electric Lightnings as a member of 56 Squadron, I had a fair amount of in-flight refuelling experience, but not at night; our commitment in Cyprus did not require this. "I guess we're what you might call half and half," my navigator had said earlier, though I was not entirely sure what he meant. "Yes...no...if you say so," I'd mumbled diplomatically, aware that the USAF did things differently. The US Boeing KC-135 Stratotanker employed a boom operator whose job it was to manoeuvre the refueller's boom onto the receiver's probe – the exact reverse of the RAF method whereby the receiving pilot had to carry out the manoeuvring.

I'm uncertain at what point the full significance of our task struck me on that night in April 1970, but earlier, when my navigator and I had been awaiting news from our squadron duty operations officer, the original plan had not involved in-flight refuelling. The squadron engineers – as was, frankly, not uncommon – had been struggling to produce enough serviceable aircraft to meet the night's planned flying programme.

Meantime, as one does, although perhaps as one shouldn't, I was making less than complimentary comments about the engineering effort though my navigator remained tactfully non-committal. Nevertheless, we talked together about life in general, about this and that, including, by the way, one's considerable anxiety following yesterday's drama on the Apollo 13 spacecraft. Evidently an oxygen tank had exploded and the crew were forced to abort their mission to land on the moon. With reports of hardship on board the command module due to limited power, loss of cabin heat, shortage of water and other problems, there was much ongoing worry about the ability of James Lovell, the commander of the flight, and his crew to return safely to earth.

We worried, too, about the incident of a few days ago when Israeli air force Phantom 11s aimed bombs and missiles at an Egyptian military installation – or what they claimed to have taken as a military installation. In fact, the building was occupied by schoolchildren and nearly fifty of the children had been killed in the calamitous attack. "Why does it always happen?" asked my navigator.

"Why does what always happen?" I said.

"You know...the endless problems over there."

"Good question," I said. "With their entrenched attitudes there seems to be little room for compromise."

"It's real bad. Everybody blames everybody else."

"The waters have become muddied – what's known, I suppose, as constructive ambiguity. Sometimes it's best not to know stuff."

"Gee."

To accompany such philosophical meanderings we heard muted chatter from a radio in one corner of the crewroom. A professor had started to speculate about the goings-on connected with Apollo 13. He attempted to explain something about pencils in space but when, unfortunately, his attempts at clarification began to drift towards gallimaufry, the presenter seemed keen to change the subject. In place of space-talk, listeners would be entertained by the American singing duo Simon and Garfunkel with their current chart topper Bridge over Troubled Water. The lyrics '...I'm on your side when times get rough and friends just can't be found...' seemed eerily apposite at present. In the distance, we heard the raised voice of the duty operations officer, evidently still striving to make the best of a bad job. With just one serviceable Phantom at his disposal, his options were becoming progressively less encouraging as the night wore on.

"It's not looking too hopeful," I said to my navigator. He glanced at me with a sudden smile but said nothing. His eyes appeared to refocus and his jaw twitched. Clearly he was accustomed to the USAF doing things on a rather grander scale. In an attempt to cheer him up and by way of polite conversation I asked him: "What's this news about cigarettes in the States?" "Yeah," he said, "the dreaded weed's killing too many Americans. President Nixon's decided to ban cigarette adverts on TV from next year." "Is that a good idea?" "Hmmm. Maybe. Who can say?"

I nodded knowingly and stood up. "Coffee?" I asked.
"Sure - thanks," he said.
"I'll put the kettle on."
"You'll what?"
"I'll...I'll make you some coffee."
"Thanks."

We lapsed into silence while I dealt with the makings. The aircraft serviceability situation, I reflected, seemed to be turning into quite an embarrassment. I dared not surmise what our American exchange officer was making of the efforts of his NATO ally, and as his expression remained inscrutable I reckoned that it might be best not to ask him. But I couldn't avoid feeling a little ashamed by the way our squadron's shortage of serviceable Phantoms had become an all-too-familiar event. It seemed an intractable problem. Outside, the yellowy glow of sodium lighting cast slanting beams that reflected into the room and it was with a sense of woe that I gazed up at the ceiling, looked down at the floor, then studied some of the room's Scandinavian flat-pack furniture. Perhaps, I thought, the Scandinavians could invent a flat-pack Phantom. Brilliant! Regretfully, though, the idea was driven from my mind when, just as the kettle came to the boil, the duty operations officer suddenly appeared in the doorway. "Good news!" he cried.

"The engineers have finally produced another aircraft?"
"No. Not exactly that."
"What then?"

"There's still just one serviceable Phantom but a Victor tanker has become available. To make use of our one and only Phantom, therefore, I want you to get airborne and join up with the Victor. You can practise some in-flight refuelling. The Victor's setting up on Towline 'Bravo', by the way."

"Bravo!" I said. The operations officer stared at me. "But there's one small difficulty," I added.
"There is?"
"I haven't been given the required briefing on night-time in-flight refuelling."
"You had plenty of practise in the Lightning force didn't you?"
"Yes I did, but not at night."

There was a slight pause as the operations officer mulled this over. I knew, of course, that we were caught between two certainties: I was keen to fly, so was my navigator, and this would be our one and only opportunity of the night, however without that detailed briefing on the complexities of night in-flight refuelling in a Phantom we could find ourselves in trouble – big trouble. A faraway look came into my navigator's eyes. I could almost read his thoughts: this was the sort of thing that had to be done right otherwise we might end up as toast. For a moment or two I gazed dispassionately at the operations officer. I was struck by his wearied look. How grave were the issues he had to resolve, how stooped and shuffling was his gait. But his eyes were aflame again as he went on:

"There's no problem really," he said. "It's exactly the same as refuelling in daylight only...only..." he shifted uneasily on his feet.
"Only what?"
"Only it's dark!"

And so it was that, spurred on by this observational triumph, we turned blind eyes to the lack of our all-important briefing as my navigator and I set off to confront the world of the great unbriefed. He walked ahead directly to the squadron's sole serviceable Phantom while I signed the authorisation sheet and the aircraft technical log. Outside, a Scottish wind that nipped the buds of spring blossom stormed across the airfield. I hastened to the flood-lit Phantom and carried out the external walk-around checks before I climbed into the front cockpit. In practically no time at all, having completed the cockpit checks and started the Phantom's Rolls-Royce Spey engines, I called air traffic control for clearance to taxi. It was a quiet night so clearance was soon approved and I taxied the Phantom at a fairly fast pace towards the take-off point. "There's currently no other circuit traffic," went on the controller. "You're clear to enter the runway and take off."

When lined-up for take-off, I glanced at the Phantom's cockpit instruments while I eased both engines into full reheat then concentrated on the runway centre line as the aircraft accelerated. On either side of me, the runway lights shot past at an increasing rate until, as the Phantom lifted into the air, I was struck by the sudden contrast; the night was an uncommonly dark one. As we climbed up we seemed to penetrate an unusually intense darkness – a solid mass of unbroken blackness, the heart of nowhere that lacked the smallest glimmer of moonlight and even the starlight appeared enervated.

My navigator worked away at his radar set while we climbed and it was not long before we made radio contact with the crew of the Victor tanker. As we closed up to a position behind the Victor, the captain said: "You're clear astern the centre hose."

"That's acknowledged," I said routinely, "clear astern centre hose." After a pause I continued: "Could you switch off your anti-collision lights, please?" On a dark and dirty night, the flashing red beacons could induce a sense of disorientation, especially on a night as dark and dirty as this one.

"No problem," said the Victor's captain and soon I was left with nothing but dim illumination from a few low-watt bulbs placed around the refuelling basket's perimeter. The challenge was about to commence but I continued to feel unprepared – almost out-of-place, as if, in an unfortunate juxtapositional quirk, a stringy-haired hippy with faded jeans and dark glasses should stumble into a meeting of Quakerly-types in sensible shoes and cardigans. I could almost feel the fall-out of failure flutter in the dark air. But if I was about to face my own juxtapositional quirks, I knew that dogged, even though dog-eared, determination would prove key. Motivated, therefore, with thoughts of stern resolve as if King Arthur himself was observing, I manoeuvred the Phantom for my first attempt.

For this, I flew the Phantom to a position some way back from the refuelling basket. I'd already agreed with my navigator that it would be best for him not to rabbit on and on as we moved up to make contact with the basket. Instead, he would stay silent while I manoeuvred, but if I failed – if the Phantom's probe missed the refuelling basket – he would call out the clock-code and distance of the miss.

"Okay, Jim," I said to my navigator. "Moving forward now."
"Sure. Good luck, Roger."

With bated breath and trying to ignore extraneous distractions – including, I seem to recall, bizarre and unhelpful images of mother's home-made plum wine – I focused on the refuelling basket as I inched the Phantom's throttles forward. From my Lightning days I was conscious that this was not a good technique; it was generally much better, I knew, to concentrate on holding formation on the Victor's wing or fuselage; staring hard at the refuelling basket tended to induce over-control, especially in turbulent conditions. That night, however, there was no alternative: other than the basket's low-watt perimeter bulbs, I was surrounded by nothing but dismal pitch blackness.

Perhaps it was almost inevitable, therefore, that my navigator's next call – "You missed! Ten o'clock at eighteen inches" – a call that made my heart sink – was followed by another attempt...then another...and another...and yet another. After some ten minutes of successive failures, with my morale declining exponentially with each new failure, an unexpected distraction suddenly came to the rescue.

"Victor captain," said a chirpy voice on the radio, "this is a Lightning aircraft, do you read?"

"Loud and clear," said the captain.

"I understand that you may have some spare fuel to give away?"

"Affirmative," said the captain. "We're currently on Towline Bravo and can offer you some fuel."

"Copied. I'll join you in three minutes."

"Understood. We have one Phantom in tow but he'll hold off to our starboard side while you refuel."

So it was that the Lightning, exactly on schedule, appeared on the Victor tanker's left side while my navigator and I observed proceedings from the other side. The Lightning pilot, when cleared astern the centre refuelling hose, wasted no time. I was impressed by the slick and professional manner in which he manoeuvred his aircraft. There's a certain *je ne sais quoi*, I mused nostalgically, about the dash and élan of a Lightning pilot. I was surprised, however, by his next radio call. "Lights please!" he said. At this, recessed floodlights on the Victor's underside promptly lit up the tanker.

"Look at that," I said to my navigator who emitted a low whistle of amazement.

"Why didn't the Victor crew turn on the lights for us?"

"Maybe," I said, "they were too busy chattering amongst themselves. Or perhaps they were enjoying their air force sandwiches."

"Great!"

The Lightning pilot soon filled his aircraft's fuel tanks after which it was our turn once more. When the Lightning had shot off into the wide blue/black yonder, the Victor captain cleared us to resume our position behind the centre hose. At least he had the grace to apologise –"Sorry about the lights, 43 Squadron," he said. And so it was that, with the Victor tanker lit-up like a Christmas tree, in what felt like no time at all I had achieved the required fifteen contacts and was able to bid goodnight to the Victor crew.

The following day I met up with the officer in charge of my training programme. "I hear that you managed okay last night, Roger," he said. "We had our moments," I said. "But we got there in the end."

"It's a bit late now, but I suppose we'd better cover the required briefing anyway. We'll need to put a tick in the box. Besides, you may still find the briefing helpful – dispel a few myths and all that."

"Right-oh," I said. "Fair enough, I have to admit that we had one or two problems – more hits than misses until I got the hang of it."

"Oh dear," he said. "That doesn't sound good. Not too good at all. In fact, frankly, it sounds to me like a worrying case of hit or myth."

CHAPTER 17

CLOSE SHAVES

Alan Winkles, 17 Squadron RAF Brüggen, 1971.

ALAN WINKLES
RECOLLECTS A
BIRD STRIKE

I stared silently ahead. My front windscreen, smeared in blood and greasy bird remains, was barely usable apart from a small section on the left-hand side. This, though, was just one of my problems. I'd already reduced the Phantom's airspeed and now, as I flew at an altitude of around 2,000ft, I tried to ask my navigator for a heading to steer for our nearest diversion airfield. My navigator, however, was not responding. I had no idea about his state of health. He may have been injured; he may even be dead. It was possible that he could have ejected – the Phantom's canopy had been shattered by the bird strike and the consequent wind racket could have masked the noise of an ejection. I had no option, therefore, but to fly on in the hope that I'd recognise a ground feature from where I could turn towards RAF Gütersloh for an emergency landing.

The weather that day was reasonable although visibility was reduced significantly in local showers. Earlier, when we had taken off from our home base at RAF Brüggen, the aim of the mission was to fly a singleton 'strike' sortie towards East Germany before turning left to take up an anti-clockwise route. Eventually, we had made for the Nordhorn Range situated close to the West German/Netherlands border where we carried out a practise toss-bombing run. The approach to a toss-bombing run involved very low-level flying before, at a pre-determined distance from the target, I executed a sharp pull-up to release a bomb at the apex of a ballistic arc. This was followed by a rapid escape before the Phantom overflew point defences. The toss or loft attack, although more complex than a dive-bombing or level-bombing approach, was a particularly appropriate technique in a nuclear weapons environment.

Following our 'attack' of the Nordhorn Range, we headed due south towards Cologne before turning left on a north-easterly course. Still at low level, we flew above the colourful patchwork of German countryside, a mix of farmland and tracts of forest interspersed with towns and villages. In the rawness of that showery day I had to manoeuvre around the rain clouds from time to time, otherwise we kept to our planned route, the final part of which took us over Osnabrück ridge – a line of hills with occasional radio masts positioned on the hilltops.

As we crested the ridge, I looked left then right to try to spot an adjacent radio mast but it was obscured by one of the rain showers. It was as I looked ahead again that I saw something else. Perhaps, on impulse, I tried to take avoiding action for I knew that the consequences of a collision with that great creature would be drastic. At that instant, time became distorted; events seemed to happen in slow motion. The buzzard, wings outstretched, was craning its neck in the eagerness of its passage. The typical wingspan of a common buzzard, in the order of four feet, exceeded that of an AIM-7 Sparrow missile, but any form of avoiding action proved ineffective in view of the Phantom's airspeed of 420 knots. When the bird struck, the impact was explosive. There was a sudden crash and a hollow *crumph* almost as if someone had burst a giant paper bag. The windscreen directly in front of me, just eighteen inches from my face, was immediately covered in the creature's remains. Dust and debris began to swirl around me and I knew at once that the Phantom's canopy had shattered. The armoured windshield at the forward part of the cockpit had held firm but its flexing had thrown off the canopy itself.

At this point, while I continued to fly straight on, I tried to concentrate on the small area to the windshield's left-hand side – the only area which offered some sort of view ahead. My cockpit, normally cosy and familiar, had abruptly become wild and alien. In anticipation of an ejection, I pulled back the Phantom's control stick and was tempted to close the throttles but realised this would be imprudent in view of possible engine damage from ingested bird remains. However, approaching an altitude of around 2,000ft, just below the main cloud base, I eased back the throttles a little and was more than relieved when the engine instruments showed no signs of serious trouble although one engine was running a little hot. To help reduce the Phantom's airspeed as I levelled off, I selected the airbrakes out. Simultaneously, I transmitted a Mayday distress call on the aircraft radio.

Now, as I struggled to take stock of the situation, a deep dread gripped my thoughts. I still had heard nothing from my navigator. The rush of wind was buffeting me from side to side and despite the sound-proofing of my bone dome the din from wind blast was almost overwhelming. I lowered my seat fully and kept my face as low as possible in the cockpit, even so the violence of the slipstream restricted any head movement. I tried shouting to my navigator but with no result. I hoped that my call had been received by air traffic control but, with the level of wind noise, I'd heard no response. I therefore transmitted a further 'blind' Mayday call, gave the Phantom's estimated position of some 25 miles south-west of RAF Gütersloh and stated my intention to divert there.

By this stage, as I headed towards the general direction of Gütersloh, the Phantom's airspeed had settled at around 270 knots. At that airspeed I was able to peep carefully from side to side as far as I dared before the slipstream struck. So it was that, in addition to gazing through the windshield's small left-hand section, I managed to identify key navigational features. Before long I became reasonably confident that we were heading in the right general direction for Gütersloh. I made a further attempt to shout to my navigator: "Bob!" I yelled, "Bob, can you hear me?" As before, though, there was no reply. I became increasingly worried about his condition and my anxiety seemed all the more poignant when I remembered how we'd been crewed together for a long time – nearly two tours. We'd been through a lot in that period.

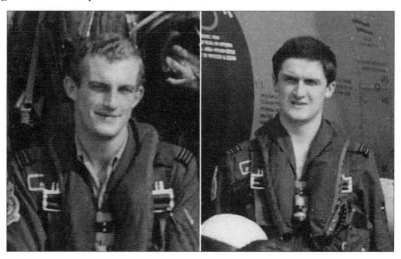

Alan Winkles and Bob Woodward (navigator).

An ex-English Electric Canberra man, Bob had joined the Phantom force at the same time as me and we'd been crewed-up more-or-less from day one at the operational conversion unit at RAF Coningsby. When flying in the venerable Canberra he'd been accustomed to lying prone on his stomach in the nose of the aircraft. The change from this to gyrating around the sky in the back seat of a Phantom had, for him, been a traumatic transition. Perhaps, as an ex-Lightning pilot, I'd been rather cack-handed with little concept of the consideration needed for another crew member, but whatever the reason the end result had always been the same: poor Bob had been violently airsick on every sortie. This was before the days of sympathetic medical treatment when an individual susceptible to motion sickness would be placed on a turntable to re-programme the ears' semi-circular canals. Instead, we both knew that if Bob was to continue with his service career, the condition had to be concealed from prying eyes.

Supplied with suitable plastic bags by his wife, and with me as co-conspirator, Bob's stalwart attitude had helped him to cope. On our air-to-ground practise strikes at Holbeach, Wainfleet, Cowden and other firing ranges, in a dozen or more diving attacks we'd loose off rockets or bombs, or fire the Phantom's Gatling gun. On each sortie, after about five or six such attacks, Bob would throw up. It seemed like an insoluble problem yet after just a few seconds he'd manage to carry on with his duties. I was full of admiration for the way in which he appeared to recover so rapidly. He must have felt like death warmed up and yet he was still able to call out instructions and key parameters. The efficiency of our task was not compromised – indeed, we honed our skills to achieve good results. Nowadays I grimace when I think about it and frankly I don't know how he managed. After landing, he would conceal the plastic bags carefully and no-one was the wiser. This went on for several months until one day, on our return from a sortie on the Cowden range, he announced that he had survived the flight without being airsick. As far as I'm aware, he was not sick again. His solid determination had cured the condition.

Not long after this we were tasked to fly to the Otterburn range in Northumberland to fire 68mm SNEB rockets. The target, an old Centurian tank, was hard to find on that bleak winter's day in 1969. Flying up towards the range, we had passed traces of snow on fields by the coast, and on the range itself the shapes of hills and other features were obscured by blankets of snow. We made radio contact with the army's forward air controller (a minor miracle in those days) who briefed us on his plan. Soon, we were ready to set course from the 'initial point' to the target. Our aim was to pull up just before reaching the target and to turn hard right before adopting a ten-degree dive onto the target. At a pre-calculated height, Bob would call 'pickle' (i.e. fire the weapons). That, as they say, was the plan.

At first, all went well. The run from our initial point was as anticipated and some fifteen seconds before the pull-up point I looked to the right to try to spot the target. All I could see, though, was snow-covered terrain. I pulled up anyway and, with the forward air controller's high-velocity instructions in my ears, I promptly spotted the target – or what I thought was the target. I pulled hard to the right to bring a black object into the Phantom's sight-glass then, just as I heard the call from Bob, I glimpsed the real target way off to our right. I had no option but to call "missed target" and to overshoot for another attempt.

The next 'attack', as before, went well initially. However, following the planned pull-up, in my zealousness to keep the tank in sight I started our turn to the right prematurely. As a result, the necessary parameters were never quite achieved – we were too shallow in the dive, our airspeed was too high and I struggled to place the pipper accurately on the target. At least I had found the correct target this time, although distance and height were hard to judge in the snowy surroundings. When Bob called "Pickle!" I was still trying to steady my aim so, for a second or two, delayed before pressing the 'pickle' button. The resultant barrage of rockets on either side of the Phantom was startling. Half-a-second seemed a long, long time and I was enthralled by the mass of crimson rocket exhausts and the way they enshrouded the target. When I heard the urgent shout: "Pull out! Pull out!" and when it dawned on me that this call from my navigator was in an uncharacteristically anguished tone, I suddenly understood just how close we were to the ground.

My pull-out was energetic – so much so that six-and-a-half 'g' was registered on the aircraft's 'g' meter. The Phantom had flown so close to the ground that a mass of debris was stirred up and I was aware of gravel and other hazardous detritus striking the windshield. My vision ahead was diminished by the layer of dirt that now covered the Phantom's windshield, nonetheless I reckoned that I could see sufficiently well to carry out an emergency landing. I therefore set heading for RAF Leuchars and declared a Pan urgency call. During the twenty-minute transit flight to reach Leuchars my mind was in turmoil: I knew well enough that if I had been on my own in the range, if Bob had not been there to make that crucial pull-out call then...

Suddenly, as I sat in my canopy-less Phantom following the bird strike, I was aware of another aircraft. In the difficult conditions it was hard to discern, but to my right, beyond the Phantom's wing tip, I reckoned that I saw something. For a second or so I thought that it might be the black shadow of our own aircraft against the whiteness of the nearby rain shower. However, I soon realised that it was not a shadow but another Phantom. I could make out the dark bulk of the machine which gradually drew closer as the pilot flew in formation on us. The crew must have heard our Mayday call and now, as I gazed at the pilot's cockpit, I could spot his reassuring hand signal to indicate that Gütersloh was ahead. Later, I learnt that our shepherd had been my squadron commanding officer, Wing Commander Paddy Hine.

I decided to make a further effort to communicate with my navigator: "Bob!" I yelled once more. "Can you hear me at all Bob?" I sat, with muscles tensed, in my cockpit, listening. It was no use, though: I heard nothing apart from the dominant, high-pitch shriek from slipstream. On and on it went like a madness.

My heart seemed to stand still. I knew that with that huge, violent motion of airstream just inches from my head, my nerve had to hold if we were to survive.

It was not long, however, before I began to distinguish the outline of an airfield ahead. Just as lights in fog can be hallucinatory and mesmeric, so the first signs of hoped-for sanctuary can be treacherous, nevertheless I started to realise that this was indeed an airfield, furthermore it was one that I was able to identify as RAF Gütersloh. My sense of relief was profound. I positioned the Phantom for a left turn onto final approach to the airfield's westerly runway. Even though I knew that any verbal reply would be drowned-out by wind noise, I made a radio call to air traffic control and was gratified to spot a green flare fired from the runway caravan.

The Phantom's remaining fuel level meant that the aircraft was overweight for landing. My touchdown at Gütersloh, therefore, was firm and fast. I forced myself to concentrate on trying to hold the white centre line although my peripheral vision picked up the runway edges flash past in a blur. Insufficient, though, was the combination of tail 'chute and hard braking when the end of the runway started to hurtle towards the Phantom. Without delay, I lowered the Phantom's tail-hook as, with a sudden feeling of alarm, I realised the danger of decapitation from the top wire of the crash barrier. "Lower the barrier...lower the barrier," I cried on the aircraft radio. The controller reacted swiftly for I saw the barrier go down at once before, within seconds, I felt robust retardation and a great rush of relief as the Phantom's tail-hook caught the over-run cable.

At this juncture, however, any sense of relief proved short-lived. I tried again to establish contact with my navigator. "Bob!" I shouted. "Are you there? Are you okay?" "I'm here," he replied. Thank God, I thought. "But I can't see," he went on, "my eyes are bad." I was still strapped into my ejection seat, nevertheless I was able to turn around sufficiently to gain an image of the scene behind me. What I could see made me gasp. My navigator's oxygen mask and his bone dome's inbuilt visor were covered in gruesome remains. Despite his lowered visor, shards of canopy and bits of bird had bounced off his oxygen mask and slithered up into both of his eyes. The cold, fresh air appeared to grow heavy with the sickly-sweet stench of grime and blood that covered him as well as the windshield and parts of the cockpit. I struggled to comprehend the implications and rued a sense of impotence at my inability to offer the help that he needed urgently. The weight of responsibility seemed to bear down on me and I was afflicted by a feeling of utter isolation. As though by a raptor's claw I was seized and clutched by a sensation of emptiness – a dark mood of dread and weariness that was hardly helped when I noticed another problem: the headrest of my Martin Baker ejection seat was covered in bird splatters and the seat's drogue 'chute was in shreds. The seat was still 'live' and therefore was in a perilously unstable state.

By now, fire engines had raced up to deal with the incident. A fireman with a ladder ran to my cockpit. "What do you want me to do, sir?" he asked. "My ejection seat is in a dangerous state," I spoke in an anxious, sibilant voice, "so move away from the front cockpit just now. But get the doctor to help the navigator." "Okay," said the fireman and slid down his ladder to pass on instructions to his colleagues and to the doctor. The good doctor, though, was having problems of his own. Just as the chief fireman ordered the fire engine driver to back away from the Phantom, a Land Rover ambulance with the doctor on board careered up to the scene and skidded to a halt behind the fire engine. The timing was such that the heavy fire engine now began to reverse into the side of the ambulance. The ambulance was consequently tipped over onto two wheels. The doctor, as he tried to leap clear of the ambulance, was nearly crushed by the fire engine. The ambulance's rear door, dislodged by the proceedings, fell to the ground as if in an act of outrage.

Despite this apparent real-life performance of a game of consequences, the doctor managed to extricate himself from the chaos before he ran to the Phantom's rear cockpit to apply first aid to my navigator. Meanwhile, I unstrapped and gingerly – very gingerly – stood up on the ejection seat, turned around and judiciously vacated the Perspex-less cockpit. I noticed that virtually every scrap of canopy Perspex was missing. When my feet touched terra firma I removed my bone dome to find that the turbulent excitement had left my hair as well as the palms of my hands wetted with perspiration. My face felt black and puffy, and I had an ongoing sense of enervation as I gazed up at the Phantom's rear cockpit while the doctor did his best to administer first aid to my navigator.

At length the two of them – doctor and navigator – stepped down the rear cockpit's access ladder to head for the mangled ambulance where I joined them. Inside the vehicle I gazed uneasily at my navigator who was clearly still in a great deal of pain. His discomfort, however, was hardly assuaged when the German ambulance driver set off at high speed to take us to the medical centre. Undaunted by the rutted grassy surface, the driver took a direct route and I almost expected the vehicle's remaining doors to be cast off by the roughness of the ride. If the doctor asked the driver to ease up, his pleas went unheeded. Perhaps the driver could not speak English, maybe he harboured old resentments but whatever the reason I have abiding images of three passengers holding on for dear life while we spent most of that hair-raising journey in a state of unwelcome weightlessness.

When, finally, the ambulance reached its destination, the passengers stumbled into the medical centre while the vehicle itself appeared to limp off somewhere to be scrapped or repaired, I was unsure which. Inside the building, I sat in a reception area for what felt like a long time while my navigator received medical attention. I read magazines, stared up at the ceiling, listened to distant voices. While waiting for news, if I felt an unexpected emotional tug perhaps that was no great surprise.

Suspense built while I sat there but eventually I heard a door click. Conversation from the half-opened door drifted across. When a telephone rang, I watched the receptionist lift the receiver and tap her fingertips delicately while she spoke. At last, though, my navigator emerged from his consultation and walked over to where I sat. He moved with an air of steadfast unconcern but I could tell that he was still suffering. "The corneas of both of my eyes have been scratched," he said in reply to my enquiring look, "but the doctor reckons that they should repair themselves in due course." No doubt, I thought, that brutal, self-willed pluck of his had been recognised by the doctor. "How long is that likely to be?" I asked. "A few weeks," he replied with a shrug of the shoulders. And so it turned out; after a few weeks he was allowed to return to flying.

When I look back, I recall some of the feelings which the incident had induced, including a sense of bitter loneliness as events began to unfold. The necessary levels of courage and resolve had been great – so great, indeed, that perhaps they'd not been fully appreciated to the deserved degree. If the run of events had occurred in a way and to an extent which had thrown doubts on a number of procedures, of one thing I had no doubts at all: both this affair and the one at the Otterburn firing range had involved the closest of close shaves. That much, at least, was clear to me.

*

Author's note: When my draft for this chapter was seen by Alan Winkles he asked if I would like to receive an input from his navigator on that day, Flight Lieutenant Bob Woodward. The following is reproduced verbatim:

Many thanks for sight of the draft Chapter 17. I must say that Sylvia (my wife) was aghast at what had taken place, since that was the first time she had heard the full story. Personally, I had to go and lay down in a darkened room to get over the flashbacks of that eventful day (4 May 1971) and to thank, whoever, that I was in the hands of such a competent and superb pilot. Here are my thoughts on the day:

My logbook shows 'XV901 low-level area 3/bird strike – divert Gütersloh'; as bland as that and certainly no true reflection on what took place. The heart-stopping 'bang!' when it came, was like a mortar bomb landing in one's trench. Then, almost worse than the bang, came the howling 400 mph gale from your cockpit accompanied by all the detritus, debris and muck from the buzzard and the cockpit floor. Instantly, my face was full of buzzard, my eyes were useless and the sense of confusion was total. I instinctively leant right forward in my seat (head on the AWG 12 radar) to minimise the horrendous wind tunnel effect and try to make sense of what had happened. I recall grabbing the seat pan firing handle, more for comfort than anything else, and wondering if I should depart the scene. However, ejecting from that doubled-up position would have done nothing for my back and might have taken the back of my head off on the combing.

I could hear nothing in my headset and my eyes were really starting to hurt badly but I retained a feeling that you still had control of the aircraft; these were pre-command ejection days. I kept my head fully down until we ultimately landed (somewhere; I knew not where) and then I recall my canopy being opened. I was still sightless and so missed the pantomime between the fire tender and the ambulance, although I don't suppose anybody was laughing at the time. The journey back via Pembroke (Percival Pembroke light transport aircraft), RAF Hospital Wegberg and thence directly home to Roermond, passed in a complete blur.

Later that evening, as I lay in bed at home with Sylvia valiantly trying to apply eye drops, we had a phone call from the squadron to ask if I was fit for the air officer commanding's parade the following day, as I was apparently due to carry the standard!

It was a man's life in those days, obviously!

The underlying moral of this story is to take care when about to crest a wooded ridge and allow a bit more clearance to avoid the 'rising' birds. A life lesson that Alan and I carried forward in future sorties.

Bob Woodward.

CHAPTER 18

CRAFTY COMBAT

KEITH SKINNER AT DECIMOMANNU

"Look!" cried Jeff, my navigator. "Up there!" For a moment he'd glanced away from his radar picture. "You're right!" I said. "It's their contrails!" By this stage I had taken our Phantom to ultra-low level, an untraditional fighter aircraft tactic. I was well aware that, more-or-less from the year nineteen-o-dot, the urgent aim normally was to gain height above an adversary. Our situation, however, was far from normal.

"They're currently just over fifty miles from us," said Jeff as he returned his gaze to the small radar screen. "Okay," I said. "Standby." I checked to the right to ensure that my wingman was still in position. Then, with a positive nod of my head, I indicated our pre-briefed plan: turn off radars and other radio emitters now. Simultaneously, I eased my Phantom's throttles forward to select reheat on the Rolls-Royce Spey engines. My wingman did the same and soon the two aircraft were streaking along at supersonic airspeed above the surface of the Mediterranean Sea. In the bright March weather on that day in 1981, shimmers of reflected light rebounded through our cockpits. The very air appeared to become electric with anticipation. The Phantoms were buffeted by turbulence as we continued to fly at ultra-low altitude and I could picture the patterns that swirled around our wings and airframe in the potent yet invisible streams of air stirred up by supersonic flight. Below, it seemed as if we could reach out to touch the surface of the water – those cool seas with mysterious currents and streams of another kind, a curious contrast to our cockpit worlds.

Meanwhile, our opponents, two USAF McDonnell Douglas F-15 Eagle aircraft detached from Bitburg in Germany (a US base, incidentally, where Buzz Aldrin, the second man to step on the moon after Neil Armstrong, had served as a flight commander), were approaching head-on as part of an air combat training flight.

For this and other exercises, our 92 Squadron Phantom FGR2s had been detached from their home base at RAF Wildenrath in Germany to the Italian air force station at Decimomannu in the southern reaches of Sardinia. The facility at Decimomannu was unique. Using an in-flight recording system with the somewhat un-catchy title of air combat manoeuvring instrumentation (ACMI), each engagement could be analysed by computer during post-flight debriefs. Gone were the days when such debriefs relied on experiential accounts with liberal use of a pilot's fingers and hands. The computer's frame-by-frame evaluation would determine whether a missile had been launched within design parameters, and whether the missile would have found the target.

All of this, however, did not help our problem on that day, for our Phantoms, developed in the 1950s and which had first entered service in 1960, were no match for the modern technological capabilities of the F-15 Eagle. The Eagle had first entered service over fifteen years after the Phantom and we were, in truth, outdated and outclassed. Almost by the time the Phantom's flaps had been raised after take-off, the Eagle's high thrust-to-weight ratio (1.04 nominally loaded versus the F4's 0.86) would enable the aircraft to climb towards some 30,000ft – indeed the twin Pratt and Whitney F100 axial-flow turbofan engines allowed the Eagle to accelerate in a vertical climb.

This remarkable thrust-to-weight ratio meant that the F-15 could out-climb and out-turn us, furthermore the fighter's novel digital central computer system contained an overload warning device which permitted the pilot to fly his machine at up to 9 'g' at all weights, a limit well beyond that of the Phantom. The F-15's single pilot workload was reduced by computer technology with new controls and displays as well as a 'look-down/shoot-down' radar system. The latter employed X-band Pulse Doppler signal processing, and while the Phantom also was equipped with Pulse Doppler radar, the improved technology incorporated in the F-15's versatile APG-63 equipment, developed in the early 1970s and later upgraded, was significant. With the ability to detect and track high flying targets as well as aircraft at tree-top level, these radars could operate at ranges up to around 90 nautical miles, and down to close range. The F-15's radar was designed to acquire enemy aircraft and project information to the pilot's head-up display, an especially useful facility for close-in dogfights, and the pilot received threat warning as well as automatic countermeasures against selected threats.

In ten years' time, following the First Gulf War, General C A Horner, overall commander of Allied air assets, was to describe the F-15's capability thus: "During the first three days of the war, when control of the air was greatly contested, what it basically amounted to was the Iraqi aircraft would take off, pull up their landing gear and blow up." If I felt somewhat daunted by our prospects against the F-15s, this was more a reflection of pragmatic rather than defeatist notions. For while defeatism undoubtedly should form no part of a fighter pilot's psyche, pragmatism should. I learnt this at an early stage in my service career when I joined the Royal Air Force in 1965. After training, my first tour was as a qualified flying instructor on Hunting Jet Provost aircraft and my next tour, on English Electric Lightnings with 56 Squadron in Cyprus, certainly taught me a thing or two about the need for pragmatism. My time on Lightnings was followed by a four-year stint at RAF Brawdy where my job was to instruct budding fighter pilots. My posting to 92 Squadron at RAF Wildenrath followed and now I knew that, if we were to have a chance of success against the F-15s, all of my previous experience combined with a fair amount of pragmatic guile would have to be applied.

It was not exactly behind locked doors that our pre-flight briefing took place on that day, nonetheless all four of our 92 Squadron Phantom crew members were keenly aware of the need for discretion. For our plan to work out, the details had to be kept to ourselves. This plan, which amounted to flying low and fast with all emitters switched off, relied on the F-15 pilots failing to angle down their radar scanners far enough to detect us at very low altitude. While, in this way, we concealed the Phantoms, we'd use old-fashioned eyeball techniques to observe the opposition approaching at a high level. According to the morning's meteorological briefing, high-level contrails could be expected, and in this respect the fates were on our side. Our four pairs of eyes would monitor the contrails carefully then, just as the F-15s were about to fly over us, we'd pull up the Phantoms into a huge loop manoeuvre aiming to roll out in missile firing range behind the 'enemy'.

Our tactics may have been non-standard, nonetheless they appeared to be a plausible solution in view of the one-sided nature of the encounter. We knew, in other words, that unconventional methods were needed if we were to avoid becoming, as they say, duck soup. In any case, the point of the exercise was to prepare us for combat against the likes of the Soviet Mikoyan-Gurevich MiG-25 (NATO code-named Foxbat), especially the MiG-25PD variant with its Pulse Doppler Sapphire-25 radar system. Any such combat actions were likely to be one-off – a case of shoot or be shot down.

There was a curious, somewhat apprehensive mood as the Phantom and Eagle crews walked out to their respective aircraft that day. In addition to our in-house Phantom briefing, an overall briefing that had covered the complexities of a two versus two dissimilar-type air combat mission had been comprehensive. It was a training exercise, this was hardly war and yet, in a fashion, it felt a bit like war. Perhaps the two Eagle pilots harboured feelings of superiority. If that was the case, we Phantom crews were careful to adopt studiously poker-faced expressions for we were determined to avoid the smallest hint of our plan.

It was not long before all four aircraft had started up and taken off. We flew in a westerly direction initially, a route that took the formation over high ground dominated by Mount Linas at over 4,000ft high. The terrain was largely scrubland marked by spiky thorn bushes and the emerald green dots of trees. Beyond the mountains, the coastal strip led to the blue-grey waters of the Mediterranean Sea, waters which were about to witness scenes of hectic activity above. Our Phantoms' crews with their secret to keep had conflicting emotions; anxious to proceed yet wary of the hazards, for imponderables remained. As the moment of battle drew near, so the tension increased.

When it was time for the two sides to 'split', as if in a boxing match, the referee (the radar controller) directed the F-15s to the 'red' corner, while the Phantoms proceeded to the 'blue' corner. With a pre-briefed separation of at least fifty miles until we turned to face each other, this was our opportunity to descend before the fight commenced. And as we descended it was with feelings of trepidation; phase one of our plan was in progress – there was no turning back now.

By the time of the controller's next instruction – "Turn onto reciprocal headings" – the two Phantoms had reached sea level. It was during the turn that I felt a sudden sense of relief: the weather man had been correct; high-level contrails revealed the position of the F-15s. With my navigator's cry, "They're up there!" the air of expectation dominating our cockpits began to intensify. Following a positive nod of my head, the crew of the other Phantom reacted as briefed, and soon both aircraft, with radio emitters turned off and reheats selected, were skimming at supersonic airspeed just above the sea's surface. With a closing velocity of approximately one mile in three seconds, the countdown was rapid. When my navigator estimated a range of 35 miles, we knew that the time to 'collision' was about one minute and forty-five seconds. This was the range at which, in a real situation, the F-15 pilots would be likely to launch their AIM-7 Sparrows (semi-active radar homing air-to-air missiles).

With one minute to go and with the high-level contrails showing no signs of deviation, I began to feel increasingly confident that our plan would work out. At the thirty-second point I glanced at my instruments; low-level turbulence was causing the instrument panel to vibrate. At twenty seconds I re-checked that the other Phantom was holding a good position; the machine, I reckoned, looked mean, not unlike a black mamba snake about to strike – that fast, nervous, highly aggressive creature with malevolent eyes would raise its head so swiftly that the action would be invisible and the snake's body would arch upwards as it waited for the moment to attack its prey.

Fifteen seconds...the air remained heavy with angst as the last few seconds ticked by. *Ten seconds*...as our 'prey' persisted on a steady course, I knew that the F-15 pilots would be puzzled about why they had failed to spot us...*eight seconds*...our camouflaged paintwork had evidently been effective against the sea's backdrop...*six seconds*...ready for the imminent move, the other Phantom had edged closer to our aircraft...*four seconds*...my left hand still held the throttles fully forward as...*three...two...one*...in a small but positive movement I pulled back on the stick to initiate a large, lazy loop. The other Phantom followed and our altimeters became a blur of movement as they registered the rapid rate of climb. Simultaneously, the airspeed started to reduce and it was not long before we began to approach the altitude of the F-15s. Now, the distinctive landmass of Sardinia stood out to the east of us, and the fluorescent azure of the Mediterranean sky provided a dramatic contrast to our low-level world when we'd been rushing above the sea's surface.

Suddenly, his voice terse with excitement, my navigator said: "Our current range to the targets is...standby...one-and-a-half miles." "Standby, Jeff..." I said. My heart was thumping. Our judgement had been good, we'd ended up within missile-firing range. This was confirmed by the steady growl in our bone dome ear pieces – the growl from the AIM-9 Sidewinder missiles that indicated 'in range'. So it was that, with a final check of parameters and with a sense of exuberance that our plan had worked, I squeezed the trigger on my control stick and called: "Fox 2."

This call, together with a similar one from the other Phantom, caused a predictable reaction from the F-15s as they initiated a hard turn. It was too late, though. If this had been for real, my navigator and I would have been aware of a flash and a slight thump as an AIM-9 missile left its mounting. Perhaps our peripheral visions would detect a spout of flame and we'd smell the sour odour of explosives. We'd watch the missile drop slightly then accelerate on its inevitable path of destruction; even the F-15 could not out-manoeuvre an AIM-9 Sidewinder. The explosion, when it came, would be startling. In a billow of black smoke and orange flame, debris would ascend briefly until, while we observed with awe, we'd see sad scraps of F-15 residue begin an earthwards plunge. Maybe, at that point, any sense of triumph would end.

Luckily, of course, this was mere supposition. That day, when the ground controller confirmed: "Fox 2 on the left target! Fox 2 on the right target!" the sense of triumph was considerable and lasted for quite a long time. But the protagonists flew on, the controller set us up for other engagements for which, having learnt a lesson or two, the F-15s demonstrated their superior capabilities. I didn't care, though. The first engagement was the key one and during that pre-planned procedure we'd managed to demonstrate how the latest technology, good as it may be, can still be outdone by a canny opponent. The point had been made. I was well satisfied.

*

Author's note: This is dedicated to the memory of Flight Lieutenant Jeff Bell, the navigator featured in the chapter. Jeff was killed when his Phantom crashed in the Falkland Islands in October 1983.

CHAPTER 19
BOLD SPIRITS

RICHARD PIKE RECALLS INTRIGUING EVENTS

There was no applause when we finished. That's to say, if there was any applause, we were unaware. It was as if, to set the seal on our success, we had bowed and withdrawn gracefully. Perhaps the congratulations were generous, the tributes admiring for the airborne manoeuvres had gone well, our skills had been put to a tremendous test. When the display had commenced, eyes had been riveted on the four Phantoms and the crowds had watched with cheerful fascination, even stared aghast, while we cavorted around the Scottish skies. Members of the audience were thrilled, ladies swooned, strong men were breathless with emotion. The excitement of it all!

Now, though, our moment was over, our bit was done, and maybe we felt a mix of elation and deflation as we prepared to land the Phantoms at RAF Leuchars. Perhaps, after landing, we'd be asked to sign programmes as mementos and I'd enjoy the unusual opportunity to apply my best handwriting with gusto (although my wife has claimed that I have terrible handwriting – I've disputed this but she will not be persuaded).

At present, however, within the four cockpits, the calm, if tense, atmosphere was noteworthy, an aspect probably not appreciated by the crowds. During the display itself we'd said little although there had been occasional terse instructions from the formation leader. The routine had been well rehearsed; superfluous chatter was a distraction and intense concentration was needed. Probably, though, the crowds were not interested in such details and in any case their attention was swiftly diverted at the conclusion of our display; an intriguing programme had been devised for that lively Leuchars day and onlookers were keen to focus on the next planned item.

Meanwhile, other such displays were underway at various bases around the country for that Battle of Britain anniversary in September 1974. It was a memorable year – a year of political turmoil in Britain with two general elections, one change of national government, the declaration of a state of emergency in Northern Ireland, and the impact of the Three Day Week. In the United States of America, the looming impeachment of President Nixon seemed too incredible to take in. Closer to home, across the muddied waters of the Eden Estuary from Leuchars, members of the University of St Andrews, rarely averse to critical digs at a lot of things, including the military – especially the military – stepped up their flow of complaints about noisy Phantoms. There were idle rumours that the university may have sent a deputation to recommend that Royal Air Force Leuchars was declared a free state. The station authorities no doubt expressed feelings of essential sympathy and explained with great reasonableness and a good deal of historical citation that the optimum conditions for total revolution were not yet here. Undoubtedly, the wing commander went on to explain that such conditions could not be realistically anticipated for at least a dozen years and that in the interim the university deputation should go away and come back then.

For 1974 somehow represented a point in time when the issues that individuals had fretted about in years of personal struggle seemed suddenly to matter for everyone. At Leuchars, where I was a member of 43(F) Squadron, we were affected as much as everyone else by these startling shifts in outlook, nonetheless our duties did not stop. Operational commitments continued, secondary duties carried on including preparations for the annual Battle of Britain events, although these reflected, in encapsulated form, the tenor of the times with budgetary restrictions and the need for ingenuity. "One just needs brains," said one of the organisers broodingly.

"Where are we supposed to park the VIP's cars?" asked someone else practically.
"In front of the air traffic control tower, of course."
"In front? That's terrific. That's just the jolly old place for it."
"What's brought this on?"
"Brought what on?"
"Holy Moley. What the hell ails you?"
"Shhh!"

If small squabbles erupted, I couldn't help reflecting that this, in a way, was appropriate for events designed to commemorate the strains and torments of a mere thirty-four years ago when the Battle of Britain was fought. Even thinking about the preliminaries to that battle, to the spring months of 1940 when the fight in France had raged with a swiftness and ferocity that both awed and terrified, a sense of doom must have appeared inevitable. I tried to imagine how it might have felt when, on 9 June 1940, the BBC broadcasted the news that German Panzers had reached the lower reaches of the River Seine, and, just five days later, that Paris itself had fallen. In France, despair and capitulation were complete; an irritating Frenchman, a collaborationist called Pétain supposedly favoured with clarity of vision, announced that within three weeks "England would have her neck wrung like a chicken," ("Some neck! Some chicken!" Prime Minister Winston Churchill later retorted). By that stage nearly 350,000 Allied troops had been evacuated from the beaches of Dunkirk and as Churchill said in his speech to the House of Commons: "...the Battle of France is over. I expect the Battle of Britain is about to begin."

I wasn't even born then, that happy event was three years in the future, but in conversations with my mother later in life (my father, an operational Beaufighter pilot, never discussed his war experiences with me) I learned that the effect on people in Britain had been drastic. In frenzies of tireless activity, sandbags were filled, gas masks were distributed, food was stockpiled, aluminium pots were handed over to be made into Spitfires and Hurricanes, shops ran out of candles, road signs were taken down, other signs were put up ('Dig For Victory', 'Make Do And Mend', 'The Walls Have Ears'), houses were requisitioned, tangles of barbed wire were erected, air-raid sirens wailed, tempers frayed. People quarrelled over small issues and took it out on each other in various petty ways. "Oh! This terrible war," was a common conversational opening. "Good grief, what a shambles, what a bloody awful shambles. Makes you sick. Bastards..." was another line which reflected the confused, contagious, bitter sense of anxiety felt at the time.

My mother described how, at Churchill's behest, men of all ages, creeds and class began to form themselves into a volunteer defence force (the Home Guard or 'Dad's Army') whose personnel would crawl about hedgerows, farmyards, churchyards and woodlands in deadly serious if clumsy manoeuvres through the summer nights. An aura of fear was almost tangible as people waited for the inescapable onslaught. To cope with it, more and more individuals were conscripted. In places up and down the country, said my mother, there were poignant farewells. The scenario could be imagined:

"I must go now..." the young person would seem impatient, preoccupied. A shadow would darken the atmosphere of foreboding.

"Don't hurry. There's time yet."

"I really must." Affections would stir deep inside; thoughts would turn over and over. There might be a painfully solemn and tender hush; someone faced with the perils of war could seem impossibly young. Lower lips might start to tremble, throats tighten with a suffocating sense of yearning.

"Don't look at me like that. I can't bear it."

"Stay a bit longer..." A voice inside the head would cry: 'Please don't get yourself killed.' Eventually, though, that particular someone would have to leave – have to stumble off into the unknown. Their departure, as if to emphasise the cruel conundrum of war, would signify the twilight of the scene, perhaps the life.

My mother would describe other scenes too. One time, at a party in the officers' mess at RAF Tangmere in Sussex where my parents were based, someone asked: "Where's David? He'd enjoy this. Any news?" Dead silence followed. It was not, evidently, one of those accidental silences that can occur when, for a moment or two, no-one has anything to say. It was a shocked silence, a silence during which the proverbial pin might be heard to drop.

Later that evening, when my parents discussed the matter, my mother asked: "So what *has* happened to David?" My father looked pained. "The fact is – we don't know," he said. His tone was dark. "Oh God." "He was brought down by enemy fire. We're still trying to find out what went on."

As I recall her description (and history, they say, can be likened to a three-way division: what people believe happened, what historians say happened, and what *actually* happened), my mother moved to a window and stared up at the stars. How bewitching were those stars, she must have thought; how immortal and ethereal, as was the feeling brought on by the sweet scent of summer flowers that wafted in through the open window. My father joined her but apparently my parents said nothing for a time while they stood there and gazed at the night sky. Maybe, in those reflective moments, the tranquillity of the night merged with an unmistakable clarity that made words seem dreadfully inadequate.

It was before this, in August 1940, not long after the Battle of Britain had commenced (British historians date the battle as starting on 10 July 1940; German historians place the start as mid August 1940) that my mother and sisters had first-hand experience of being bombed. They had walked to a local shop not far from RAF North Weald (at that juncture my parents lived near North Weald while my father worked in the Air Ministry in London) when she became aware of the roar of numerous aircraft in the vicinity. At once, she hustled the children and herself into a roadside ditch. As they lay there, one on top of the other, they heard a whistling sound followed by a concerto of several loud crumps that shook the ground. They heard glass shatter in a nearby house. An ominous moment of quiet ensued before, within seconds, they heard a further whistling sound followed by more crumps, that time further away. At length, when the hubbub had died down, she and the children ran home where an air raid shelter had been constructed in the garden. Later, it was reported that German bombers, harassed by defending Hawker Hurricanes, had headed for North Weald airfield at around 15,000ft and proceeded to drop bombs in a straight line before the airfield was hit.

For me, it was such individual accounts which brought alive the reality of the

Battle of Britain. Sometimes it could seem that the carnival atmosphere generated at anniversary events with burger vans, hot dog stalls, jazz bands, Punch and Judy shows, fabulous flying displays, general razzmatazz, obscured the real reason for holding the event. However, notwithstanding the side-shows, few would argue that the brave men and women who fought the battle deserved to be remembered. The statistics produced after the battle were revealing, even if figures appeared to vary according to the source. ("No doubt," wrote Churchill later, "we were always over-sanguine in our estimate of enemy scalps.") In broad terms, the Allied number of serviceable aircraft committed to the battle at less than 2,000 compared adversely with the German tally of over 2,500. However, the Germans lost nearly 1,900 aircraft during the battle compared to the Allies' losses of less than 1,600. One of the more remarkable statistics concerned the number of aircrew killed – according to one source 2,698 German airmen lost their lives compared to 544 Allied aircrew.

On 15 September 1940, two waves of German attacks using vast numbers of aircraft were repulsed by the RAF with every available aircraft of 11 Group being used on that day. The statistics for this crucial day revealed that sixty Luftwaffe aircraft had been shot down, over double the number of RAF aircraft, a figure which influenced Hitler's decision to order the postponement of preparations for the invasion of Britain. This day became known as Battle of Britain Day, the day which, thirty-four years later, would be marked by our four-ship Phantom display at Leuchars.

The work-up for the display had been complex, but then the Phantom was a complex aircraft – from both the aircrew and engineering perspective. When, in the late 1960s, pilots and navigators were posted as staff members to 228 (Phantom) Operational Conversion Unit at RAF Coningsby, most of them admitted later that they'd found it hard to devise an effective course. Nearly all agreed that a year or more was needed before a course was developed that did justice to the Phantom's flexibility and potential. As one instructor noted: 'Fighter pilots are not renowned for their willingness to adapt to the ideas of others (with the possible exception of Lightning pilots who can adapt to anything), and the fundamental problem was not one of manipulating the radar and other aids but that of operating the complete weapons system, whether in the fighter or fighter-bomber role, in such a way that the crew did not limit the machine. For many crews, their greatest difficulty lay with openly demonstrating the humility which effective crew co-operation demanded. It may have been hard to accept the burden of blame for a failed intercept or a "long" bomb, but those who met their navigator or pilot halfway at least attempted properly to operate the most successful fighter/bomber aircraft of its generation.'

With crews thus encouraged to focus on their own failings, the transition for a former single-seat fighter pilot used to airborne self-sufficiency could be tricky. Tricky, too, were some of the problems that had to be solved in the event of failure of the Phantom's complex technical systems. One such affected me on a night flight almost exactly a year after the four-ship Battle of Britain display of 1974. The flight was shortly before I left the Phantom force and involved a training sortie planned for the benefit of a crew new to 43 Squadron. The pilot I knew from Lightning days. "My dear fellow," I said when he arrived at Leuchars, "you haven't changed a bit. This is great!" His voice was just the same as of old and his square, almost angular, face had not changed either.

On the night in question, the two of us, together with our navigators, converged on the briefing room for a detailed run-through of the planned flight. The room, which was fairly large, had windows that overlooked the airfield at Leuchars. Outside, the orange glow of powerful sodium floodlights penetrated the dark. Airmen could be spotted as they hastened here and there to perform necessary tasks. Nearby, huddled hangars were bathed in the floodlights' eerie glow.

During the briefing I detailed the take-off and recovery procedures as well as the night's intended exercise of practise interceptions for which, in an alternating sequence, we would take turns to act as target and interceptor. The flight should have been a straightforward training task of the type we flew regularly. After the briefing the four of us bantered our way to the locker room where we picked up bone domes and life jackets before the pilots signed the flight authorisation sheets and technical logs.

The autumnal air was chilly as we walked to our Phantoms and my navigator clambered hastily into the rear cockpit of our allocated aircraft 'S'. Meanwhile, I went through the ritual of the external checks before climbing the steps to the front cockpit. A ground crewman helped me to strap in then checked carefully that the ejection seat safety pins were stowed – a routine, if we had but known, which might have proved more than usually significant. After this he moved to a pre-positioned fire extinguisher which he manned while monitoring the engine start process. The procedures went normally, the aircraft was fully serviceable and at this stage in the proceedings I had no indications that hinted at the problems ahead.

Air traffic control now gave permission for our pair of Phantoms to taxi out for Leuchars' westerly runway. At the holding point, where I was instructed to wait for other traffic to clear the runway, I glanced at the surrounding scene. A few miles beyond the airfield boundary, the lights of St Andrews showed up as a conspicuous backdrop. To the west, I could just make out flat farmland before the ground began to rise towards the village of Balmullo where my wife would be settling our eighteen-month-old daughter at our home there. The runway itself, a black ribbon of tarmac, was flanked by rows of lights. At one side of the runway a single flickering light emitted the abbreviated Morse code signal for Leuchars.

"You're clear to enter the active runway and take off," said the controller, at which I released the Phantom's brakes and monitored behind to ensure that the number two was following. At the take-off point I applied the brakes again, checked that my number two was still in position and began to ease the throttles forward. The low whine of the Rolls-Royce Spey engines rose to a cry at which juncture, with the engine revolutions gauges each showing around 80 percent, I released the brakes, pushed the throttles to full cold power, paused, then selected reheat on both engines. The twin Speys crescendoed to a roar and the sensation of a powerful punch in the back verified that the reheats had lit. Meantime, the number two delayed his take-off by thirty seconds after which he followed in a trail position.

We climbed up through at least three layers of cloud. At lower levels a few wisps presaged the tumult on high. The next layer, made up of improbable shapes that pointed in various directions, led to the main body of cumulus that was piled in great masses that moved with the wind. With the number two still trailing by thirty seconds, both Phantoms broke out of cloud at an altitude of around 30,000ft to be met by the ghostly glow from an almost-full moon. The moonlight accentuated the cloud tops which appeared as scraps of whitish fragments like spectral clouds, lost creatures in strange transparent space.

The trouble, when it came, struck with alarming swiftness. The ground radar controller, as he set up the first practise intercept, ordered separate headings for each Phantom. I'd just taken up the required heading when, at a precise instant, I heard, and perhaps sensed, a slight metallic clunk. Simultaneously, I lost radio contact and the cockpit lights went out. Cocooned in a warm and comfortable cockpit with Perspex protection from the mega-minus temperatures outside, for a moment my mind appeared to play tricks – as if the component parts that sent messages between the brain and the body had broken down. I was aware of a brief period of hesitation, a slowness induced, perhaps, by shock. It might have lasted for one second, maybe two but that can be a long time in a fast-jet aircraft. When, eventually, a message got through to my brain, it was not a pleasant one: 'We've suffered an electrical failure,' said the message, 'do something about it.'

At once my eyes flicked down to check the two generator switches. These were on the right-hand side of the cockpit and fortunately, thanks to the moon, there was just enough ambient light for me to see what I was doing. Both switches were in their normal position; nothing wrong there. In turn I selected each switch off, then back on – but to no effect. I'd hoped to kick-start one of the generators but it hadn't worked; the electrical power was still off and I'd have to think of something else. Now I reached for a lever on the left-hand side of the cockpit and pulled it downwards firmly. This action operated a ram air turbine (RAM) system, a mini-windmill arrangement which, when deployed, rotated in the airstream to produce electricity. It was a get-you-home device designed to be basic but foolproof.

However, the supposedly infallible RAM system failed to work. With the electrical power remaining stubbornly off, my options were starting to look bleaker by the second. Thousands of formidable feet of cloud had to be penetrated, a daunting prospect for which I'd need electrical power to operate the flight instruments.

But the flight instruments, apart from a small E2B compass, were not working, not even the emergency back-up systems. The designers at McDonnell Douglas had deemed that two generators plus the RAM should provide sufficient back-up, but the flaws in this hypothesis were becoming rapidly, awfully apparent: all of these electrical systems, so I discovered later, went through a common junction and it was the junction itself that was faulty. Such a design weakness was serious enough but to compound the whole horrible business, the mark of Phantom in question, the FG1, was a naval version and as the navy, so we were told, did not like aircraft batteries on ships, the FG1 had no proper battery back-up.

It was a year or so after this incident that another Phantom suffered the same problem. To the eternal shame of those involved, action to rectify the fault was either inadequate or not taken at all. The pilot on that occasion was unable to restore electrical power, he became disorientated in cloud, lost control of the machine and both crew members were killed when the Phantom plunged into the sea. If ever there was an accident, as they say, waiting to happen, this was a dire example and the tragic outcome was surely as needless as it was outrageous.

Just now, though, in Phantom 'S', the moonlight helped me to retain sufficient orientation to turn back towards base and to maintain a straight and level attitude. With my eyes fixed on the moonlit horizon, I seemed to be floating above pure, abstract blackness. Everything was ominously quiet apart from the steady whine of the Rolls-Royce Spey engines. My sense of direction from the moon was in a geographic sense, although, in the grand scheme of things, maybe there was a deeper sense too.

In emergency situations such as this, the navigator would usually produce his emergency checklist to read aloud the necessary actions. However, in the present circumstances without electrical power I lacked the means to communicate with my navigator. I could have used a night-flying torch to read my own checklist but it was unnecessary: I knew well enough that this particular emergency was not listed. I heard a terse shout from the rear cockpit – "*RAM*" – and realised that my navigator must have removed his oxygen mask briefly to yell at me. By way of reply I removed my own oxygen mask to yell back: "I've tried, Hugh – the RAM's not working."

At this stage, aware of the growing possibility of having to eject into the North Sea, I began to pull my seat straps even tighter than normal. My heart felt in my mouth. Our present distance from the Scottish mainland meant that the Phantom was beyond the range of the rescue helicopters. The chances of rescue before morning were not good and the prospect of a long night bobbing up and down in a rubber dinghy on the surface of the North Sea appeared to be looming. It's not often that I have felt fear – real fear – but at that moment I did. It proved to be a treacherous foe, one that offered no compassion, only doubt and disbelief. Brought face to face with the prospect of one's premature end, the fear seemed to be exacerbated by not knowing what to expect.

With years of training, a pilot or a navigator or an aircrewman will acquire knowledge that will help to overcome fear. Now, though, I had that sinking sensation as if standing at the edge of a cliff with no control over what was about to happen. And conscious that something terribly wrong was going on, my system seemed to succumb to an anxiety that grew and grew until it became a sensation of dread. I learnt the need to fight hard to sustain hope. And I discovered that real fear, the type that was felt, no doubt, by those who fought in the Battle of Britain, could shake you to the core. My own experience may have been minor compared to theirs, nonetheless it was something that would fix itself within the memory cells and stay there for good.

I thought about the many survival briefings that I'd attended in the past, about the seemingly endless, tedious repetition of the required techniques. Perhaps I was about to rue my complacency. The survival priorities – protection, location, water, food – were imprinted in my mind but there were other issues too. Survival meant paying attention to what was close at hand. The survivor's mentality should be focused; to fantasise with idle hope would be tantamount to dreaming one's life away. The will to live, we'd been told, was crucial. It was not in-built; some people would give up on life with a resigned sigh, others would fight a little then lose hope, some would never give up; some would fight and fight no matter what the cost. They would fight to the end. It may be nothing more than pigheadedness or a life-hungry stupidity, but for some individuals it was not just a matter of courage but of a fundamental inability to let go. Presumably such people would see all the happiness that was theirs and all the happiness that could still be theirs and understand clearly all that they could lose.

With my face doubtless set in an expression of stony determination, I decided, in last-ditch attempts, to try switching the generators regularly off and back on despite a risk of short-circuit and fire. It was during this process that, fleetingly, a vestige of electrical life appeared. The cockpit lights flickered on then went out again. I tried again. Suddenly, after another cycle or two, the cockpit lights came on and stayed on. Now I could speak with my navigator as well as with the other Phantom – and with the rest of the world. 'Quick, man, quick', I thought; 'there's not a second to lose.' Our circumstances remained tenuous but at least, while the electrics still worked, a plan could be decided. My mind worked fast as the controller gave directions to the other Phantom and quite rapidly the aircraft appeared on the left side of ours. The pilot held a loose formation position, meanwhile I confirmed that our aircraft's flight instruments had re-erected so that I could adjust the heading for base.

Difficult decisions now had to be made. Ideally, I would have manoeuvred to hold a close formation position on the other Phantom while he led us down through the banks of cloud. Tonight, though, in a paradoxical twist, this was the other pilot's first night flight in a Phantom. With his lack of experience on the aircraft type, let alone his lack of a briefing on the difficult art of night-time close formation flying in a Phantom, this option seemed best avoided if possible.

It was at about this point that our luck seemed to change. The cloud ahead was becoming lighter in colour which signified a less dense area of cloud. This would allow the two Phantoms to maintain visual contact with each other without the need for holding close formation. I briefed the other pilot, therefore, to stay on my left side and slightly above me. In the event of difficulty, I'd move to a close formation position on him, otherwise we'd continue down as we were. It was a compromise solution, not stipulated in any manual, but it worked. As we commenced descent into the patchy cloud, the moon disappeared but the other Phantom didn't. As briefed, my number two remained in position throughout and although I was absorbed in the task of flying the approach procedure, an occasional glance over my left shoulder revealed the reassuring sight of his aircraft.

At length we reached the ragged cloud-base at which stage, like a beacon of welcome, I was able to pick up the glow of airfield lights ahead. Before long, the lights flashed past on either side of the aircraft as we touched down at Leuchars. The Phantom's electrics continued to remain online so I was able to taxi to the squadron dispersal area to complete the shut-down routine. After this, I sat still in the cockpit to reflect for a moment or two. Soon there'd be forms to fill in, engineers to debrief, operations staff who'd want to hear every detail, but just now I needed to ponder the seesaw of events, the bizarre blend of good and bad fortune. If the electrical failure had occurred in thick cloud during the climb-out, if there had been no moonlight, if I'd been unable to restore one of the generators...*if*...*if*...*if*. Perhaps the affair, like the destiny of flotsam and jetsam cast up on the shore, had the mark of pure chance although, on reflection, there seemed to be other influences too.

Eventually I stepped out of the aircraft into the chill of the September night. Everything was uncommonly quiet. When I explained what had happened to the engineers, they seemed perplexed; the operations staff looked worried; aircrew colleagues listened with sombre expressions. When the debriefs were over, I felt dispirited – almost guilty as if, in our Phantom, my navigator and I had been forced to flee, nearly blind, like wrong-doers, as we coughed and spluttered and cried foul while we struggled to escape. It had been a roller coaster ride which had stirred up severe ambiguities and dark places. I'd wrestled with fate and learned lessons, quite a few of them.

The situation, though, was exceptional and on looking back it was the positive aspects of flying the Phantom which I preferred to remember. For one thing, involvement in the Leuchars four-ship Battle of Britain display of 1974 was an exhilarating occasion. I'd been delighted and excited, if a little surprised, when the squadron commander (we were hardly the best of friends) had offered me the echelon port position in his formation. His leadership style had created fractures within the squadron, nonetheless he was an experienced formation leader.

Several practise sessions took place before the display itself. The leader would brief his team in detail after which, when asked if happy, we'd respond with thumbs up signs. "Okay," he'd say, making a circle of approval with thumb and forefinger, "let's go and do it."

Once airborne, the team soon settled into the briefed routine. When the sessions went well, as they usually did, we all felt a fine sense of satisfaction. We acted as one unit for which particular techniques were needed: while focused on the aircraft ahead, it was important to remain relaxed and not to allow the eyes to dart about like startled rabbits. From certain angles I could glimpse observers by the shore as they gazed up at the formation. I might notice a truck on a country road. When we pointed out to sea I'd be aware of the afternoon sun and a particular phosphorescence reflected from the sea's surface. As we turned inland, the background hills showed up a mix of dark green and purple. These glimpses, though, were vague and fleeting while I worked to hold a good formation position.

Eventually, with our display completed, we landed at Leuchars, closed down the four Phantoms and walked to the aircrew crewroom where family members and friends waited to greet us. My wife Sue, as she proudly clutched our 9-month-old daughter Lizzie, described how the air had visibly quivered, like the shimmer coming off a road on a hot day, when the formation swept by. The power of eight Rolls-Royce Spey engines thundering overhead had created a mighty maelstrom. Now, though, it was over and the crewroom's calm atmosphere made the experience seem distant, almost like an illusion.

Maybe, I thought, this was a sensation not so different from the way the Hurricane and Spitfire pilots and their supporting personnel might have felt in 1940. Back then, air displays were far from their minds, no doubt, nevertheless the brave souls who had fought against a Teutonic tyranny had passed on skills from one generation to the next as if touching fingertips over time. Perhaps in that respect their bold spirits lived on.

A HIGH NOTE

CHRIS STONE RECALLS A SPECIAL FLY-PAST

There it was on the nose, and with just 30 seconds to go before being over the target, the unmistakable tree-lined avenue of the Mall pointing directly towards Buckingham Palace.

Just a few seconds before this crucial sighting, I was anxiously searching the ground as it flashed past below for features that would match the maze of roads, rail and waterways on the 1:50,000 map I was holding. It was a fine day with just a few scattered cumulus clouds at 2,000 feet; although a thin layer of haze at our low altitude over the heart of London was restricting horizontal visibility to around 4 miles. On my map there was a black-inked track line that a trusty navigator back at base had carefully drawn. The map had been neatly folded and orientated on the final heading of 237° Magnetic. There were 10-second interval marks on the track line to show the distances being covered at the calculated ground speed. Flying at 420 knots indicated airspeed, and with the wind factored in, we were moving over the ground at just a little over 7 miles per minute; so things were coming up fast. With about 45 seconds to go, the distinctive gasometers at Hackney came into view. They were the first good dimensional landmarks to stand out since passing over Fairlop railway station nearly a minute earlier. Now there they were, just to the left of track precisely where they had been highlighted on the map. Looking further ahead, and with anxiety now starting to recede a little, I could just make out the final 'real-world-to-map' match I was after. It was the point where the Thames was starting a lazy meander to the left, and where the V-shape of the Hungerford and Waterloo bridges crossing the river at that point were positively indicating the position of Charing Cross. We needed to fly right over that railway station, and that's where I was heading – spot on track. Adopting as nonchalant a manner as I could, I calmly relayed this reassuring identification over the intercom. An equally comforting voice came back, "35 seconds to go Sir – timing's good – maintain this air speed".

The four boxes of four aircraft were in as close a position as I had dared brief the section leaders to adopt without disobeying a Group Headquarters tiresome edict not to fly over as I had wished in a close diamond formation. More's the pity I kept thinking to myself. Flying a perfect symmetrical pattern, when individual sections of four were spaced apart, was just as difficult to achieve, if not more so, than having all sixteen aircraft in tight formation. I was thankful, therefore, that there was no need for any aileron inputs or throttle changes to correct course or speed, thereby making matters even more challenging for section leaders holding their equidistant positions in these final seconds. I pressed the radio transmit button on the throttle to tell the formation we were "30 seconds out", and added encouraging words for all to "hold steady". I am certain many others who have led a similar fly-past, before and since, will know the feeling of relief that overcomes a leader of a large formation knowing he is certain not to miss the IP or time-on-target – not even by a yard or a second.

With lifted spirits, a fleeting temptation flashed through my mind as we approached Admiralty Arch to ease the formation down a bit below the stipulated height of 700ft. Thankfully, sanity suppressed the evil thought, even though I imagined the Royal Party on the balcony might be suitably impressed by the closer spectacle and louder roar of thirty-two Rolls-Royce Spey engines speeding overhead. So, no rules were broken and a career was kept intact. It was, after all, satisfying enough to have brought the sixteen Phantoms directly over Buckingham Palace precisely at the appointed time of 13:00. In doing so, the mission – to extend a RAF salute to Her Majesty Queen Elizabeth II in recognition of her official birthday and the Silver Jubilee year of her coronation – was accomplished.

Of course, for getting us to the right place at the right time on this important event I give much credit to the gallant wing commander who was sitting right behind me. Bob Arnott was OC 56 Squadron at the time, which was fortunate for me for two reasons. Firstly, he was a first class navigator who reassuringly kept an eagle eye on our track, timings and speed all the way; and secondly, it gave me a clear conscience in leading the Wattisham Wing without having to displace a pilot squadron commander from his rightful front seat.

Up until I commanded Wattisham, comprising 23 Squadron (the Red Eagles) and 56 Squadron (the Firebirds), each equipped with 10 Phantom FGR2 (F-4M) aircraft, all my flying had been in single-seat fighters. Of these, the English Electric Lightning was undoubtedly the most exciting aircraft to fly, but the threat for which it had been designed back in the early 1950s – to knock out Soviet bombers attacking the UK from high level – was starting to change by the time it came into front-line service. Instead, the Soviet long-range bomber force was expected to adopt a rather unsporting tactic of attacking at low level underneath UK radar coverage: an environment where the Lightning's own radar capability was also a very poor match. The Lightning Force nevertheless persevered with training for these difficult tasks. But, attempting to detect and identify intruders, especially at night or in poor weather conditions, very often both, an extremely high workload (some might say near impossible) was placed on the single occupant of a Lightning. If the air defence version of the Panavia Tornado was to be the saviour, the question was whether this hopeful entity would ever get off the drawing board and transcend development hurdles? While this would take ten years longer than anticipated to resolve, there was a stalwart in the wings that would come to the rescue and fill the void.

There could have been no better choice than the McDonnell Douglas F-4M Phantom II. A purposeful, battle-proven machine, it was arguably one of the finest aircraft designs to have emerged during the Cold War. It served the RAF well in the interdictor, strike, and reconnaissance roles until Tornado IDS aircraft entered service in the mid 1970s. Then, with Tornado ADV still nowhere in sight, the F-4M Phantoms were switched from their air-to-ground role to an air-to-air role to relieve the ageing fleet of Lightnings. In this time of need, the Phantom was a quantum leap forward for the UK air defence system. For the first time the RAF had an air-to-air fighter that could loiter for respectable periods, had Pulse Doppler radar providing a good 'look down' capability against low flying targets, and carried a sensible load of both radar-guided and heat-seeking missiles. Moreover, a comfort I particularly appreciated was a two-man crew to share the demanding workloads.

Getting up to speed in the Phantom, after having last commanded a Lightning squadron followed by a ground tour, required that I first take refresher flying courses on Jet Provosts and Hunters, before attending the Phantom Operational Conversion Unit. Senior commanders going to a flying station, but who normally had no operational role on a front-line squadron, were programmed for the short course at the OCU. This translated to just ten conversion exercises, where the first 'captain' sortie (in other words solo on type, but with a navigator in the back seat of the F-4 as opposed to a QFI) was Convex 4. The remaining six flights as 'pilot captain' would cover rudimentary intercept exercises, formation and instrument flying. The lucky thing for me was that after the conversion course I still had six weeks to spare before taking command of Wattisham, and 56 Squadron just happened to be working up to operational status at the Coningsby OCU with its new Phantoms prior to permanent deployment to Wattisham. What better way could there be to fill in time, thought I, than flying additional operational training exercises with them.

So, by the time I got to Wattisham, very shortly followed by 56 Squadron, and with thanks to its squadron commander – who clearly knew which side his bread was buttered – I had now accumulated a significant amount of hours and experience in weapons and intercept training. At least it assured me that I was not going to be a 'lame duck' station commander bothering the squadrons to do aimless continuation training in one of their valuable two-stick Phantoms with a supervising QFI. In fact, a happy situation developed where I was often in demand by the squadrons when they were short of a pilot. Thus, I was able to fly just about every type of exercise in the book, including deployments overseas and live air firing. I found the most exhilarating exercises in the Phantom involved air combat manoeuvring (ACM). Being a heavy machine, however, with a bulky fuselage, large cheek air intakes, and that unusual outer wing dihedral and tail anhedral arrangement, the Phantom did not excel in the drag coefficient league. Thus, getting into a turning fight with lighter-weight fighters was not a particularly wise course of action. Nevertheless, with judicious use of rudder leading into turns, astute use of thrust, and keeping the fight vertical, one could learn how to maintain advantageous levels of energy. As proven on occasions in Vietnam fighting against MiG-21s, when a Phantom was handled intelligently, guile could outweigh an adversary's superior turning performance.

ACM exercises were of very short duration, usually 40 minutes, since once the fight had started it seemed that the throttles rarely came out of full after-burner, and those Speys sucked fuel down fast. In contrast, I discovered that blood didn't flow so fast through the veins of an over-40-year-old as it did in one's youth, and at the end of one of these trips I felt like I had been carrying a ton of rocks around all day. But I never turned down any request to fly ACM training exercises – after all, who in their right mind would give up the opportunity to get into a good old aerial 'gun fight' in a Phantom. I just went to bed earlier (pleasantly exhausted) on those evenings.

Flash back now to the royal fly-past. To ensure all twenty Phantoms of the Wattisham Wing would be serviceable for this auspicious occasion, whilst at the same time not jeopardizing the normal squadron training leading up to the event, a heavy workload was placed on the engineers. We first flew a sixteen-aircraft formation around East Anglia on Friday 31 March 1978 to celebrate the 60th anniversary of the founding of the RAF. On this occasion I led the formation over Ipswich, and neighbouring operational airfields in East Anglia. We were also able to include a salute to Lord Stradbroke who just happened to be handing over his royal duties that day having served 30 years as Lord Lieutenant of Suffolk. It was very much a spur-of-the-moment addition to the planned route, but time was available that morning to send a small ceremonial party, comprising the station adjutant and some very smart airmen, to the venue complete with a dais on which his lordship could take the salute as we overflew. He was so taken with this unexpected tribute that he drove over to Wattisham as soon as his day's formalities were over to personally thank all the crews. It was a gracious act on his part, and much appreciated by everyone. On 31 May 1978 a full dress rehearsal for the Buckingham Palace fly-past was flown – again, all twenty aircraft were available and took to the air. The formation was flown only as far as Fairlop railway station (about two minutes flying time short of the palace), but it provided a good check on timings, and valuable formation practice.

The big day was Saturday 3 June 1978, and once more both squadrons excelled in getting all their Phantoms serviceable. Working backwards from the required 'time on target', and to allow for forming up, plus a couple of 'show the flag' runs across the airfield before setting course for London, our taxi-out time would need to begin at 12:05. A formation briefing was held in the Wing Operations building. This concluded with watches being synchronized, and the order given for crews to walk out to their aircraft at 11:30.

Having strapped in, and completed the pre-start checks, my mind momentarily drifted back to childhood days in 1944. Then, as an 11-year-old schoolboy, I remembered visiting Wattisham. The airfield at that time was occupied by American airmen of the 479th Fighter Group. I recalled the nostalgic days of harvest time that summer. A warm sun, and just the gentle clink of chains that harnessed two horses pulling a reaper, was all that broke the silence as the machine cut and sheaved wheat in a field overlooking the airfield. A scene of peaceful bliss that would suddenly be broken by the mighty roar of Merlin engines overhead as dozens of P-51 Mustangs took to the air. Thrilling times indeed for a youngster who had absolutely no idea then that one day he would be commanding this very airfield, and taking to the air himself in another kind of American fighter. But now fast forward 34 years from reminiscences to reality. It was 11:52, time for radio checks with everyone, and order engines to be started. Our take-off time would be 12:20.

The four spare aircraft took off after the sixteen were airborne, and escorted the main formation as far as Fairlop. In the event, none of the airborne spares were needed to fill empty slots that might have occurred through unserviceability in the main formation. And, as a 'belt and braces' precaution, an additional four Phantoms had been flown down to Wattisham from the OCU at Coningsby the day before to provide ground spares. They too were happily not called upon. As this was the 25th anniversary of Her Majesty's coronation, our formation carried several thousand First Day postal covers commemorating the royal event. I still

Leading out from Wattisham , 3 June 1978, 12:05 hours BST.

have two of the serially numbered 910 that were loaded in the aircraft I flew – XV482. The Queen has one!

After flying over the palace a right turn was made on to a northerly heading for home. Since Headquarters No 11 Group at Bentley Priory in Stanmore, Middlesex was not far off course in this general direction, it had occurred to me that the beleaguered staff serving their time on ground tours in our revered headquarters would rejoice with the sight of real aeroplanes (theirs to boot) flying overhead. Approval was given some days before; and I passed on a precise timing of 2 minutes and 47 seconds past the hour of 13:00 so that all would know when to watch out for us. And, by the way, I did plan to come down a bit for this one! The route and timings were duly promulgated by air traffic control in a notice to airmen (NOTAM).

Disappointingly, however, the word seemed not to have been passed around 11 Group because no one from the air staff appeared to witness the event. None, that is, except a loyal corporal photographer at Bentley Priory who captured the moment as we roared over the priory clock tower and Spitfire gate guardians. Likewise, another dutiful corporal photographer, our own from Wattisham, had been given a rail warrant and strict instructions to locate himself on the Mall that day and take an official picture as we flew overhead the palace. If he failed to get a picture, it was added that 'he might care to consider not coming back, but to join the Foreign Legion'. Of course, he came up trumps.

Sad as it is to come to the end of a flying tour, especially if the next one means

Chris Stone leading the fly-past over Buckingham Palace, 3 June 1978.

being chained to a desk; it helps if the heartbreaking last flight in one's beloved aircraft is a happy and memorable one. With the beautiful Hunter it coincided for me with winning a major air gunnery trophy; with the Lightning the happy coincidence was it being my 1,000th hour on type. And the last flight I made in the magnificent Phantom just so happened to be the flight over Buckingham Palace. Needless to say, a chilled bottle of champagne was waiting as I descended from the cockpit. There was also a nice telegram from the palace to congratulate Wattisham. I gave the station a well deserved 48-hour stand down, and more liquid flowed during the 'debriefing' held at an earlier time than usual through to Happy Hour in the officers' mess. I have little recollection of further events that occurred the rest of that day!

There cannot be anything more gratifying in one's RAF career than running a fighter station. My two allotted years had been due to end the day before the fly-past. But, rather than throw my successor into the deep end, the 'powers that be' allowed a two-week extension for me to oversee that, and yet another important royal event for Wattisham. An official visit to the station by HRH Prince Philip was announced to take place on 12 June 1978. It happened, and was a hugely successful day full of good cheer and pride for everyone at Wattisham. There couldn't possibly have been a higher note on which to finish.

SELECT BIOGRAPHIES

Jack Hamill joined the RAF in 1960. After training he flew Vulcans for six years and became the training captain on 27 Squadron at RAF Scampton. After this he became a qualified flying instructor (QFI) on the Gnat and instructed for three years at the Advanced Flying Training School at RAF Valley. This was followed by conversion to the Phantom in the air defence role and tours at Leuchars (43 Squadron), Wildenrath, Germany (19 Squadron) and Coningsby (29 Squadron).

The 29 Squadron tour was cut short by a posting to the Phantom Operational Conversion Unit (OCU) again as a flying instructor. However this only lasted for about nine months until he did a tour on loan to the Sultan of Oman's Air Force (SOAF). This was on the Hunter in the ground-attack role and also as QFI to the Omani students on their advanced flying training. On return Jack went back to the Phantom OCU and also became a display pilot on the Battle of Britain Memorial Flight flying the Spitfire and Hurricane for four years.

In the middle of this he converted to the Tornado F2/3 and remained as an instructor on the Tornado OCU. Jack joined a small unit that was set up within the OCU to train Saudi aircrew on the Tornado and after the first crews had completed their training he went to Saudi Arabia on secondment to British Aerospace to help in the set up of the Saudi squadrons. Initially he was seconded for eighteen months but this was extended and eventually Jack retired from Saudi Arabia in 1999 having spent ten years there.

Alan Winkles, born in Torquay, Devon, and became a member of the Air Training Corps at school. Aged 17, he gained a pilot's licence on Tiger Moths and joined the RAF to become a fighter pilot. His first appointment in 1966 was as a Lightning air defence pilot on 5 Squadron at RAF Binbrook. After this tour he transferred to the Phantom and became a qualified weapons instructor serving on 54 Squadron at RAF Coningsby and then on 17 Squadron at RAF Brüggen. In 1973 he became a flight commander on 43 Squadron (Phantoms) at RAF Leuchars, he then commanded the Royal Navy's Phantom training squadron and spent six months with 892 Naval Air Squadron on HMS *Ark Royal*.

After a tour on the weapons staff at HQ 38 Group RAF Upavon, he attended Staff College at RAF Bracknell and was posted to army staff duties at the MOD London. Following promotion, he took up duties as wing commander training at HQ 11 Group at RAF Bentley Priory. From there he was posted to assume command of 43 Squadron (Phantoms) at RAF Leuchars.

From 1987 onwards he was posted to the Sultan of Oman's Air Force, returned to the RAF Staff Collegein 1990 as a memeber of the directing staff. In 1993 Alan went to HQ USCENTCOM at MacDill Air Force Base in Tampa Florida as the first and sole British exchange officer. In January 1996, he was then posted to the Defence Evaluation and Research Agency (now QinetiQ) at Malvern and eventually retired from the RAF in 2001, having flown more than 5,000 hours. In retirement he became an A2 flying instructor with the Air Training Corps flying Vigilant (Grob 109) motor gliders. Alan also enjoys conventional gliding.

John Walmsley joined the RAF in 1963 aged 17 and was one of the very few teenage Lightning pilots. After a tour on Lightnings with 5 Squadron, he transferred to ground attack with the new Phantom on 54 Squadron at Coningsby. Qualifying as a fighter weapons instructor (FWI), he returned to 54 Squadron until becoming an instructor with 228 OCU. During a four-year tour he qualified as an electronic warfare officer and qualified weapons instructor (QWI [AD]) serving on the QWI staff. A tour as QWI with 56 Squadron at RAF Wattisham was followed by becoming a USAF instructor pilot on the staff of the USAF Central Instructor School at Luke AFB, Arizona, flying the F-4C in air-to-air and air-to-ground roles.

After a brief tour with the Central Tactics and Trials Organisation (CTTO) and Staff College, he became a flight commander with 43 Squadron in 1983, followed by 23 Squadron in the Falklands. He then had another tour with the CTTO as AD (air-to-air missiles) and AD (fighters), flying trials of missile firings and Phantom modifications. In 1989 he was promoted to wing commander and commanded the Phantom OCU/64 Squadron at RAF Leuchars until its demise in 1991. Of his 4,500 flying hours, over 3,000 were on the F-4 Phantom.

After a tour in the Plans Branch of HQSTC at High Wycombe, he became the defence and air attaché at the British embassy in Stockholm, Sweden. He retired from the RAF in 1994. He supports the Lightning Preservation Group at Bruntingthorpe.

Steve Gyles joined as a direct entry pilot in August 1965. He went through the normal training; Chipmunk (South Cerney), Jet Provost (Syerston), Gnat (Valley), Hunter (Chivenor), Lightning (Coltishall).

1968 to 1971   11 Squadron Lightnings Leuchars.
1971 to 1972   Lightning simulator instructor Gütersloh.

1972 to 1974	19 Squadron Lightnings Gütersloh.
1974 to 1977	TWU Brawdy Hunter tactics instructor.
1977 to 1980	43 Squadron F-4 Leuchars (Ejected on take-off on 21 Nov 1977)
1980 to 1982	RAF Handling Squadron at Boscombe Down.
1982 to 1987	27 Squadron Tornado GR1 at Marham (mud moving).
1987	Promoted squadron leader.
1988 to 1990	Squadron leader Operation Marham (kept current on Tornado).
Oct 1990	Retired.

Roger Colebrook was born in 1946. Roger left school at sixteen, determined to be an RAF pilot and worked on a farm until old enough to join. In 1964 he began an eight-year short service commission and trained on the Jet Provost (3 FTS 1964-5), Folland Gnat (4 FTS 1965-6), Hawker Hunter (229 OCU 1966), then the Lightning (226 OCU 1966-7).

Roger joined 56(F) Squadron, Lightning F3, March 1967, based at RAF Wattisham, Suffolk, then RAF Akrotiri, Cyprus. In July 1969 he was posted to CFS for QFI training, but requested a further air-defence tour of duty, flying the Phantom OCU (700[P] Squadron, RNAS Yeovilton, September 1969) then joined 43(F) Squadron, Phantom FG1, November 1969, based at RAF Leuchars. In 1972 he took his 'eight-year option' to leave.

For the next thirty years Roger worked for a number of airlines including British Caledonian Airways, Air Europe, Korean Air, Air 2000, and EVA Airways of Taiwan operating, amongst others, Beech 18, Piper Aztec, Britten-Norman Trislander, the DC10-30, Boeing 757, Boeing 767 and Fokker 100. His final appointment was on the Thomas Cook B757 fleet before retiring in 2006.

Les Hurst joined the RAF in 1960. After officer training he started basic flying training in February 1961 and soloed on the Jet Provost MK 3 but was transferred to navigation training in May 1961. He undertook the basic and advanced navigation courses on Varsity and Meteor before attending the Bomber Command Bombing school to train as a V Force navigator radar on the Hastings. This was followed by the Victor B1 Conversion Course at 232 OCU in 1963, before posting to 55 Squadron at RAF Honington.

After RAF Honington closed in 1966, he transferred to 57 Squadron which was converting from the bomber role to an in-flight refuelling squadron at RAF Marham. He served as a navigation instructor at RAF Cranwell on Varsity, Dominie and Jet Provost from 1969-1972. After a short period as a flight commander at the Apprentice School at RAF Halton he undertook in 1973 a Phantom FGR2 Ground Attack/Air Defence Course at 228 OCU RAF Coningsby.

From 1973-1975 he served with 892 Naval Air Squadron, HMS *Ark Royal*, on the Phantom FG1. On returning to the RAF he served for a short period with 29

(Air Defence) Squadron at RAF Coningsby. From 1975-1979 Les instructed at 228 (Phantom) OCU, attended electronic warfare and qualified weapons instructor (AD) courses and served as a QWI(AD) at 228 OCU.

After leaving the RAF, Les obtained a CAA flight navigator's licence and joined the Warton flight operations test team on 2 July 1979 as a Tornado test navigator. He spent the next fourteen years testing both variants of the Tornado and was appointed chief test navigator in 1990. Les made his last flight on 23 April 1992 having flown 899 Tornado test flights, amounting to 1,192 flying hours on the Tornado, out of a career total of 6,500 hours.

Rick Peacock-Edwards was educated in South Africa from where he joined the RAF in 1965. He spent over thirty years in the RAF and retired as an air commodore in 1999. RAF appointments included station commander RAF Leeming, deputy commander RAF Staff Washington, inspector of flight safety and director of Eurofighter.

The son of a Battle of Britain pilot his flying career has been spent mainly on fighters and he has over 1,000 hours on each of the Lightning, Phantom and Tornado. He also has over 1,000 hours on the Gnat and has flown many other types including the Hawk and Hunter. He introduced the Tornado F2/3 into RAF service and commanded the first squadron. He led the fly-past for the Queen's 60th birthday and also the opening of the 1986 Commonwealth Games. Whilst he has had an involvement in display flying on a number of aircraft he will be best remembered as the Tornado element in the unique Tornado F3/Spitfire display combo in the mid 1980s.

He is actively involved with the supervision of air displays and in this capacity he is currently chairman of the Imperial War Museum Duxford Flying Control Committee (FCC). He is also a member of the FCC for a number of other air displays. On leaving the RAF, Rick first joined General Dynamics UK as director of government relations/military advisors and then moved on to become managing director of Vector Flying Training Services, a consortium that bid for the UK Military Flying Training System contract. Awarded the AFC in 1987 and appointed Commander of the British Empire in 1993 he was Master of the Honorable Company of Air Pilots in 2008/9, and is currently vice chairman of the RAF Club and the chief operating officer of In Command Ltd.

Ian Hartley joined through the RAF College in 1965 and began his first tour on 23 Squadron Lightnings at Leuchars in early 1970 and then a second Lightning tour with 56 Squadron at Akrotiri. Next came a ground tour on the HQ 11 Group air staff looking after the TWU at Brawdy followed aptly by four years at Brawdy on 79 Squadron flying both the Hunter and Hawk. 92 Squadron Phantoms at Wildenrath came next including a stint in the Falklands then in 1985 it was back to TWU instructing, now at Chivenor.

In 1987 he went to St Athan for five years as OC Flying/chief test pilot flying all marks of Tornado, Phantom, Hawk, Jet Provost, Bulldog and Chipmunk – quite a variety! A change of pace followed with five and a half years at Lyneham on 70 Squadron, the final part as the tactical training captain. From here he was seconded to DERA Boscombe Down on the Heavy Aircraft Test Squadron primarily involved in the assessment of the then new C130J Hercules. He left the RAF in June 1999 and moved to Suffolk where he managed GP practices before becoming a school bursar in 2008. Ian retired in 2012.

Keith Skinner joined the RAF in 1965. He trained on the Chipmunk at South Cerney, Jet Provost at Church Fenton and Gnat at RAF Valley. 'Creamed off' to become an instructor for first tour and arrived at RAF Leeming as a pilot officer QFI in 1968. Three years later he was selected to fly Lightning fighters and converted first to Hunters at RAF Chivenor and then the Lightning at Coltishall.

He spent six weeks on 111 Squadron at Wattisham before joining 56(F) Squadron at RAF Akrotiri in Cyprus. Followed by four years (1974–1978) instructing on the Hunter at the TWU unit at Brawdy before converting to the Phantom and joining 92(F) Squadron at Wildenrath as squadron QFI. Staff tours followed at HQ 11 Group, UK Taceval and UKMOD Air Team in Riyadh, Saudi Arabia interspersed by a wonderful two years at RAF Scampton as wing commander Red Arrows. He retired in 1999 and took full-time reserve commission serving as 'Squadron Uncle' with 4 Squadron Harriers at RAF Cottesmore until 2007. Now a director of an aerospace consultancy (www.resource.aero) with particular interest in satellite surveillance and maritime oil spill control.

INDEX

OTHER BOOKS BY RICHARD PIKE

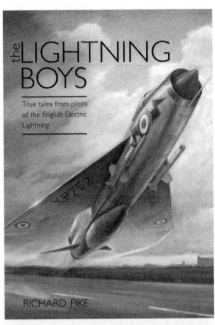

Richard Pike relates the highs and lows, the dramas and the demands of those who operated this iconic aircraft at the sharp end.

Flypast

Richard Pike is to be congratulated on this fascinating compilation of true tales.

Aeroplane

An enlightening canter around the crew room. I recommend it as a good read both to aviators in general and to the Lightning fraternity in particular.

Royal Air Force Historical Society

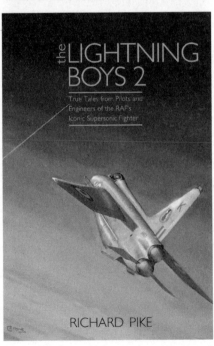

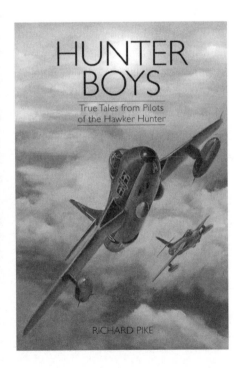